Finding the Right Path:

Researching Your Way to Discovery

By Lynne and Herman Sutter

PROFESSIONAL
GROWTH
SERIES®

A Publication of THE BOOK REPORT & LIBRARY TALK
Professional Growth Series

Linworth Publishing, Inc.
Worthington, Ohio

Library of Congress Cataloging-in-Publication Data

Sutter, Lynne.
      Finding the right path: researching your way to discovery/by
Lynne and Herman Sutter
          p. cm.–(Professional growth series)
      Includes biographical references (p.) and index.
      ISBN 0-938865-76-5 (Perfectbound)
      1. Children's literature, English Bibliography. 2. Library
research. I. Sutter, Herman II. Title. III. Series.
Z1037.S965 1999
011.62–dc21   99-20829
                                        CIP

Published by Linworth Publishing, Inc.
480 East Wilson Bridge Road, Suite L
Worthington, Ohio 43085

Copyright©1999 by Linworth Publishing, Inc.

Series Information:
      From The Professional Growth Series

ISBN 0-938865-76-5

5 4 3 2 1

Table of Contents

- -

Table of Contents continued

Table of Contents continued

Table of Contents continued

for Lucia and Isabel

Introduction

▷ CHILDREN AND THEIR NATURAL SENSE OF WONDER

Children have a natural sense of wonder. At a young age a stream of questions begins flowing from their lips. What are clouds made of? Why do flowers grow? How are mummies made? What do bugs eat? And, in time these questions grow to become genuine interests in atmospheric conditions, agriculture, ancient history, and the environment. By nurturing children's questioning minds, their natural wonder flourishes.

Younger children will depend on parents, teachers, librarians, and other important figures in their lives to create an environment of discovery. But as children mature they become increasingly more self-sufficient, able to locate resources on their own and fuel their own expanding imagination.

The pages of this book can be used as a guide in this discovery process. Through carefully selected books, journals, and multimedia resources, children will begin to find answers and to formulate new questions about the world in which we live.

▷ ABOUT THE AUTHORS

Herman Sutter is a poet/playwright and high school library media specialist with an M.S. in Library Science from the University of North Texas. He reviews for *School Library Journal, The Book Report,* and *Library Talk.* In 1988 Herman received the Innisfree Prize for poetry and in 1991 his poem for voices, "The World Before Grace," was honored and performed at the Texas Playwright's Festival. He is currently at work on a play based on Dostoyevsky's *The Possessed.*

Lynne Sutter, having previously worked with high school and undergraduate students, is currently involved in a cooporative learning program with the couple's young daughters, Lucia and Isabel. Lynne received a B.A. from the University of Saint Thomas and a M.Arch. from the University of Houston. She dreams of moving to a house in the woods.

CHAPTER 1

Getting Started

▶ WHO CAN USE THIS BOOK: TEACHERS, LIBRARIANS, PARENTS, AND THE YOUNG RESEARCHER

This book is a guide; it provides a path to discovery. Our point in writing it was to help young researchers get started down the research path. We wanted our paths to inspire exploration and to open up into new vistas—and to avoid doubling back on themselves. The Pathfinder section, for instance, contains a broad collection of subjects which young, elementary-aged children find most interesting. Each subject is followed by a brief description, the Dewey decimal numbers (DDC 21) and subject headings associated with it, search terms, bibliographies of reference, nonfiction and fiction books, Web sites, CD-ROMs, and video recordings on that subject. The materials selected for these bibliographies are generally appropriate for the elementary-aged child, however, some will be more suitable for younger children, while others will appeal to the older child.

This book is intended for teachers, librarians, parents, and students. Teachers may find this book most useful in planning unit studies for a particular subject. Using these lists as a starting point, a variety of resources can be brought together for an in-depth study of a favorite subject.

The elementary school and children's librarian may use these pages to guide a student's research or broaden a child's interest base. The librarian may also find this book an aid in collection development, using lists of materials to help create a balanced collection on subjects that are covered repeatedly. For example, if the second graders study endangered species every fall, a librarian may want to use the Endangered Species pathfinder to create a balanced variety of resources on the subject.

Parents may also find this book useful as a tool to nurture their child's budding interests. Simply surrounding children with books on their favorite subjects, or guiding them to a shelf in the library, may be all that is needed to help their newly forming interests grow.

For the older elementary-aged child, this book may become a tool for independent research. As children mature, their natural, free-flowing desire to know begins to find points of focus and to become more organized. Now, they want to know not just what clouds are made of, but how they occur and what they do. No longer are they satisfied with knowing just how mummies were made, but they begin to wonder why, which leads to deeper questions about the culture of the Ancient Egyptians, asking not only how, but why mummies were made.

▶ WHAT'S INSIDE

The largest section of this book contains the "pathfinders." Pathfinders are a collection of resources—a bibliography, in part—on a given topic. The topics in this book were selected based on the interests of elementary-aged children and contain lists of print and multimedia resources available for young children.

> **Pathfinders are a collection of resources— a bibliography, in part— on a given topic.**

Following the pathfinders is a section on methods of research. Teachers, librarians, and older students will find helpful approaches to the research task.

For teachers and librarians, Appendix A: Research Methods and Library Skills Bibliography includes a listing of books on research projects and methods, and on teaching library skills. These books are primarily directed toward the classroom teacher and school librarian but may prove useful to older students, as well.

Appendix B: Researching on the Internet and Evaluating Web Sites is helpful in approaching the tangled web of the Internet and its ever-changing Web sites. Appendix C: Creative Citations gives a unique approach to teaching and to noting the variety of resources available. The final three appendices offer information on additional resources: children's magazines and periodical indexes for children's literature.

CHAPTER 2

An Introduction to the Pathfinders

➤ HOW THE PATHFINDERS PAGES ARE ORGANIZED

In the pathfinders section, the topics are organized alphabetically. Each topic includes a description of the subject; the Dewey numbers specific to that topic; search terms to use when researching the topic; a selection of nonfiction, reference, and fiction books; a list of Web sites appropriate for student or teacher use; and a list of multimedia materials. Bibliographic lists, including videos and CD-ROMs, are organized alphabetically by title.

➤ THE PATHFINDER PAGE

Title

A brief description of each topic is intended to pique the interest of students and give suggestions toward broadening their knowledge base and refining their approach to research. These descriptions were adapted from a variety of sources, including **The**

Encyclopedia Americana (Grolier Incorporated, 1996); **The Dorling Kindersley Big Book of Knowledge** (Dorling Kindersley, 1994); **The Dorling Kindersley Visual Encyclopedia** (Dorling Kindersley, 1995); **The Golden Book Illustrated Dictionary** (Golden Press, 1961); the **Picturepedia** series (Dorling Kindersley, 1993); and **Webster's New Twentieth Century Dictionary** (Simon & Schuster, 1983).

Dewey Decimal Call Numbers and Search Terms

200s 300s 400s The call number and search term lists begin with the most specific terms followed by related terms. Refer to the descriptions next to the call numbers to determine the best place to start searching. A quick review of the list will help locate the area of interest within the general subject. The search terms will be useful when doing keyword and subject searches in online catalogs, periodical indexes, and electronic and print encyclopedias.

Nonfiction/Reference Books and Fiction Books

There is a great distance between the reading level of a first grader who is reading picture books and of a fifth grader who is able to finish short novels. Titles were selected with that in mind, therefore each topic has a selection of titles appropriate for readers at any level.

While making selections, we occasionally found activity and craft books appropriate to a topic. These books were included in the lists whenever possible, to add a hands-on dimension to a student's research.

Web Sites

Most Web sites selected are more appropriate for older students. However, teachers and librarians may be able to select certain pages of a site that younger children can enjoy. Unfortunately, Web sites may be frequently modified. The dynamic nature of the Internet can be very exciting, with its constant flow of new information, but it can also be frustrating. You may find what appears to be a perfect oasis of information on your topic one day, but when you return to it a week later, that information may have vanished, and something new is in its place!

Multimedia

As with the bibliographic section, the multimedia selection spans a broad range of interest levels. The video selections are generally well balanced between the younger and

older elementary student. The CD-ROM selections, however, more often than not are geared toward the older student.

▶ HOW THE PATHFINDER PAGES WERE COMPILED

Topics

We queried elementary educators and librarians across the United States to obtain our topics list. The pathfinder topics in this book are a collection of their students' favorite themes and topics to learn about.

Books and Audiovisual Materials

We used personal knowledge, library catalogs, publisher catalogs, online booksellers, and a database of library resources on CD-ROM, to help us compile a list of titles. We looked for books that are considered classics, books that have received awards or exceptional reviews, and books by respected authors. We also made every effort to create a sense of diversity, in viewpoint and approach, for each topic. On occasion we struggled to simply find a good selection of materials.

Often, for the younger reader, information is imparted in the form of a story. Therefore, our fiction lists may occasionally seem heavy with picture books appealing to early readers, while the nonfiction lists seem weighted more toward the older child. This seemed to occur naturally, flowing from the needs of children at different stages of learning.

> You may find what appears to be a perfect oasis of information on your topic one day, but when you return to it a week later, that information may have vanished, and something new is in its place!

Web Sites

Lists of Web sites proved the most difficult to compile. First, there are just so many, and second, though print and online guides to the Internet are available and some Professional publications (*School Library Journal, The Book Report* and *Library Talk,* etc.) are reviewing Web sites, there is no standard reviewing mechanism for gleaning the good, the useful, and the kid-friendly out of the morass of mediocrity, idiosyncrasy, and obscurity. Therefore, in our search for useful Internet sites, we often turned to Web pages created for educators, the American Library Association's Web page, and public library kid's pages. Each has compiled lists of sites recommended for kids and their teachers. However, the ever-changing nature of the Internet makes these lists of Web sites somewhat unreliable. Some Web pages are so idiosyncratic, a citing on the Internet may be only slightly more reliable than a sighting of Elvis.

On occasion, however, like trailblazing path finders of old, we, too, wandered out into the great untamed wilderness of the World Wide Web armed with only a few years of experience, 12 oz. of raw nerve, and a broad-reaching search engine!

> **Some Web pages are so idiosyncratic, a citing on the Internet may be only slightly more reliable than a sighting of Elvis.**

Multimedia CD-ROMs

The CD-ROM selections range from interactive games to information-filled databases. For instance, role-playing games such as *Oregon Trail* or *Pilgrim Quest* can be very valuable teaching tools. They offer students insight into what it meant to try to cross the prairie in a covered wagon or to survive a bitter winter without supplies in a foreign land. Such games can bring history to life for students in ways that books and videos cannot.

Other CD-ROMs included in the bibliography are more strictly informational. They were either selected for their specialized content or for their encyclopedic nature. For example, a CD-ROM which covers the history of the world will appear on nearly all of the topic bibliographies that are historical in nature. Some topics do not have CD-ROM selections. These topics may have been too specific or not "mainstream" enough for the interactive multimedia industry. Occasionally, for certain topics, we were unable to find suitable CD-ROM programs for elementary-aged children.

CHAPTER 3

The Pathfinders

Adventure

Anything that involves courage, daring, boldness, or a sense of excitement can be considered adventure. Adventure may include exploring the unknown and experiencing unforeseen events. Some adventures, like space exploration or mountain climbing, for example, involve an element of risk and danger.

 DEWEY DECIMAL CALL NUMBERS

(Most will be found in the fiction section, however, some may be cataloged as literature in the 800s. See also: 809.3 Literary forms.)

920	Collective biographies
921	Individual biographies
910s	Geography & travel
629.4	Astronautics (space travel)

 SEARCH TERMS

Adventure
Exploration
Action
Suspense
Mystery
Western
Space travel
Science fiction

Search by names of adventurous activity, for example: *Mountain climbing*

 NONFICTION/REFERENCE BOOKS

Adventure in Space: The Flight to Fix the Hubble by Elaine Scott. Hyperion, 1995.

Alice Ramsey's Grand Adventure by Don Brown. Houghton Mifflin Co., 1997.

Dolphin Adventure by Wayne Grover. Beech Tree Books, 1993,

Hudson River: An Adventure from the Mountains to the Sea by Peter Lourie. Boyds Mills Press, 1998.

Into the Deep Forest with Henry David Thoreau by Jim Murphy. Clarion Books, 1995.

One Day in the Alpine Tundra Books by Jean Craighead George. Crowell, 1984.

The Outdoor Adventure Handbook by Hugh McManners. Dorling Kindersley, 1996.

Space Camp: The Great Adventure for NASA Hopefuls by Anne Baird. Beech Tree Books, 1995.

The Story of Three Whales by Giles Whittell. Gareth Stevens Children's Books, 1989.

Trapped by the Ice: Shackleton's Amazing Antarctic Adventure by Michael McCurdy. Walker & Co., 1997.

The True Adventure of Daniel Hall by Diane Stanley. Dial Books, 1995.

FICTION

All Aboard! by James Stevenson. Greenwillow Books, 1995.

Cold Shoulder Road by Joan Aiken. Bantam Books Doubleday Dell, 1997.

The Five Sisters by Margaret Mahy. Viking, 1997.

Friends Go Adventuring by Helme Heine. Margaret K. McElderry Books, 1995.

Jumanji by Chris Van Allsburg. Houghton Mifflin Co., 1981.

The Lion, the Witch and the Wardrobe by C. S. Lewis. HarperCollins, 1997.

The Rattlebang Picnic by Margaret Mahy. Dial Books, 1994.

Santa Calls by William Joyce. HarperCollins, 1993.

The Seven Voyages of Sinbad by Quentin Blake. Margaret K. McElderry Books, 1997.

Stuart Little by E. B. White. Harper & Row, 1973.

Tintin: 3 Complete Adventures in 1 Volume by Herge. Little, Brown & Co., 1994.

Treehouse Tales by Anne Isaacs. Dutton Children's Books, 1997.

The Whipping Boy by Sid Fleischman. Troll Assoc., 1987.

The Wind in the Willows by Kenneth Grahame. Scribner, 1983.

MULTIMEDIA

 CD-ROMS:

Amazon Trail II. MECC, 1996.

Curious George Comes Home Interactive. Houghton Mifflin Co., 1997.

The Magic School Bus Interactive (series). Microsoft, 1995.

Oregon Trail II. MECC, 1995.

 VIDEOS:

Balto. MCA Home Video, 1995.

Christopher Columbus and the Great Adventure. Video Knowledge, 1992.

City Boy (Wonder Works). Bonneville Worldwide Entertainment, 1993.

The Lion, the Witch and the Wardrobe. Bonneville Worldwide Entertainment, 1988.

Wallace and Gromit: The Wrong Trousers. BBC Video Production, 1993.

 WEB SITES

(See also: Web pages of particular writers, i.e., Brian Jacques, Gary Paulsen, etc., or book series, such as American Girl)

Biography.Com (Bios of historic figures) www.biography.com/bio_main.html

Discoverers Web (Lots of good links) www.win.tue.nl/cs/fm/engels/discovery/

Explorers of the World www.bham.wednet.edu/explore.htm

➤ SEE ALSO THESE RELATED PATHFINDERS
Explorers & Exploration; Heroism; Mythology; Space Travel and Outer Space

Ancient Civilizations

Several different ancient civilizations are well known for their complex social systems and broad range of knowledge: the Mayan civilization, the civilizations of Ancient Rome and Greece, Imperial China, and Ancient Egypt. These cultures are known for their progress in the arts and sciences, for their extensive use of writing, and for their highly developed political and social institutions.

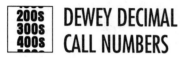 **DEWEY DECIMAL CALL NUMBERS**

930s Ancient world
290s Religion and mythology

 SEARCH TERMS

Ancient civilization
Ancient history
Ancient Rome
Ancient Greece
Imperial China
Ancient Egypt
Greek mythology
Roman mythology

 NONFICTION/REFERENCE BOOKS

Ancient China by Judith Simpson. Time-Life Books, 1996.

The Ancient Greeks by Charles Freeman. Oxford University Press, 1996.

The Ancient World of the Bible by Malcolm Day. Viking, 1994.

The Arabs in the Golden Age by Mokhtar Moktefi. Millbrook Press, 1992.

Dateline Troy by Paul Fleischman. Candlewick Press, 1996.

The Grandchildren of the Incas by Matti Pitkanen. Carolrhoda Books, 1991.

How People Lived by Anne Millard. Dorling Kindersley, 1993.

The Kingfisher Books Book of the Ancient World. Kingfisher Books, 1995.

The Master Builders by Philip Wilkinson. Chelsea House, 1994.

The Maya by Pat McKissack. Children's Press, 1985.

The Mediterranean by Philip Wilkinson. Chelsea House, 1994.

The Romans by Peter Hicks. Thomson Learning, 1994.

Smithsonian Timelines of the Ancient World. Dorling Kindersley, 1993.

Vietnam: The Culture by Bobbie Kalman. Crabtree Pub. Co., 1996.

The Visual Dictionary of Ancient Civilizations. Dorling Kindersley, 1994.

FICTION

I Am the Mummy Heb-Nefert by Eve Bunting. Harcourt Brace & Co., 1997.

The Jade Horse, the Cricket, and the Peach Stone by Ann Tompert. Boyds Mill Press, 1996.

Maya's Children by Rudolfo Anaya. Hyperion, 1997.

The Same Sun Was in the Sky by Denise Webb. Northland Pub., 1994.

The Waiting Day by Harriett Diller. Green Tiger Press, 1994.

MULTIMEDIA

CD-ROMS:

Ancient Civilizations. Entrex, [nd].

Ancient History Series. Thomas S. Klise Co., [nd].

Ancient Times: People and Places. Queue, [nd].

Eyewitness History of the World. Dorling Kindersley Multimedia, [nd].

First Connections Interactive: The Golden Book Encyclopedia. Jostens Learning, 1996.

How Would You Survive. Grolier Kids, 1995.

VIDEOS:

Ancient Civilizations for Children (Nine titles in series). Schlessinger, 1998.

The Lost Kingdom of the Maya. National Geographic Society, 1993.

Mystery of the Ancient Ones. PBS Video, 1996.

This Old Pyramid. NOVA, 1993.

WEB SITES

Ancient City of Athens (Good pictures of historic sites, virtual tours) www.indiana.edu/~kglowack/athens/

Ancient Greek World (Depicts life in Ancient Greece using artifacts. Some pictures, lots of text—may not appeal to younger students.) www.museum.upenn.edu

Ancient World Web (Compendium of Internet sites highlighting or discussing the Ancient World) www.julen.net/aw/

Life in Ancient Egypt (This Carnegie Museum of Natural History exhibit gives short descriptions of daily life, religion, funeral practices, and more in Ancient Egypt. Some pictures, lots of text—may not appeal to younger students) www.clpgh.org

➤ *SEE ALSO THIS RELATED PATHFINDER*
Ancient Egypt

Ancient Egypt

The civilization of Ancient Egypt began developing in the valley of the Nile more than 5,000 years ago. This period lasted for 3,000 years and is divided into three kingdoms: Old Kingdom; Middle Kingdom; and New Kingdom. Ancient Egypt was ruled by pharaohs. Their beliefs in the afterlife and their process of mummifying the body were a very important part of their culture. Also during this period the great pyramids of Giza were built. A high culture developed early, and the use of writing was introduced. During the New Kingdom Ancient Egyptian civilization reached its peak. A vast empire was established, and the cities of Thebes and Memphis became the political, commercial, and cultural centers of the world.

DEWEY DECIMAL CALL NUMBERS

932 Ancient Egypt

962 Egypt (These books may have chapters on Ancient Egypt)

299 Religion and mythology

SEARCH TERMS

Ancient Egypt
Egypt
Ancient civilizations
Pharaoh
Mummies
Nile
Pyramids

NONFICTION/REFERENCE BOOKS

Ancient Egypt (Cultural Atlas for Young People Series) by Geraldine Harris. Facts on File, 1990.

Ancient Egypt (Eyewitness, No. 23) by George Hart. Knopf, 1990.

Ancient Egypt by Robert Nicholson. Chelsea House, 1994.

The Ancient Egypt Pack: A Three-Dimensional Celebration of Egyptian Mythology, Culture, Art, Life and Afterlife by Christos Kondeatis. Bullfinch Press, 1996.

The Ancient Egyptians: Life in the Nile Valley (People's of the Past) by Viviane Koenig. Millbrook Press, 1996.

Cat Mummies by Kelly Trumble. Clarion Books, 1996.

Cleopatra by Diane Stanley. William Morrow Junior Books, 1994.

The Curse of Tutankhamen by Elaine Landau. Millbrook Press, 1996.

How Would You Survive As an Ancient Egyptian? (How Would You Survive) by Jacqueline Morley. Franklin Watts, 1996.

Mummies Made in Egypt by Aliki. Harper & Row, 1985.

Pyramid by David Macaulay. Houghton Mifflin Co., 1975.

Pyramids by Anne Millard. Kingfisher Books, 1996.

Tutankhamen's Gift by Robert Sabuda. Atheneum, 1994.

Unwrap the Mummy: A Four Foot Long, Fact Filled Pop-up Mummy to Explore by Ian Dicks. Random House, 1995.

FICTION

Croco'nile by Roy Gerrard. Farrar Straus Giroux, 1994.

Cry of the Benu Bird: An Egyptian Creation Story (adapted by C. Shana Greger). Houghton Mifflin Co., 1996.

The Egyptian Cinderella by Shirley Climo. HarperCollins, 1992.

I am the Mummy Heb-Nefert by Eve Bunting. Harcourt Brace & Co., 1997.

The Mystery of King Karfu by Doug Cushman. HarperCollins, 1996.

The Myth of Isis and Osiris by Jules Cashford. Barefoot Books, 1994.

A Place in the Sun by Jill Rubalcaba. Clarion Books, 1997.

Pepi and the Secret Names by Jill Paton Walsh. Lothrop, Lee & Shepard, 1995.

MULTIMEDIA

 ### CD-ROMS:

Annabel's Dream of Ancient Egypt Interactive. Texas Caviar, 1991. (Presents Ancient Egypt's history and the music of the opera *Aida*)

Destination, Pyramids Interactive. Edmark, 1996.

How Would You Survive? Interactive (Based on How Would You Survive book series). Grolier Kids, 1995.

The Road to Ancient Egypt (Ancient History). Thomas S. Klise Co, [nd].

 ### VIDEOS:

Ancient Egypt (laser disc). Voyager, 1987.

Biography: Cleopatra—Destiny's Queen. A&E Entertainment, 1996.

The Giant Nile. Acorn Media, 1990.

Pyramid. PBS Video, 1988.

This Old Pyramid. NOVA, 1993.

Who Built the Pyramids. National Geographic Educational, 1992.

 ## WEB SITES

Ancient World Web main index (Compendium of Internet sites highlighting or discussing the Ancient World) www.julen.net/aw/

Egypt and the Ancient Near East (Web resources for young people and teachers, includes virtual walking tours) www.asmar.uchicago.edu/OI/DEPT/RA/ABZU/YOUTH_RESOURCES.HTML

Life in Ancient Egypt (This Carnegie Museum of Natural History exhibit gives short descriptions of daily life, religion, funeral practices and more of Ancient Egypt. Some pictures, lots of text—may not appeal to younger students) www.clpgh.org

> ## SEE ALSO THIS RELATED PATHFINDER
Ancient Civilizations

Animals

There are more than a million species of animals. They include any living organism that is not a plant, from a tiny flea to an enormous whale. Most of the animals on earth are either insects or worms. Animals are divided into two major groups: vertebrates and invertebrates.

 DEWEY DECIMAL CALL NUMBERS

590 Animals
592 Invertebrates
595.7 Insects
597 Fish
598.2 Birds
598.9 Birds of prey
598.29 Water birds
599 Mammals
636.088 Domesticated animals

 SEARCH TERMS

Animals
Birds
Water birds
Birds of prey
Fish
Insects
Spiders
Arachnids
Mammals

Domesticated animals
Farm animals
Invertebrates
Herbivores
Carnivores
Search by names of specific animals, for example: Platypus

 NONFICTION/REFERENCE BOOKS

101 Questions & Answers about Backyard Wildlife by Ann Squire. Walker & Co., 1996.

African Animals ABC by Philippa-Alys Browne. Sierra Club Books for Children, 1995.

African Wildlife by Warren Halliburton. Crestwood House, 1992.

All Eyes on the Pond by Michael J. Rosen. Hyperion for Children, 1994.

The Amateur Zoologist: Explorations and Investigations by Mary Dykstra. Franklin Watts, 1994.

An American Safari: Adventures on the North American Prairie by Jim Brandenburg. Walker & Co., 1995.

Animals on the Inside: A Book of Discovery & Learning by Andres Llamas Ruiz. Sterling Pub., 1994.

Biggest, Strongest, Fastest by Steve Jenkins. Ticknor & Fields Books for Young Readers, 1995.

Birds (Picturepedia). Dorling Kindersley, 1997.

Do You Know the Difference? by Andrea and Michael Bischhoff-Miersch. North-South Books, 1994.

The Dorling Kindersley Visual Encyclopedia. Dorling Kindersley, 1995.

NONFICTION/REFERENCE BOOKS CONTINUED

Encyclopedia of the Animal World (series). Facts on File. See these titles in the series: **Birds** (1989); **Birds: The Plant-and-seed-eaters** (1989); **Birds: The Aerial Hunters** (1989); **Fish** (1990); **Insects and Spiders** (1990); **Mammals: The Small Plant-eaters** (1988); **Pets and Farm Animals** (1989); **Simple Animals** (1989).

Eyewitness Natural World by Steve Parker. Dorling Kindersley, 1994.

Fearsome Fish by Steve Parker. Raintree/Steck Vaughn, 1994.

A Gaggle of Geese: The Collective Names of the Animal Kingdom by Philippa-Alys Browne. Atheneum Books for Young Readers, 1996.

Horses by Dorothy Hinshaw Patent. Carolrhoda Books, 1994.

Insects and Spiders (Picturepedia). Dorling Kindersley, 1997.

Jungle Animals (Picturepedia). Dorling Kindersley, 1997.

The Kingfisher Books First Encyclopedia of Animals by David Burnie and Linda Gamlin. Kingfisher Books, 1994.

The Kingfisher Books Illustrated Encyclopedia of Animals: From Aardvark to Zorille—and 2,000 Other Animals edited by Michael Chinery. Kingfisher Books, 1992.

Koko's Kitten by Francine Patterson. Scholastic, 1985.

Lies (People Believe) about Animals by Susan Sussman and Robert James. Albert Whitman & Co., 1987.

Life Cycles of a Dozen Diverse Creatures by Paul Fleisher. Millbrook Press, 1996.

Little Giants by Seymour Simon. William Morrow & Co., 1983.

Mammals (Picturepedia). Dorling Kindersley, 1997.

My Visit to the Zoo by Aliki. HarperCollins, 1997.

Peaceful Kingdom: Random Acts of Kindness by Animals by Stephanie Laland. Conari Press, 1997.

Primates: Apes, Monkeys, and Prosimians by Thane Maynard. Franklin Watts, 1994.

Sea Life (Picturepedia). Dorling Kindersley, 1997.

Sponges Are Skeletons by Barbara Esbensen. HarperCollins, 1993.

Toad Overload: A True Tale of Nature Knocked off Balance in Australia by Patricia Seibert. Millbrook Press, 1996.

The Usborne Illustrated Encyclopedia: The Natural World edited by Lisa Watts. Usborne Pub., 1995.

What Does the Crow Know?: Mysteries of Animal Intelligence by Margery Facklam. Sierra Club Books for Children, 1994.

FICTION

Aardvarks, Disembark! by Ann Jonas. Greenwillow Books, 1990.

Advice for a Frog by Alice Shertle & Norman Green. Lothrop, Lee & Shepard, 1995.

Baboon by Kate Banks. Farrar Straus Giroux, 1997.

Beast Feast by Douglas Florian. Harcourt Brace Jovanovich, 1994.

The Beauty of the Beast: Poems from the Animal Kingdom selected by Jack Prelutsky. Knopf, 1997.

Farmer Duck by Martin Waddell. Candlewick Press, 1992.

If Anything Ever Goes Wrong at the Zoo by Mary Jean Hendrick. Harcourt Brace Jovanovich, 1996.

In the Small, Small Pond by Denise Fleming. Henry Holt & Co., 1993.

In the Tall, Tall Grass by Denise Fleming. Henry Holt & Co., 1992.

The Incredible Journey by Sheila Burnford. Bantam Books, 1984.

Mean Margaret by Tor Seidler. HarperCollins, 1997.

The Three Little Wolves and the Big Bad Pig by Eugenios Trivizas. Aladdin Paperbacks, 1993.

Time to Sleep by Denise Fleming. Henry Holt & Co., 1997.

Tuba Lessons by T. C. Bartlett. Creative Editions, 1997.

MULTIMEDIA

CD-ROMS:

Animal Planet Interactive: The Ultimate Wildlife Adventure. Discovery Channel Multimedia, 1996.

Animals in Their World Interactive. Edunetics, 1996.

Eyewitness Encyclopedia of Nature 2.0. DK Multimedia, 1997.

Multimedia Bugs Interactive Multimedia: The Complete Interactive Guide to Insects. Inroads Interactive, 1996.

Rand McNally Children's Atlas of World Wildlife Interactive. GameTek, 1995.

U*X*L Science. Gale, 1997.

VIDEOS:

Amazing Animals (series). Dorling Kindersley, 1997.

Creatures of the Blue. Sierra Club for Kids, 1995.

Deep Sea Dive (Really Wild Animals). National Geographic Home Video, 1994.

Desert Wildlife. Natural History Educational, 1995.

Eyewitness Natural World (series). Dorling Kindersley, 1995.

Insects (Tell Me Why). Bennett Marine Video, 1987.

Insects: Little Things that Run the World. Unapix Entertainment, 1989.

Prairie Wildlife. Natural History Educational, 1995.

Rocky Mountain Wildlife. Natural History Educational, 1995.

WEB SITES

Audubon Society
www.audubon.org

The Electronic Zoo
www.netvet.wustl.edu/e-zoo.htm

National Wildlife Federation—Endangered Species and Habitats
www.igc.org/nwf/endangered/index.html

Wildlife Links (Links to wildlife images, sounds, endangered species, zoos, and more) www.selu.com/~bio/wildlife/links/index.html

➤ *SEE ALSO THESE RELATED PATHFINDERS*

Biomes; Birds; Dolphins; Insects; Penguins; Pets; Reptiles; Sea Animals; Sharks; Whales; Zoo Animals

Apache Indians

The Apache Indians are the Native American people of the Southwest. Apaches lived on wild game, seeds and fruit, and livestock. The Apaches were known as fierce fighters, and they led strong efforts to stop the white man's westward expansion. Today they live on reservations in Arizona and New Mexico and still keep many of their tribal customs.

DEWEY DECIMAL CALL NUMBERS

970.1 Indians of North America
301.45 Ethnic groups (American Indians)
970.004 History, North America (1800-1900)
973 History, United States
976 South central United States
979 Pacific Coast states
398.2 Folk literature

SEARCH TERMS

Apache Indians
Indians of North America
Indians of New Mexico
Apache Indian legends
Apache Indian folklore
Geronimo
Cochise

NONFICTION/REFERENCE BOOKS

The Apache (A New True Book) by Patricia McKissack. Children's Press, 1984.

The Apache Indians (Native Peoples) by Bill Lund. Bridgestone Books, 1998.

The Apache Indians (The Junior Library of American Indians) by Nicole Claro. Chelsea House, 1992.

Apache Rodeo by Diane Hoyt-Goldsmith. Holiday House, 1995.

The Apaches: People of the Southwest by Jennifer Fleischner. Millbrook Press, 1994.

The Apaches (A First Americans Book) by Virginia Driving Hawk Sneve. Holiday House, 1997.

The Apaches and Navajos by Craig A. Doherty and Katherine M. Doherty. Franklin Watts, 1989.

Children of the Sun: The Pueblos, Navajos, and Apaches of New Mexico by Maudie Robinson. J. Messner, 1983.

Cochise, Apache Chief by Melissa Schwarz. Chelsea House, 1992.

Encyclopedia of Native American Tribes by Carl Waldman. Facts on File, 1988.

The Encyclopedia of North American Indians. Marshall Cavendish, 1997.

Geronimo (American Indian Stories) by David Jeffery. Raintree, 1990.

The Gift of Changing Woman by Tryntje Van Ness Seymour. Henry Holt & Co., 1993.

FICTION

Antelope Woman: An Apache Folktale by Michael Lacapa. Northland, 1992.

The Flute Player: An Apache Folktale by Michael Lacapa. Northland, 1990.

The Legend of Red Horse Cavern (World of Adventure) by Gary Paulsen. Bantam Books, 1994.

Run Away Home by Pat McKissack. Scholastic, 1997.

Runs With Horses by Brian Burks. Harcourt Brace Jovanovich, 1995.

Three Fools and a Horse by Betty Baker. Collier Macmillan Pub., 1987.

Walks Alone by Brian Burks. Harcourt Brace Jovanovich, 1998.

VIDEOS:

Apache (Indians of North America). Schlessinger, 1993.
Gourd Masks. Lifebase Team, 1995.

➤ SEE ALSO THESE RELATED PATHFINDERS

Native Americans; Westward Expansion

Architecture

Any building can be called architecture, but usually the word "architecture" refers to buildings designed for a special purpose and in a particular style. Throughout history, as building methods and technology developed, the styles of architecture responded and changed accordingly. Styles of architecture and the types of buildings built during any period in history were also influenced by the values and interests of society at that time. Some styles of architecture include Gothic Architecture, Renaissance Architecture, and Modern Architecture.

 200s 300s 400s DEWEY DECIMAL CALL NUMBERS

720 Architecture
724 Modern Architecture
725 Public structures
728 Residential Architecture

 SEARCH TERMS

Architecture
Buildings
Skyscrapers
Historic buildings
Architecture history
Dwellings
Civil engineering
Building
Construction
Residential architecture

 NONFICTION/REFERENCE BOOKS

Architects Make ZigZags: Looking at Architecture From A to Z by Roxie Munro. Preservation Press, 1986.

Architecture by Richard Wood. Thomson Learning, 1995.

Cathedral: The Story of Its Construction by David Macaulay. Houghton Mifflin Co., 1973.

The Empire State Building (Building America) by Craig A. Doherty and Katherine M. Doherty. Blackbirch Press, 1998.

Frank Lloyd Wright for Kids by Kathleen Thorne-Thomsen. Chicago Review Press, 1994.

Great Buildings (Discoveries Library) by Anne Lynch. Time-Life Books, 1996.

The House I Live In: At Home in America by Isadore Seltzer. Maxwell Macmillan International, 1992.

The Homes We Live In (Have You Noticed?) by Sally Hewitt and Jane Rowe. Raintree/Steck Vaughn, 1997.

Super Structures by Philip Wilkinson. Dorling Kindersley, 1996.

Unbuilding by David Macaulay. Houghton Mifflin Co., 1980.

Waiting for Filippo: The Life of Renaissance Architect Filippo Brunelleschi: A Pop-Up Book by Michael Bender. Chronicle Books, 1995.

Wonders of the World (See & Explore Library) by Giovanni Caselli. Dorling Kindersley, 1992.

FICTION

Anno's Journey by Mitsumasa Anno. Collins-World, 1978.

Building a House with Mr. Bumble by John Wallace. Candlewick Press, 1996.

The Do-It-Yourself House That Jack Built by John Yeoman.
Atheneum Books for Young Readers, 1995.

Frankie's Bau Wau Haus by Melanie Brown and Anthony Lawlor. Rizzoli, 1995.

The Great Wonder (Odyssey) by Annabelle Howard. SoundPrints, 1996.

The Little House (Sandpiper Books) by Virginia Lee Burton. Houghton Mifflin Co., 1978.

MULTIMEDIA

CD-ROMS:

Davidson's Kid CAD Interactive Multimedia. Davidson & Assoc., 1994.

SimCity 2000 Interactive Multimedia. Maxis Kids, 1996.

SimTown Interactive Multimedia. Maxis Kids, 1996.

VIDEOS:

Building Skyscrapers. David Alpert Assoc., 1994.

Cathedral. PBS Video, 1988.

Dig Hole, Build House. Real World Video, 1994.

Let's Build a House! Video Connections, 1996.

This Old Pyramid. NOVA/WGBH Video, 1993.

WEB SITES

Images of Medieval Art and Architecture
www1.pitt.edu/~medart/index.html
SPIRO (Architecture slide library)
www.mip.berkeley.edu/query_forms/
browse_spiro_form.html
Monuments In Egypt
www.interoz.com/egypt/monument.htm
Medieval Architecture
www.cua.edu/www/hist/netserf/architec.html
The Seven Wonders of the Ancient World
www.pharos.bu.edu/Egypt/Wonders/
Castles on the Web
www.fox.nstn.ca/~tmonk/castle/castle.html
The Pyramids—The Inside Story (PBS/NOVA
site) www.pbs.org/wgbh/nova/pyramid/
Architecture in Education
www.whyy.org/aie/page2.html
The Skyscraper's Page (Links to buildings
and architects) www.iit.edu/~boonchv/
**Architecture and Interior Design for 20th
Century America** (Photographic images)
www.lcweb2.loc.gov/ammem/gschtml/
gotthome.html

➤ SEE ALSO THESE RELATED PATHFINDERS
Artists; Ancient Civilizations; California Missions; Middle Ages; Shelter

Artists

An artist is a person who expresses ideas and emotions creatively. Often artists are influenced by the culture and society in which they live. Visual artists may paint, draw, sculpt, carve, or create using a variety of other medium. Some of the best know artists include Botticelli, Leonardo da Vinci, Michelangelo, Roudin, Manet, Picasso, Goya, Andy Warhol, and Frida Kahlo.

DEWEY DECIMAL CALL NUMBERS

700s Fine and decorative arts
730s Sculpture
740s Drawing
750s Painting
920   Collective biographies
921   Individual biographies

SEARCH TERMS

Artists
Art
Painter
Sculptor
Illustrator
Search by names of individual artists, for example: Vincent Van Gogh.

NONFICTION/REFERENCE BOOKS

Alexander Calder (Getting to Know the World's Greatest Artists) by Mike Venezia. Children's Press (1998). Also see additional titles in this series: **Andy Warhol** (1997); **Botticelli** (1994); **Da Vinci** (1994); **Diego Rivera** (1995); **Edward Hopper** (1994); **El Greco** (1998); **Francisco Goya** (1994); **Georgia O'Keeffe** (1993); **Grant Wood** (1995); **Henri De Toulouse-Lautrec** (1995); **Henri Matisse** (1997); **Jackson Pollock** (1994); **Mary Cassatt** (1994); **Michelangelo** (1994); **Monet** (1994); **Cezanne** (1998); **Paul Gauguin** (1994); **Paul Klee** (1994); **Picasso** (1988); **Pierre Auguste Renoir** (1996); **Pieter Brueghel** (1994); **Rembrandt** (1988); **Salvador Dali** (1994); **Van Gogh** (1994); **Frida Kahlo** (1999).

The Amazing Paper Cuttings of Hans Christian Andersen by Beth Brust. Ticknor & Fields Books for Young Readers, 1994.

Artist in Overalls: The Life of Grant Wood by John Duggleby. Chronicle Books, 1995.

Ezra Jack Keats: A Biography with Illustrations by Dean Engel and Florence Freedman. Silver Moon Press, 1995.

Inspirations: Stories about Women Artists: Georgia O'Keeffe, Frida Kahlo, Alice Neel, Faith Ringgold by Leslie Sills. Albert Whitman & Co., 1989.

Leonardo da Vinci by Diane Stanley. Morrow Junior Books, 1996.

Li'l Sis and Uncle Willie: A Story Based on the Life and Paintings of William H. Johnson by Gwen Everett. Hyperion, 1994.

Lives of the Artists: Masterpieces, Messes (and What the Neighbors Thought) by Kathleen Krull. Harcourt Brace Jovanovich, 1995.

Looking at Pictures: An Introduction to Art for Young People by Joy Richardson. Harry N. Abrams, 1997.

Redoute: The Man Who Painted Flowers by Carolyn Croll. G. P. Putnam's Sons, 1996.

FICTION

All I See by Cynthia Rylant. Orchard Books, 1994.

The Art Lesson by Tomie dePaola. G. P. Putnam's Sons, 1989.

The Boy Who Drew Cats by Arthur Levine. Dial Books, 1993.

The Dreamer by Cynthia Rylant. Scholastic, 1993.

The Fantastic Drawings of Danielle by Barbara McClintock. Houghton Mifflin Co., 1996.

Hands by Lois Ehlert. Harcourt Brace Jovanovich, 1997.

Josefina by Jeanette Winter. Harcourt Brace Jovanovich, 1996.

Linnea in Monet's Garden by Christina Bjork. R.&S. Books, 1987.

Little Mouse's Painting by Diane Wolkstein. Morrow Junior Books, 1992.

My Painted House, My Friendly Chicken and Me by Maya Angelou. C. Potter, 1994.

The Paper Dragon by Marguerite Davol. Atheneum, 1997.

A Weekend with Matisse by Florian Rodari. Rizzoli, 1994.

MULTIMEDIA

CD-ROMS:

The Art Lesson Interactive (Based on book by Tomie dePaola). MECC, 1996.
Artrageous!: The Amazing World of Art. Softkey, 1995.
A Love of Art (Five-CD collection). 1998.
With Open Eyes. Voyager, 1995.

VIDEOS:

Daniel and the Towers (Wonderworks). Bonneville Video, 1987.
Ezra Jack Keats Library. Weston Woods, 1993. (Features a documentary introducing the artist.)
Leonardo da Vinci (Animated Hero Classics Video). Schlessinger, 1996.
Linnea in Monet's Garden. Linneafilm, 1993.
Meet Leo Lionni. SRA School Group, 1992.
The Mystery of Picasso. Voyager, 1957.
Norman the Doorman. Weston Woods, 1971.
Sister Wendy's Story of Painting. Twentieth Century Fox, 1997.
When I Grow Up I Want to Be an Artist. Five Points South, 1995.

WEB SITES

A&E Biography series (Searchable database with brief biographical entries) www.biography.com

Exploring Leonardo (da Vinci—of course) www.mos.org/sln/Leonardo/

KinderArt (Lesson plans) www.bconnex.net/~jarea/lessons.htm

Web Museum (Very brief bios, but lots of art) www.sunsite.unc.edu/wm/

➤ *SEE ALSO THIS RELATED PATHFINDER*
Architecture

Aviation

Aviation is the science of building and flying heavier-than-air aircraft. In 1903, Orville and Wilbur Wright were the first people to successfully fly a motor-powered airplane. Since this time, the field of aviation has made significant advances. Today, aircraft are used in the military, to transport things and people, and for pleasure. There are two basic types of airplanes: planes with propellers and planes powered by a stream of hot gases, called jet planes.

DEWEY DECIMAL CALL NUMBERS

629.13 Aeronautics
629.132 Principles of flight
629.133 Aircraft
629.134 Aircraft components (design, construction, maintenance, repairs)
629.136 Airports

SEARCH TERMS

Aviation
Airplane
Pilot
Biplane
Jet
Jet Plane
Glider

NONFICTION/REFERENCE BOOKS

Aircraft (20th Century Inventions) by Ole Steen Hansen. Raintree/Steck Vaughn, 1997.

The Aircraft: Lift-The-Flap Book by Gerard Browne. Lodestar Books, 1992.

The Aircraft Encyclopedia by Roy Braybrook. Simon & Schuster, 1985.

Airplanes and Other Things That Fly by Steven Kelley. Western Pub. Co., 1990.

Amelia Earhart: Challenging the Skies (Great Lives) by Susan Sloate. Fawcett Books, 1995.

At the Controls: Women in Aviation (Space and Aviation Series) by Carole S. Briggs. Lerner Pub. Co., 1991.

Aviation: Reaching for the Sky (Innovators) by Don Berliner. Oliver Press, 1997.

Before the Wright Brothers (Space & Aviation) by Don Berliner. Lerner Pub. Co., 1990.

Beryl Markham: Never Turn Back (Barnard Biography Series) by Catherine Gourley and Rosellen Brown. Conari Press, 1997.

Black Eagles: African Americans in Aviation by Jim Haskins. Scholastic Professional, 1995.

Bombers by Malcolm V. Lowe, Tony Bryan, and Tony Gibbons. Lerner Pub. Co., 1991.

Charles Lindbergh: Hero Pilot (Discovery Biographies) by David R. Collins and Victor Mays. Chelsea House, 1991.

The Fantastic Cutaway Book of Flight (Fantastic Cutaway Series) by Jon Richards. Copper Beech Books, 1998.

The First Air Voyage in the United States: The Story of Jean-Pierre Blanchard by Alexandra Wallner. Holiday House, 1996.

Flight (Make It Work! Science) by Jack Challoner and Andrew Haslam. World Book, 1995.

Flight: An Interactive Guide to Aircraft and Flight (DK Action Packs) by Deni Bown. Dorling Kindersley, 1996.

Flight: The Journey of Charles Lindbergh by Robert Burleigh. Philomel Books, 1991.

NONFICTION/REFERENCE BOOKS CONTINUED

How Do Airplanes Fly?: A Book About Airplanes (Discovery Readers) by Melvin Berger and Gilda Berger. Hambleton-Hill Pub., 1996.

Jets (The Usborne Young Scientist Series) by Mark Hewish. E D C Pub., 1977.

Learn About Flight: A Fascinating Fact File and Learn-It-Yourself Project Book (Learn About Series) by Peter Mellett. Lorenz Books, 1997.

Planes Gliders Helicopters and Other Flying Machines (How Things Work) by Terry Jennings. Kingfisher Books, 1993.

Super Paper Airplanes: Biplanes to Space Planes by Norman Schmidt. Sterling Pub., 1996.

Up in the Air: The Story of Bessie Coleman (Trailblazers) by Philip S. Hart and Barbara O'Connor. Carolrhoda Books, 1996.

The Wright Brothers: Pioneers of American Aviation (Landmark Books) by Quentin Reynolds. Random House, 1981.

FICTION

The Airplane Alphabet Book by Jerry Pallotta, Fred Stillwell. Charlesbridge Pub., 1997.

Angela's Airplane (Munsch for Kids Series) by Michael Martchenko. Firefly Books, 1988.

The Berenstain Bears Fly-It!: Up, Up and Away (Berenstain Bears Big Chapter Do-It Books) by Stan and Jan Berenstain. Random Library, 1996.

Coast to Coast by Betsy Cromer Byars. Yearling Books, 1994.

The Magic School Bus Takes Flight. Scholastic, 1994.

MULTIMEDIA

CD-ROMS:

Inventor Labs: Transportation. Houghton Mifflin Co., 1996.

Way Things Work 2.0. Dorling Kindersley, 1996.

VIDEOS:

All About Helicopters. Bill Aaron Productions, 1995.

Flight (Tell Me Why). Bennett Marine Video, 1987.

Flight (Eyewitness). Dorling Kindersley, 1997.

Let Me Tell You about Planes. Traditional Images, 1994.

Magic School Bus Takes Flight. Kid Vision, 1997.

WEB SITES

National Air and Space Museum (Exhibits, information, and links) www.nasm.edu/NASMpage.html/

National Aviation Hall of Fame (Bios) www.nationalaviation.org/inductee.html

➤ SEE ALSO THESE RELATED PATHFINDERS

Birds; Inventions; Space Travel and Outer Space; Technology

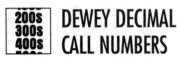

Bees and Beekeeping

There are thousands of different types of bees. Some types of bees live alone, but social bees, like honey bees, live together in hives. During the spring and summer, bees fly from flower to flower collecting pollen. Bees then turn the pollen into food. By dancing in patterns, bees are able to communicate with each other, usually to indicate where food may be found. Some farmers build bee hives in their orchards and depend on bees to pollinate their trees so that fruit will grow.

200s 300s 400s DEWEY DECIMAL CALL NUMBERS

595.79 Bees
595 Invertebrates
638 Insect culture

SEARCH TERMS

Bees
Bee culture
Bumblebee
Honeybee
Africanized honeybee
Pollination

NONFICTION/REFERENCE BOOKS

A Beekeeper's Year by Sylvia A. Johnson. Little, Brown & Co., 1994.

Amazing Bugs by Miranda MacQuitty. Dorling Kindersley, 1996.

Animals and Nature: Scholastic Reference. Scholastic, 1995.

Exotic Invaders: Killer Bees, Fire Ants, and Other Alien Species are Infesting America! by Jeanne Lesinski. Walker & Co., 1996.

The Honey Makers by Gail Gibbons. Morrow Junior Books, 1997.

Honeybee by Barrie Watts. Silver Burdett Press, 1989.

Killer Bees by Kathleen Davis and Dave Mayes. Dillon Press, 1993.

Killer Bees by Bianca Lavies. Dutton Children's Books, 1994.

The Life and Times of the Honeybee by Charles Micucci.
Ticknor & Fields Books for Young Readers, 1995.

Life of the Honeybee by Heiderose Fischer-Nagel. Carolrhoda Books, 1986.

A Wasp is Not a Bee by Marilyn Singer. Henry Holt & Co., 1995.

FICTION

The Bee Tree by Patricia Polacco. Philomel Books, 1993.

Cloud Eyes by Kathryn Lasky. Harcourt Brace Jovanovich, 1994.

Gran's Bees by Mary Thompson. Millbrook Press, 1996.

King Solomon and the Bee by Dalia Hardof Renberg. HarperCollins, 1994.

The Magic School Bus Inside a Beehive by Joanna Cole. Scholastic, 1996.

MULTIMEDIA

 VIDEOS:

Beekeeper (When I grow up...). Five Points South, 1995.

Bug City: Bees. Schlessinger, 1998.

Honey Bee Profile. AIMS Media, 1972.

Insects (Tell Me Why). Bennett Marine Video, 1987.

 WEB SITES

Honey.Com (Beekeeping site with good stuff for kids)
www.honey.com/kids/

Raising Bees
www.farminfo.org/bees/bees.htm

➤ *SEE ALSO THESE RELATED PATHFINDERS*
Animals; Insects

Biographies

A biography is the true story of someone's life. Usually biographies are written about famous people: heroes, presidents, athletes, authors, and movie stars. When a person writes their own biography it is called an autobiography.

DEWEY DECIMAL CALL NUMBERS

200s 300s 400s

920 Collective biographies
921 Individual biographies

SEARCH TERMS

Biography
Search by names of particular people, for example: Davey Crockett
Search also by the activity the person is famous for, for example: Texas Independence *or* Alamo

NONFICTION/REFERENCE BOOKS

Topic-based biography series include: **Basketball Legends** (Chelsea House); **Getting to Know the World's Greatest Artists** (Children's Press); **Historical American Biographies** (Enslow).

An Actor's Life for Me by Lillian Gish. Viking Kestrel, 1987.

After the War was Over by Michael Foreman. Arcade, 1996.

Ann Frank, Beyond the Diary: A Photographic Remembrance by Rian Verhoeven. Viking, 1993.

Bard of Avon: The Story of William Shakespeare by Diane Stanley and Peter Vennema. Morrow Junior Books, 1992.

Baseball's Greatest Hitters by Sydelle Kramer. Random House, 1995.

Big Annie of Calumet: A True Story of the Industrial Revolution by Jerry Stanley. Crown, 1996.

Biography for Beginners edited by Laurie Lanzen Harris. Omnigraphics, 1995.

Comeback!: Four True Stories by Jim O'Connor. Random House, 1992.

Francis, the Poor Man of Assisi by Tomie de Paola. Holiday House, 1982.

The Glorious Flight: Across the Channel with Louis Bleriot, July 25, 1909 by Alice Provensen. Puffin Books, 1987.

Harriet Beecher Stowe and the Beecher Preachers by Jean Fritz. G. P. Putnam's Sons, 1994.

Leonardo da Vinci by Diane Stanley. Morrow Junior Books, 1996.

Lives of the Artists: Masterpieces, Messes (and What the Neighbors Thought) by Kathleen Krull. Harcourt Brace Jovanovich, 1995.

Margaret, Frank, and Andy: Three Writers' Stories by Cynthia Rylant. Harcourt Brace Jovanovich, 1996.

Minty: A Story of Young Harriet Tubman by Alan Schroeder. Dial Books, 1996.

My First Book of Biographies by Jean Marzollo. Scholastic, 1994.

Parallel Journeys by Eleanor Ayer. Atheneum, 1995.

The U.S. Space Camp Book of Astronauts by Anne Baird. Morrow Junior Books, 1996.

Walt Whitman by Catherine Reef. Clarion Books, 1995.

You Want Women to Vote, Lizzie Stanton? by Jean Fritz. G. P. Putnam's Sons, 1995.

FICTION

Carry On, Mr. Bowditch by Jean Lee Latham. Houghton Mifflin Co., 1983.

Hugh Glass, Mountain Man: Left for Dead by Robert McClung. Beech Tree Books, 1993.

Stradivari's Singing Violin by Catherine Deverell. Carolrhoda Books, 1992.

Trail Fever: The Life of a Texas Cowboy by D. J. Lightfoot. Lothrop, Lee & Shepard, 1992.

MULTIMEDIA

CD-ROMS:

Biographies Interactive Multimedia. Gale, 1996.

Encarta Multimedia Encyclopedia. Microsoft, 1998.

Great Artists Interactive Multimedia. Attica Cybernautics, 1994.

The Guide to Classical Music. Cambrix, 1996.

His Name Was Lincoln Interactive. Sunburst, 1996.

Infopedia Interactive (Includes *Webster's New Biographical Dictionary*). Future Vision, 1995.

People Behind the Holidays. National Geographic Society, 1994.

World Book Multimedia Encyclopedia. World Book, 1998.

VIDEOS:

A&E Biography (series). A&E Entertainment, [dates vary].

American Women of Achievement (series). Schlessinger, 1995.

Black Americans of Achievement (series). Schlessinger, 1992.

Famous Americans of the 20th Century (series). Questar Inc., 1991.

Hispanic and Latin American Heritage (series). Schlessinger, 1995.

WEB SITES

A&E Biography Series (Searchable database with brief biographical entries) www.biography.com

American History 102-Who's Who in American History (102 biographies of famous Americans listed by name, era, and occupation; sources cites) www.hum.lss.wisc.edu/hist102/bios/bios. html

Biographies of Scientists Available on the Internet www.asap.unimelb.edu.au/hstm/ hstm_bio.htm

➤ SEE ALSO THESE RELATED PATHFINDERS

Artists; Black History in America; Famous People; Famous Women; Inventors; Explorers and Exploration; U.S. Presidents

Biomes

A biome, or ecosystem, is a community of plants and animals living together in an environment. Biomes are defined by their climate, altitude, latitude, water and soil characteristics, and other physical conditions. These factors support a unique group of interdependent plants and animals, specific to their particular biome.

 DEWEY DECIMAL CALL NUMBERS

577 General nature of life (conditions needed for life)

574 Biology

508 Geography, descriptions (travels and surveys)

551 Physical geology

 SEARCH TERMS

Biome
Ecosystem
Ecology
Environment
Forest ecology
Nature

Natural history
Search by biome or habitat name, for example:
Grasslands

 NONFICTION/REFERENCE BOOKS

Chaparral (Biomes of the World) by Edward R. Ricciuti. Benchmark Books, 1996. Additional titles in this series include: **Desert** (1996); **Grassland** (1996); **Ocean** (1996); **Rainforest** (1996); **Taiga** by Elizabeth Kaplan (1996); **Temperate Forest** (1996); **Tundra** (1996).

Caring for Our Animals by Carol Greene. Enslow, 1991.

Children's Illustrated Encyclopedia. Dorling Kindersley, 1998.

Coral Reef (Exploring Earth's Biomes) by April Pulley Sayre. Twenty First Century Books, 1996. Additional titles in this series include: **Desert** (1994); **Grassland** (1994); **Lake and Pond** (1996); **Ocean** (1996); **River and Stream** (1996); **Seashore** (1996); **Taiga** (1994); **Temperate Deciduous Forest** (1994); **Tropical Rain Forest** (1994), **Tundra** (1994); **Wetland** (1996).

Crinkleroot's Guide to Knowing Animal Habitats by Jim Arnosky. Simon & Schuster, 1997.

Earthworms by Elaine Pascoe. Blackbirch Press, 1997.

Explore the Wild: A Nature Search-and-Find Book by Beverly Duncan. HarperCollins, 1996.

Ecology (A Child's First Library of Learning). Time-Life Education, 1994.

Habitats: Where the Wild Things Live by Randi Hacker and Jackie Kaufman. J. Muir Pub., 1992.

My First Nature Treasury by Lizann Flatt. Sierra Club Books for Children, 1995.

Our Natural Homes: Exploring Terrestrial Biomes of North and South America by Sneed B. Collard. Charlesbridge Pub., 1996.

Rebuilding Prairies and Forests by Natalie Goldstein. Children's Press, 1994.

Richard Orr's Nature Cross-sections by Moira Butterfield. Dorling Kindersley, 1995.

Underwater Animals by Helen Cooney. Time-Life Books, 1996.

Worm's Eye View by Kipchak Johnson. Millbrook Press, 1991.

FICTION

Coral Reef Hideaway: The Story of a Clown Anemonefish by Doe Boyle. SoundPrints, 1995.

Desert Voices by Byrd Baylor. Scribner, 1981.

In the Forest by Marie Hall Ets. Puffin Books, 1978.

Jaguar by Helen Cowcher. Scholastic, 1997.

On the Trail of the Grizzly by Carol Amato. Barron's Educational, 1997.

Polar Bear Rescue by Jill Bailey. Steck Vaughn, 1991.

Sawgrass Poems: A View of the Everglades by Frank Asch. Harcourt Brace Jovanovich, 1996.

We Hide, You Seek by Jose Aruego. Greenwillow Books, 1979.

MULTIMEDIA

 ### CD-ROMS:

Animal Planet Interactive: The Ultimate Wildlife Adventure. Discovery Channel Multimedia, 1996.

Animals in Their World Interactive. Edunetics, 1996.

Earth's Endangered Environments Interactive Multimedia. National Geographic Society, 1994.

U*X*L Science. Gale, 1997.

Wild Africa Interactive Multimedia: Ngorongoro, Serengeti, Tarangire. Sumeria, 1995.

 ## WEB SITES

Ecosystems of Our World
www.tqd.advanced.org/2988/ecosystems.htm

The Electronic Zoo
www.netvet.wustl.edu/e-zoo.htm

National Wildlife Federation—Endangered Species and Habitats
www.igc.org/nwf/endangered/index.html

World Wide Biome Project
www.qesn.meq.gouv.qc.ca/ssn/Projects/biome.htm

VIDEOS:

Desert (Eyewitness). Dorling Kindersley, 1996. Additional videos in this series: **Pond & River** (1996); **Ocean** (1997); **Seashore** (1996); **Jungle** (1995).

Magic School Bus Hops Home. Kid Vision, 1995.

The Nature Connection Series: Buying a Rainforest/Urban Ecology: Vol. 1; Fishing the Ocean/Where Our Food Comes From: Vol. 2; Merv's Forest/Water Works: Vol. 3; The Badlands/A Winter Walk: Vol. 4; Carmanah/Grasslands: Vol. 5; Tide Pools/Cattail Country: Vol. 6. Discovery Channel, 1991.

What is a Habitat? Coronet/MTI/Centron, 1991.

What is an Ecosystem? Understanding Ecology, 1992.

What's It Like Where You Live? (Video, CD-ROM package series) MBG Videos, [nd].

➤ SEE ALSO THESE RELATED PATHFINDERS

Coral Reef; Desert; Ecology; Endangered Species; Everglades; Food Chain; Forest; Habitats; Ocean; Prairie; Rain Forest

Birds

Birds are vertebrate animals that grow feathers and have wings. Most birds can fly, but there are a few species that cannot fly. All birds lay eggs and most birds build some kind of nest for their eggs. Birds vary in size from the tiny hummingbird to the large, land-bound ostrich. It is believed that birds evolved from reptiles.

DEWEY DECIMAL CALL NUMBERS

598 Aves (birds)
568 Fossil Aves
590 Animals

SEARCH TERMS

Bird
Birding
Birdwatching
Aves (birds)
John James Audubon
Migration
Flight
Search by names of species, for example:
Eastern Blue Bird

NONFICTION/REFERENCE BOOKS

Bird Life: A Guide to the Behavior and Biology of Birds. Golden Books, 1991.

Birds of North America. Golden Books, 1983.

Birds, Birds, Birds (Ranger Rick's Naturescope Guides) by the Natural Wildlife Federation. McGraw-Hill, 1997.

Birds in the Bushes: A Story About Margaret Morse Nice by Julie Dunlap, illustrated by Ralph Ramstad. Carolrhoda Books, 1996.

Taking Flight: A Book About Flight. Scholastic, 1997.

What Makes a Bird a Bird by May Garelick illustrated by Trish Hill. Mondo Pub., 1995.

Picturepedia: Birds edited by Sarah Miller. Dorling Kindersley, 1993.

Backyard Birds of Summer by Carol Lerner Pub. Co.. William Morrow & Co., 1996.

Sharing the Wonder of Birds with Kids by Laura Erickson. Pfeifer-Hamilton Pub., 1996.

FICTION

Anna's Rain by Fred Burstein, illustrated by Harvey Stevenson. Orchard Books, 1990.

Flute's Journey: The Life of a Wood Thrush by Lynne Cherry. Gulliver Books, 1997.

Feathers For Lunch by Lois Ehlert. Harcourt Brace Jovanovich, 1990.

Magic School Bus Takes Flight. Scholastic, 1996.

Wing It! Riddles About Birds by Scott K. Peterson and Susan Slattery Burke. First Avenue Ed., 1991.

Dancers in the Garden by Joanne Ryder, illustrated by Judith Lopez. Sierra Club, 1992.

The Bird Tree by Hans Van Anrooy. Harcourt Brace & World, 1966.

MULTIMEDIA

 ### CD-ROMS:

Birds Interactive Multimedia. ICE Integrated Communications & Entertainment, 1996.

Eyewitness Encyclopedia of Nature 2.0. DK Multimedia, 1997.

U*X*L Science. Gale, 1997.

Virtual Reality Birds. DK Multimedia, 1996.

 ### VIDEOS:

Birds of Prey (Amazing Animals). Dorling Kindersley, 1997.

Tropical Birds (Amazing Animals). Dorling Kindersley, 1997.

Birds of Prey. Rainbow Educational Video, 1987.

Exploring the World of Birds. Video Treasures, 1992.

Bird (Eyewitness). Dorling Kindersley, 1994.

 ## WEB SITES

Audubon Society
www.audubon.org

FeederWatch/Cornell University Department of Ornithology
www.birdsource.cornell.edu/pfw

Internet Field Trip for Children
www.hed2.info.apple.com/education/curric/parents/pfet/artic.html

Jean Craighead George (Children's author—animals, birds, and ecosystems)
www.jeancraigheadgeorge.com

Local bird feeder study (Offers students chance to share their discoveries)
www.jason.org/fieldstudy

Ornithology Website
www.mgfx.com/bird/

Peterson Online (Offers bird identification tips) www.petersononline.com/

Wildlife in My Window: Birds (Video-based educational curriculum)
www.aprosti.com

> **SEE ALSO THIS RELATED PATHFINDER**
Animals

Black History in America

Black history in America is the history of African Americans in America, from the time they were first brought across the ocean in slaveships to the present. It includes many important and famous figures, such as: George Washington Carver, Frederick Douglass, Marian Anderson, Sojourner Truth, Harriet Tubman, Langston Hughes, and Martin Luther King.

200s 300s 400s DEWEY DECIMAL CALL NUMBERS

323.4 Civil rights
370 Education
920 Collective biographies
921 Individual biographies
973 History, United States
973.921-923 History, United States (1950s-1968)

SEARCH TERMS

African Americans   Civil War
Black Americans   Reconstruction
Negro   Slavery
Civil Rights   Black American folklore
movement
Search by names of people, for example:
Louis Armstrong
Search by events, for example: Desegregation

NONFICTION/REFERENCE BOOKS

Also see these series: **Great African Americans Series** by Pat McKissack, Enslow, 1991; **Gateway Civil Rights** [authors vary], Millbrook Press [dates vary]; **Contemporary African Americans** [authors vary], Raintree/Steck Vaughn, 1995.

African-Americans in the Thirteen Colonies (Cornerstones of Freedom) by Deborah Kent. Children's Press, 1996.

Buffalo Soldiers: The Story of Emmanuel Stance by Robert H. Miller. Silver Press, 1995.

Coming Home: From the Life of Langston Hughes by Floyd Cooper. Philomel Books, 1994.

From Slave to Civil War Hero: The Life of Robert Smalls by Michael Cooper. Lodestar Books, 1994.

Jump at de Sun: The Story of Zora Neale Hurston by A. P. Porter. Carolrhoda Books, 1992.

Li'l Sis and Uncle Willie: A Story Based on the Life and Paintings of William H. Johnson by Gwen Everett. Hyperion Paperbacks for Children, 1994.

Mary Church Terre: Leader for Equality by Patricia and Fredrick McKissack. Enslow, 1991.

Master of Mahogany: Tom Day, Free Black Cabinetmaker by Mary E. Lyons. Scribner, 1994.

Matthew Henson & Robert Peary: The Race for the North Pole by Laurie Rozakis. Blackbirch Press, 1994.

Maya Angelou: Journey of the Heart by Jayne Pettit. Lodestar Books, 1996.

The Real McCoy: The Life of an African-American Inventor by Wendy Towle. Scholastic, 1993.

Stitching Stars: The Story Quilts of Harriet Powers by Mary E. Lyons. Scribner, 1993.

Teammates by Peter Golenbock. Harcourt Brace Jovanovich, 1990.

Wilma Unlimited: How Wilma Rudolph Became the World's Fastest Woman by Kathleen Krull. Harcourt Brace Jovanovich, 1996.

FICTION

The Great Migration by Jacob Lawrence. HarperCollins, 1993.

Her Stories: African American Folktales, Fairy Tales, and True Tales by Virginia Hamilton. Scholastic Trade, 1995.

Little Tree in the Shade by Camille Yarbrough. G. P. Putnam's Sons, 1996.

More Than Anything Else by Marie Bradby. Orchard Books, 1995.

The People Could Fly: American Black Folktales by Virginia Hamilton. Knopf, 1994.

Tar Beach by Faith Ringgold. Crown, 1991.

Washington City is Burning by Harriette Robinet. Atheneum, 1996.

William Parker: Rebel Without Rights by John Rosenberg. Millbrook Press, 1996.

MULTIMEDIA

 ### CD-ROM:

African-American History Interactive: Slavery to Civil Rights. Queue, 1995.

 ### VIDEOS:

African American (American History for Children). Schlessinger, 1996.

African-American Heritage (American Cultures for Children). Schlessinger, 1997.

African and African American Folktales. United Learning, 1993.

And the Children Shall Lead (WonderWorks). Bonneville Worldwide Entertainment, 1987.

Black is My Color: The African American Experience. Rainbow Educational Video, 1992.

Booker T. Washington: Educator (Black Americans of Achievement). Schlessinger, 1992.

Martin Luther King, Jr.: Civil Rights Leader (Black Americans of Achievement). Schlessinger, 1992.

Race Movies: The Early History of Black Cinema. OnDeck Home Entertainment, 1996.

Roll of Thunder, Hear My Cry. SRA School Group, 1994.

WEB SITES

Black History Month (Bios on 60 important African Americans) www.gale.com/gale/bhm/bhmbios.html

Black History Month Resources www.kn.pacbell.com/wired/BHM/AfroAm.html

Negro Baseball League Online Archives www.nc5.infi.net/~moxie/nlb/nlb.html

➤ SEE ALSO THESE RELATED PATHFINDERS

Civil War, American; Famous People; Famous Women

Caldecott Books

The Caldecott Medal is an award given to artists of American children's picture books selected for their exceptional illustrations. Named in honor of the 19th-century English illustrator Randolph Caldecott, it is awarded every year by the Association for Library Service to Children, a division of the American Library Association. A Caldecott Book is a book that has been awarded the Caldecott Medal.

 DEWEY DECIMAL CALL NUMBERS

(Most Caldecott books will be found in the easy fiction section. A few may also be found in the 390s catalogued as folklore.)
028 Bibliographies
741 Illustrators
807 Literature

 SEARCH TERMS

Caldecott Medal
Children's books
Illustrator
Book design, awards
Children's literature, American awards
Awards for children's book illustrations

 NONFICTION/REFERENCE BOOKS

Art and Design in Children's Picture Books: An Analysis of Caldecott Award-Winning Illustrations by Lyn Ellen Lacy. American Library Assoc., 1986.

The Caldecott Award: The Winners and the Honor Books by Bertha Woolman. T. S. Denison, 1978.

A History of the Newbery and Caldecott Medals by Irene Smith. Viking, 1957.

The Newbery and Caldecott Awards: A Guide to the Medal and Honor Books. American Library Assoc., 1997.

Newbery and Caldecott Medal Books, 1976-1985: With Acceptance Papers, Biographies, and Related Material Chiefly from the Horn Book Magazine. Horn Book, 1986.

The Randolph Caldecott Treasury edited by Elizabeth T. Billington; with an Appreciation by Maurice Sendak. F. Warne, 1978.

CALDECOTT BOOKS

1998: **Rapunzel** by Paul O. Zelinsky (Dutton)

1997: **Golem** by David Wisniewski (Clarion Books)

1996: **Officer Buckle and Gloria** by Peggy Rathmann (G. P. Putnam's Sons)

1995: **Smoky Night**, illustrated by David Diaz; text by Eve Bunting (Harcourt Brace Jovanovich)

1994: **Grandfather's Journey** by Allen Say; text edited by Walter Lorraine (Houghton Mifflin Co.)

1993: **Mirette on the High Wire** by Emily Arnold McCully (G. P. Putnam's Sons)

1992: **Tuesday** by David Wiesner (Clarion Books)

1991: **Black and White** by David Macaulay (Houghton Mifflin Co.)

1990: **Lon Po Po: A Red-Riding Hood Story from China** by Ed Young (Philomel Books)

1989: **Song and Dance Man**, illustrated by Stephen Gammell; text by Karen Ackerman (Knopf)

1988: **Owl Moon**, illustrated by John Schoenherr; text by Jane Yolen (Philomel Books)

1987: **Hey, Al**, illustrated by Richard Egielski; text by Arthur Yorinks (Farrar Straus Giroux)

1986: **The Polar Express** by Chris Van Allsburg (Houghton Mifflin Co.)

1985: **Saint George and the Dragon**, illustrated by Trina Schart Hyman; text retold by Margaret Hodges (Little, Brown & Co.)

1984: **The Glorious Flight: Across the Channel** with Louis Bleriot by Alice and Martin Provensen (Viking)

1983: **Shadow**, translated and illustrated by Marcia Brown; original text in French by Blaise Cendrars (Scribner)

1982: **Jumanji** by Chris Van Allsburg (Houghton Mifflin Co.)

1981: **Fables** by Arnold Lobel (Harper)

1980: **Ox-Cart Man**, illustrated by Barbara Cooney; text by Donald Hall (Viking)

1979: **The Girl Who Loved Wild Horses** by Paul Goble (Bradbury Press)

1978: **Noah's Ark** by Peter Spier (Doubleday)

1977: **Ashanti to Zulu: African Traditions**, illustrated by Leo & Diane Dillon; text by Margaret Musgrove (Dial Books)

1976: **Why Mosquitoes Buzz in People's Ears,** illustrated by Leo & Diane Dillon; text retold by Verna Aardema (Dial Books)

1975: **Arrow to the Sun** by Gerald McDermott (Viking)

1974: **Duffy and the Devil**, illustrated by Margot Zemach; retold by Harve Zemach (Farrar Straus Giroux)

1973: **The Funny Little Woman**, illustrated by Blair Lent; text retold by Arlene Mosel (Dutton)

1972: **One Fine Day**, retold and illustrated by Nonny Hogrogian (Macmillan)

1971: **A Story A Story** retold and illustrated by Gail E. Haley (Atheneum)

1970: **Sylvester and the Magic Pebble** by William Steig (Windmill Books)

1969: **The Fool of the World and the Flying Ship**, illustrated by Uri Shulevitz; text retold by Arthur Ransome (Farrar Straus Giroux)

CALDECOTT BOOKS CONTINUED

1968: **Drummer Hoff,** illustrated by Ed Emberley; text adapted by Barbara Emberley (Prentice-Hall)

1967: **Sam, Bangs & Moonshine** by Evaline Ness (Henry Holt & Co.)

1966: **Always Room for One More,** illustrated by Nonny Hogrogian; text by Sorche Nic Leodhas, pseud. [Leclair Alger] (Henry Holt & Co.)

1965: **May I Bring a Friend?** illustrated by Beni Montresor; text by Beatrice Schenk de Regniers (Atheneum)

1964: **Where the Wild Things Are** by Maurice Sendak (Harper)

1963: **The Snowy Day** by Ezra Jack Keats (Viking)

1962: **Once a Mouse** retold and illustrated by Marcia Brown (Scribner)

1961: **Baboushka and the Three Kings,** illustrated by Nicolas Sidjakov; text by Ruth Robbins (Parnassus)

1960: **Nine Days to Christmas,** illustrated by Marie Hall Ets; text by Marie Hall Ets and Aurora Labastida (Viking)

1959: **Chanticleer and the Fox,** illustrated by Barbara Cooney; text adapted from Chaucer's *Canterbury Tales* by Barbara Cooney (Crowell)

1958: **Time of Wonder** by Robert McCloskey (Viking)

1957: **A Tree Is Nice,** illustrated by Marc Simont; text by Janice Udry (Harper)

1956: **Frog Went a-Courtin',** illustrated by Feodor Rojankovsky; text retold by John Langstaff) (Harcourt Brace Jovanovich)

1955: **Cinderella, or the Little Glass Slipper,** illustrated by Marcia Brown; text translated from Charles Perrault by Marcia Brown (Scribner)

1954: **Madeline's Rescue** by Ludwig Bemelmans (Viking)

1953: **The Biggest Bear** by Lynd Ward (Houghton Mifflin Co.)

1952: **Finders Keepers,** illustrated by Nicolas, pseud. (Nicholas Mordvinoff); text by Will, pseud. [William Lipkind] (Harcourt Brace Jovanovich)

1951: **The Egg Tree** by Katherine Milhous (Scribner)

1950: **Song of the Swallows** by Leo Politi (Scribner)

1949: **The Big Snow** by Berta and Elmer Hader (Macmillan)

1948: **White Snow, Bright Snow,** illustrated by Roger Duvoisin; text by Alvin Tresselt (Lothrop, Lee & Shepard)

1947: **The Little Island,** illustrated by Leonard Weisgard; text by Golden MacDonald, pseud. [Margaret Wise Brown] (Doubleday)

1946: **The Rooster Crows** by Maude and Miska Petersham (Macmillan)

1945: **Prayer for a Child,** illustrated by Elizabeth Orton Jones; text by Rachel Field (Macmillan)

1944: **Many Moons,** illustrated by Louis Slobodkin; text by James Thurber (Harcourt Brace Jovanovich)

1943: **The Little House** by Virginia Lee Burton (Houghton Mifflin Co.)

1942: **Make Way for Ducklings** by Robert McCloskey (Viking)

1941: **They Were Strong and Good,** by Robert Lawson (Viking)

CALDECOTT BOOKS CONTINUED

1940: **Abraham Lincoln** by Ingri and Edgar Parin d'Aulaire (Doubleday)

1939: **Mei Li** by Thomas Handforth (Doubleday)

1938: **Animals of the Bible, A Picture Book,** illustrated by Dorothy P. Lathrop; text selected by Helen Dean Fish (Lippincott)

MULTIMEDIA

 ### CD-ROM:

Polar Express (CD-ROM adaptation of Chris Van Allsburg's book). HMI, 1997.

 ### VIDEOS:

Abraham Lincoln. Spoken Arts, 1987.

Drummer Hoff. Weston Woods, 1969.

Ezra Jack Keats Library. Weston Woods, 1992.

Fables. SRA School Group, 1985.

Frog Went a-Courtin'. Weston Woods, 1961.

Glorious Flight. Live Oak Media, 1987.

Jumanji. SRA School Group, 1987.

Make Way for Ducklings. Weston Woods, 1991.

Maurice Sendak. Weston Woods, 1992.

Noah's Ark (Stories to Remember). Lightyear, 1989.

Officer Buckle and Gloria. Scholastic, 1997.

Owl Moon. Weston Woods, 1993.

Ox-Cart Man. Live Oak Media, 1988.

Paddle to the Sea. Lightyear, 1966.

Polar Express. SRA School Group, 1987.

Sam, Bangs & Moonshine. Random House Video, 1986.

Song and Dance Man. SRA School Group, 1989.

Sylvester and the Magic Pebble. Weston Woods, 1990.

Time of Wonder. Weston Woods, 1991.

Tuesday. SRA School Group, 1992

 ## WEB SITES

Caldecott Medal Home Page
www.ala.org/alsc/caldecott.html

Caldecott Medal (Children's Literature Web Guide)
www.acs6.acs.ucalgary.ca/~dkbrown/caldecott.html

➤ *SEE ALSO THIS RELATED PATHFINDER*

Newbery Awards

California Gold Rush

In 1848 gold was discovered at the sawmill of John A. Sutter in California. This discovery created a migration of settlers and gold prospectors from around the world. Some settlers came by sea, but many were American pioneers, traveling west across the American continent.

DEWEY DECIMAL CALL NUMBERS

978 Western United States
979.4 Great Basin & Pacific Slope region
917.94 Geography and travel, United States

SEARCH TERMS

Gold rush
California gold discoveries
California history, 1846-1850
Gold mines
Westward expansion
Frontier and pioneer life, Western United States
Western United States

NONFICTION/REFERENCE BOOKS

The California Gold Rush (Cornerstones of Freedom) by Richard Conrad Stein. Children's Press, 1995.

The California Gold Rush (World History Series) by Tom Ito. Lucent Books, 1998.

The California Gold Rush: West With the Forty-Niners (A First Book) by Elizabeth Van Steenwyk. Franklin Watts, 1991.

Gold Fever! (Step into Reading) by Catherine McMorrow. Random House, 1996.

The Gold Rush by Liza Ketchum. Little, Brown & Co., 1996.

The Gold Rush of 1849: Staking a Claim in California (Spotlight on American History) by Arthur Blake and Pamela Dailey. Millbrook Press, 1995.

Striking It Rich: The Story of the California Gold Rush (Ready-To-Read) by Stephen Krensky, illustrated by Anna Divito. Simon & Schuster Books for Young Readers, 1996.

FICTION

The Ballad of Lucy Whipple by Karen Cushman. HarperCollins Juvenile Books, 1998.
Boom Town by Sonia Levitin. Orchard Books, 1998.
By the Great Horn Spoon! by Sid Fleischman. Little, Brown & Co., 1988.
California Gold Rush: Search for Treasure (Adventures in Frontier America) by Catherine E. Chambers. Troll Assoc., 1998.
Carrie's Gold (American Dreams) by Cheryl Zach. Avon Flare, 1997.
Treasure In the Stream: The Story of a Gold Rush Girl by Dorothy and Thomas Hoobler. Silver Burdett Press, 1991.

MULTIMEDIA
 VIDEOS:

New Nation/Expansionism [Laser disc] (U.S. History collection). Schlessinger, 1997.
Adventures of the Old West—49ers and the California Gold Rush. U.S. News & World Report, 1994.
Settlement of the United States—Gold Rush and Settlement of California. Encyclopaedia Britannica, 1990.
United States Expansion (American History for Children). Schlessinger, 1996.

 WEB SITES

And the Rush Was On... California Gold Rush (Good, simple illustrated history of the gold rush)
www.sjmercury.com/goldrush/
Gold Rush History (Good information, documented, easy to read)
www.malakoff.com/gorh.htm
The Great American Gold Rush (Has a hyper-linked time line of the gold rush)
www.acusd.edu/~jross/goldrush.html

➤ SEE ALSO THESE RELATED PATHFINDERS
Pioneer Life; Westward Expansion

California Missions

During the late 1700s and early 1800s Spain sought to occupy the Pacific Coastal area now know as California. Taking advantage of the religious fervor of the Franciscan religious order, Spaniards built 21 missions ranging up the coast from San Diego (1769) to Sonoma (1823). Each mission was built a day's journey apart. The missions were founded by the Franciscan Father Junipero Serra, and they were intended to be used to convert the native Indian population in the area to the Christian faith. In addition, they became centers of agricultural and cultural development. Most of the original missions have been preserved and are now historical landmarks.

DEWEY DECIMAL CALL NUMBERS

979.4 California Missions
979 Pacific Coast states (Pacific Slope region)

SEARCH TERMS

California missions
Missions, California history
Spanish mission buildings
Spanish colonialism
California history to 1846
Junipero Serra (1713-1784)
Missionaries
Diegueno Indians, missions
Franciscan missions of California (18th century)

NONFICTION/REFERENCE BOOKS

The California Missions by Elizabeth Van Steenwyk. Franklin Watts, 1995.

California Missions Fact Cards. Toucan Valley Pub., 1995.

Never Turn Back: Father Serra's Mission (Stories of America) by Jim Rawls. Raintree/Steck Vaughn, 1993.

The Story of Junipero Serra: Brave Adventurer (Famous Lives) by Florence Meiman White. Gareth Stevens Pub., 1996.

Missions of the Southern Coast (California Missions) by Nancy Lemke. Lerner Pub. Co., 1996.

FICTION

Song of the Swallow by Leo Politi. Scribner, 1949.

MULTIMEDIA

VIDEO:

Mormon Trail and California's Mission Trail (America's Historic Trails). Questar, 1997.

WEB SITES

Junipero Serra and the California Missions (Some good information, but no documentation) www.home.earthlink.net/~foghorn1/

California Missions Interactive (An Internet Field Trip, actually a report from two cyclists who toured the Missions. Informative, asks good questions, has Q&A section with a fourth grade class [under construction]) www.tsoft.net/~cmi/

California Mission Internet Trail (Hyper-linked map, informative, includes teacher resources) www.escusd.k12.ca.us/MissionTrail.html

California Missions (Looks like a personal site, but good overview of history) www.geocities.com/TheTropics/6788/missions.html

California Missions Web Site (Links to brief informative screens—basic facts—on all missions, using a map to point and click) www.bgmm.com/missions/

Careers

A career is a chosen pursuit, profession, or occupation. People choose careers based on their personal interests. There are many different types of careers in many different fields, such as sports, business, science, design, performance, or politics.

DEWEY DECIMAL CALL NUMBERS

331   Labor economics
331.7   Choice of vocation
370.11   Vocational training

SEARCH TERMS

Careers
Occupation
Vocation
Vocational guidance
Search by names of career, for example:
Fashion designer

NONFICTION/REFERENCE BOOKS

There are also several career book series appropriate for this age group, including: Benchmark's **If You Were A...**, Harcourt's **I Want to be a..., Our Neighborhood** by Children's Press, Crestwood House's **Now Hiring**, and Troll's **What's it like to be a...**

Career as a Video Game Designer by Bill Lund. Capstone Press, 1998.

Career Discovery Encyclopedia. Ferguson Pub., 1997.

Choosing a Career in Law Enforcement by Claudine G. Wirths.
Rosen Pub. Group, 1997.

Choosing a Career in Transportation by Bruce McGlothlin.
Rosen Pub. Group, 1997.

CLICK!: A Story of George Eastman by Barbara Mitchell. Carolrhoda Books, 1986.

Doctors Help People by Amy Moses. Child's World, 1997.

I'm Gonna Be... by Wade Hudson. Just Us Books, 1992.

Pilots Fly Planes by Fay Robinson. Child's World, 1997.

You Can Be A Woman Engineer by Judith Cohen. Cascade Press, 1992.

You Can Be A Woman Zoologist by Valerie Thompson. Cascade Press, 1992.

FICTION

Pig Pig Gets a Job by David McPhail. Dutton Children's Books, 1990.

Broadway Chicken by Jean-Luc Fromental. Hyperion, 1995.

Jeffrey Lee, Future Fireman by Marcia Leonard. Silver Press, 1990.

Mr. Griggs' Work by Cynthia Rylant. Orchard Books, 1989.

Newton, Nell, and Barney: Someday I Want to Be— by Virginia Esquinaldo. Barron's, 1993.

No-job Dad by James Hiram Malone. Victory Press, 1992.

On the Road with Poppa Whopper by Marianne Busser and Ron Schroder. North-South Books, 1995.

Richard Scarry's Busy Workers by Richard Scarry. Western Pub. Co., 1987.

While You are Asleep by Gwynne L. Isaacs. Walker & Co., 1991.

Worksong by Gary Paulsen. Harcourt Brace & Co., 1997.

MULTIMEDIA

CD-ROMS:

Eyewitness Children's Encyclopedia. Dorling Kindersley, 1997.

I Can Be an Animal Doctor. Cloud 9 Interactive, 1995.

World Book Multimedia Encyclopedia. World Book, 1997.

You Can Be A Woman Engineer Interactive. Cascade Press, 1997.

You Can Be A Woman Marine Biologist Interactive. Cascade Press, 1997.

VIDEOS:

The Cat in the Hat; Maybe you should fly a jet! Maybe you should be a vet! Random House Home Video, 1997. (Second segment of video is a rhyme about career choices)

First Look At Careers. Meridian Education, 1991.

How to Be a Ballerina. Sony Wonder, 1995.

Welcome to Math: You Gotta Start Somewhere. PBS Video, 1995.

What Do You Want to be When You Grow Up? (Series). Tapeworm, 1995.

Work (Adventures from *The Book of Virtues*). PBS/Turner Home Video, 1996.

WEB SITE

Kids and Careers Web Site
www.bcit.tec.nj.us/childcareer/default.htm

➤ SEE ALSO THESE RELATED PATHFINDERS

Biographies; Explorers & Exploration; Famous People; Famous Women; Inventors; Sports

Cherokee Indians

The Cherokee Indians are a Native American people who originally lived in the southern Appalachian Mountains from the western Carolinas and eastern Tennessee to northern Georgia. They hunted and farmed, growing corn, squash, and beans. Today, many Cherokee live in northeast Oklahoma and western North Carolina.

DEWEY DECIMAL CALL NUMBERS

970.1   Indians of North America
970.004 History, North America (1800-1900)
394   Customs
398.2   Folk literature
973   History, United States
975   Southeastern United States

SEARCH TERMS

Cherokee Indians
Indians of North America
Indians of North America, Southern States
Sequoyah, 1770?-1843
Cherokee Indians folklore
Cherokee Indians rites and ceremonies
Cherokee Indians social life and customs
Trail of Tears, 1838

NONFICTION/REFERENCE BOOKS

The Cherokee (A New True Book) by Emilie U. Lepthien. Children's Press, 1985.

The Cherokee Indians (The Junior Library of American Indians) by Nicole Claro. Chelsea House, 1992.

The Cherokees (A First Americans Book) by Virginia Driving Hawk Sneve. Holiday House, 1996.

Itse Selu: Cherokee Harvest Festival by Dan Pennington. Charlesbridge Pub., 1994.

Only the Names Remain: The Cherokees and the Trail of Tears by Alex W. Bealer. Little, Brown & Co., 1996.

The Trail of Tears (Cornerstones of Freedom) by R. Conrad Stein. Children's Press, 1993.

Wilma Mankiller by Linda Lowery. Carolrhoda Books, 1996.

FICTION

Ahyoka and the Talking Leaving by Peter and Connie Roop.
Lothrop, Lee & Shepard, 1994.

The First Strawberries: A Cherokee Story retold by Joseph Bruchac.
Dial Books for Young Readers, 1993.

How Rabbit Tricked Otter: And Other Cherokee Trickster Stories by Gayle Ross.
HarperCollins, 1994.

On the Long Trail Home by Elisabeth Jane Stewart. Clarion Books, 1994.

The Story of the Milky Way: A Cherokee Tale by Joseph Bruchac and Gayle Ross.
Dial Books for Young Readers, 1995.

MULTIMEDIA

 ### VIDEOS:

Cherokee (Indians of North America). Schlessinger, 1993.
People of the Forest (Native Americans). Rainbow Educational Video, 1994.

 ## WEB SITE

The Cherokee Nation
www.powersource.com/powersource/
nation/default.html

➤ SEE ALSO THIS RELATED PATHFINDER

Native Americans

China

China is a country of eastern Asia. It has the world's largest population and is the world's third largest country. Shanghai is its largest city. Since 1949, China has been divided, with two governing bodies and two capital cities: The People's Republic of China, whose capital is Beijing; and The Republic of China, whose capital is Nanking, on Taiwan. China has the longest continuous history of any nation and is especially known for its highly advanced ancient civilization. China is also known for its landmark, The Great Wall.

 DEWEY DECIMAL CALL NUMBERS

951 China
931 Ancient China
950 Asia

 SEARCH TERMS

China
Taiwan
Chinese
Asia
Communist China
Imperial China
Great Wall of China

 NONFICTION/REFERENCE BOOKS

Ancient China by Judith Simpson. Time-Life Books, 1996.

Cat and Rat: The Legend of the Chinese Zodiac by Ed Young. Henry Holt & Co., 1995.

China by David Flint. Raintree/Steck Vaughn, 1994.

China, the Culture by Bobbie Kalman. Crabtree Pub. Co., 1989.

The Great Wall of China by Leonard Everett Fisher. Macmillan, 1986.

Growing up in Ancient China by Ken Teague. Troll Assoc., 1994.

Learning from the Dalai Lama: Secrets of the Wheel of Time by Karen Pandell. Dutton, 1995.

The Little Lama of Tibet by Lois Raimondo. Scholastic, 1994.

Made in China: Ideas and Inventions from Ancient China by Suzanne Williams. Pacific View, 1996.

The Silk Route: 7,000 Miles of History by John S. Major. HarperCollins, 1995.

FICTION

The Ch'i-lin Purse: a Collection of Ancient Chinese Stories (retold by Linda Fang). Farrar Straus Giroux, 1994.

Lon Po Po: a Red-Riding Hood Story from China by Ed Young. Philomel Books, 1989.

The Seven Chinese Brothers by Margaret Mahy. Scholastic, 1990.

Two of Everything: A Chinese Folktale by Lily Toy Hong. Albert Whitman & Co., 1993.

MULTIMEDIA

CD-ROMS:

Asia Alive. Queue, 1994.

Ancient Civilizations. India and China Interactive Multimedia. National Geographic Society, 1996.

China: Home of the Dragon. Orange Cherry New Media, [nd].

Rand McNally Children's World Atlas. GameTek, 1995.

Rand McNally Quick Reference Atlas. Rand McNally, 1995.

Eyewitness Children's Encyclopedia. DK Multimedia, 1997.

The First Emperor of China. Voyager, 1994.

VIDEOS:

Children of Other Lands (Part II). United Learning, 1987. (Daily life of children in China and other countries)

Homesick: My Own Story. SRA School Group, 1991.

Introducing East Asia. Educational Video Network, 1993.

WEB SITES

China Today (Information on contemporary China)
www.chinatoday.com/

Art of China Homepage
www.pasture.ecn.purdue.edu/%7Eagenhtml/agenmc/china/china.html

➤ SEE ALSO THIS RELATED PATHFINDER

Ancient Civilizations

Christmas Around the World

Christmas is a Christian festival celebrating the birth of Jesus. Christmas Day is on December 25. However, the entire Christmas season occurs during the months of December and early January. There are many customs and traditions for this seasonal celebration that vary from country to country. The customs of the yule log, caroling, mistletoe, and gifts at Christmas are English. In other countries, gifts are given at other times, as at Epiphany or Three Kings Day in Spain and Mexico, respectively. The Christmas tree was first a medieval German tradition that later spread to America. Christmas cards and the image of a jolly Santa Claus first appeared in New York City in the 19th century. Many people go to church as part of their Christmas celebration, while others regard Christmas as a special winter celebration and a time to be with their families.

DEWEY DECIMAL CALL NUMBERS

394.2 Holidays
226.4 Jesus Christ—Nativity

SEARCH TERMS

Christmas
Social life and customs
Search for Christmas by region, for example: Christmas Mexico

NONFICTION/REFERENCE BOOKS

Christmas Around the World by Emily Kelley. Carolrhoda Books, 1986.

Christmas Around the World by Mary D. Lankford. Morrow Junior Books, 1995.

Christmas in England (Christmas Around the World) by Cheryl L. Endelein. Hilltop Books, 1998.

Christmas in Mexico (Christmas Around the World) by Cheryl L. Endelein. Hilltop Books, 1998.

Christmas in the Big House, Christmas in the Quarters by Patricia McKissack. Scholastic, 1994.

Christmas in the Philippines (Christmas Around the World) by Cheryl L. Endelein. Hilltop Books, 1998.

Christmas in Brazil (Christmas Around the World from World Book Series). World Book, 1991. Regions and publication dates for Christmas Around the World from World Book series: **Britain** (1996), **Canada** (1994), **Denmark** (1986), **France** (1996), **Ireland** (1996), **Italy** (1996), **Mexico** (1996), **Russia** (1992), **Spain** (1996), **Switzerland** (1995), **American Southwest** (1996), **Holy Land** (1987), **Philippines** (1990), **Today's Germany** (1993), **Washington, D.C.** (1988).

The Story of Christmas by Barbara Cooney. HarperCollins, 1995.

What a Morning: The Christmas Story in Black Spirituals (selected by John Langstaff). Aladdin Paperbacks, 1996.

FICTION

Papa's Christmas Gift: Around the World on the Night Before Christmas by Cheryl Harness. Simon & Schuster Books for Young Readers, 1995.

The Bells of Christmas by Virginia Hamilton. Harcourt Brace Jovanovich, 1989.

The Christmas of the Reddle Moon by J. Patrick Lewish.
Dial Books for Young Readers, 1994.

An Early American Christmas by Tomie dePaola. Holiday House, 1987.

Nine Days to Christmas by Marie Hall Ets and Aurora Labastida. Puffin Books, 1991.

O Christmas Tree by Vashanti Rahaman. Boyds Mills Press, 1996.

Too Many Tamales by Gary Soto. G. P. Putnam's Sons, 1993

MULTIMEDIA

CD-ROMS:

Eyewitness Children's Encyclopedia. Dorling Kindersley, 1996.

The Polar Express Interactive Multimedia. HMI, 1997.

Richard Scarry's Busytown: Best Christmas Ever. 1998.

World Book Multimedia Encyclopedia. 1998.

VIDEOS:

Charlie Brown Christmas. Paramount Home Video, 1965.

Christmas (Holidays for Children). Schlessinger, 1994.

Christmas Carol. MGM/UA, 1951. (Alastair Sims as Scrooge; best film version, but colorized)

Christmas in America: A Great Grandmother Remembers. Chip Taylor Prod., 1996.

Christmas in Spain. Gessler Pub. Co., 1988.

Elmo Saves Christmas. Sony Wonder, 1996.

Multicultural Christmas. United Learning, 1993.

Savior is Born. Rabbit Ears, 1992.

Story of the Nativity. Sony Wonder, 1995.

WEB SITES

Christmas Around the World
www.peders.com/christmas/christmas.html

Holidays Around the World (Information, songs, and recipes)
www.santasworkshop.org/language1.html

Merry Christmas (An Advent calendar of Christmas traditions created by students)
www.algonet.se/~bernadot/christmas/calendar.html

Santa's Favorites: Around the World
www.santas.net/aroundtheworld.htm

WorldView Christmas: Christmas Around the World
www.christmas.com/christmas.html

➤ *SEE ALSO THIS RELATED PATHFINDER*
Holidays Around the World

Civil War, American

The American Civil War was fought from 1861 to 1865, during the presidency of Abraham Lincoln. It was a conflict that originated when 11 Southern states withdrew from the Union of the United States. The Southern states were organized as the Confederate States of America and the Northern states continued to be called the Union. There were many factors that fueled the conflict between the North and the South, but the most significant issue was the Southern state's dependence on slavery.

 DEWEY DECIMAL CALL NUMBERS

973.7   United States History ,Civil War, 1861-1865
973.8   Reconstruction

 SEARCH TERMS

Civil War
American Civil War
United States history
Battle of Antietam (Md.), 1862
Battle of Chancellorsville (Va.), 1863
Battle of Gettysburg (Pa.), 1863
Abraham Lincoln
Presidents
Slavery
Reconstruction
Search by names of specific figures, for example: Robert E. Lee

 NONFICTION/REFERENCE BOOKS

Abraham Lincoln: Sixteenth President of the United States by Jim Hargrove. Children's Press, 1988.

The Battle of Antietam (Cornerstones of Freedom) by Zachary Kent. Children's Press, 1992.

The Battle of Chancellorsville (Cornerstones of Freedom) by Zachary Kent. Children's Press, 1994.

Civil War by Martin W. Sandler. HarperCollins, 1996.

The Day Fort Sumter Was Fired On: A Photo History of the Civil War by Jim Haskins. Scholastic, 1995.

Honest Abe by Edith Kunhardt (Malcah Zeldis, Ill.). Greenwillow Books, 1993.

If You Lived at the Time of the Civil War by Kay Moore. Scholastic, 1994.

Gettysburg by Catherine Reef. Dillon Press, 1992.

From Slave to Civil War Hero: The Life and Times of Robert Smalls by Michael L. Cooper. Lodestar Books, 1994.

FICTION

The Blue and the Gray by Eve Bunting. Scholastic, 1996.

Cecil's Story by George Ella Lyon. Orchard Books, 1991.

Culpepper's Cannon by Gary Paulsen. Dell, 1992.

Emma Eileen Grove: Mississippi, 1865 by Kathleen Duey. Aladdin Paperbacks, 1996.

Pink and Say by Patricia Polacco. Philomel Books, 1994.

Sally Bradford: The Story of a Rebel Girl by Dorothy and Thomas Hoobler. Silver Burdett Press, 1997.

Shades of Gray by Carolyn Reeder. Avon, 1991, c1989.

Thunder at Gettysburg by Patricia Lee Gauch. Bantam Books, 1991, c1975.

MULTIMEDIA

 ### CD-ROMS:

The Civil War Interactive Multimedia. National Geographic Society, 1996.

Fateful Lightning: A Narrative History of the Civil War by David Inglehart. Troubador Interactive, 1998.

African-American History Interactive Multimedia: Slavery to Civil Rights. Queue, 1995.

American Heritage History of the United States for Young People. Simon & Schuster, [nd].

 ### VIDEOS:

American Civil War Series. United Learning, 1996.

A&E Biography (series). **Abraham Lincoln** (1997); **Stonewall Jackson** (1998); **Robert E. Lee** (1998). A&E Entertainment.

Causes of the Civil War (United States History). Schlessinger, 1996.

Civil War (United States History). Schlessinger, 1996.

The Civil War (Video series) by Ken Burns. PBS Video, 1991.

 ## WEB SITES

American Civil War Ethnographithy (Examines the culture that existed in the United States during the Civil War Era, with links)
www.concentic.net/~tcaswell/cw/home.html

The American Civil War Homepage (Goods links and access to primary sources)
www.sunsite.utk.edu/civil-war/

American History Sources for Students (Civil War page)
www.cl.ais.net/jkasper/civwar.html

➤ **SEE ALSO THESE RELATED PATHFINDERS**

Black History in America; U.S. Presidents; War

Clouds

Clouds give us the best clues about our weather. They can indicate if it will be a warm, dry day or a stormy one. Clouds are made primarily of water droplets that form as rising air cools and condenses. There are three basic types of clouds: cumulus, stratus, and cirrus.

 DEWEY DECIMAL CALL NUMBERS

551.5   Meteorology
551.48   Hydrologic cycle

 SEARCH TERMS

Clouds
Meteorology
Weather
Hydrologic cycle
Precipitation

 NONFICTION/REFERENCE BOOKS

The Cloud Book by Tomie de Paola. Holiday House, 1975.

Down Comes the Rain (Let's-Read-And-Find-Out Science. Stage 2) by Franklyn. M. Branley. HarperCollins, 1997.

Experiments with Weather by Miranda Bower. Lerner Pub. Co., 1994.

How's the Weather?: A Look at Weather and How it Changes (Discovery Readers) by Melvin and Gilda Berger. Chelsea House, 1998.

Rain & Hail (Let's-Read-And-Find-Out Science) by Frankly M. Branley. Crowell, 1983.

Water Up, Water Down: The Hydrologic Cycle by Sally M. Walker. Carolrhoda Books, 1992.

Weather (Eyewitness Explorers) by John Farndon. Dorling Kindersley, 1992.

Weather (Discoveries Library) by Sally Morgan. Time-Life Books, 1996.

What Makes It Rain?: The Story of a Raindrop by Keith Brandt. Troll Assoc., 1982.

Where Do Puddles Go? (Rookie Read-About Science) by Fay Robinson. Children's Press, 1995.

FICTION

Cloud Nine by Norman Silver. Clarion Books, 1995.

Cloudland by John Burningham. Crown, 1996.

Little Cloud by Eric Carle. Philomel Books, 1996.

Water Dance by Thomas Locker. Harcourt Brace & Co., 1997.

The Magic School Bus Wet All Over: A Book About the Water Cycle by Pat Relf. Scholastic, 1996.

MULTIMEDIA

CD-ROM:

Introduction to Science Interactive Multimedia. Queue, 1997.

VIDEOS:

Clouds (Now I Know). Troll Assoc., 1993.

Precipitation (2nd Ed.) Understanding Weather. Coronet/MTI/Centron, 1992.

Atmosphere in Motion (Exploring Weather). United Learning, 1993.

Weather (Eyewitness). Dorling Kindersley, 1996.

Investigating Weather. United Learning, 1995.

Magic School Bus Kicks Up a Storm. Kid Vision, 1995.

What Makes the Weather (Know I Know). Troll Assoc., 1988.

WEB SITES

The Cloud Catalogue—Univ. of Illinois
www.covis.atmos.uiuc.edu/guide/clouds/html/cloud.home.html

The Cloud Boutique - Plymouth State College Weather Center
www.vortex.plymouth.edu/cloud.html

➤ SEE ALSO THESE RELATED PATHFINDERS
Hurricanes; Natural Disasters; Weather

Colonial Life, American

Colonists are a group of emigrants or their descendants who settle in a distant territory but remain under the rule of the country they came from. American colonists came from England in the 1600s and settled the Atlantic coastal areas of America. The customs, artisanship, and ideals of the American colonialist were shaped by their British heritage, their pioneer spirit, and the hardships of living in a new land.

200s 300s 400s DEWEY DECIMAL CALL NUMBERS

973.2   United States history, Colonial period, ca. 1600-1775 sources

973.2   United States social life and customs to 1775

398.2   Folklore, United States

390   Customs, etiquette, folklore

641   Cookery, American

972.3   United States History French and Indian War, 1755-1763

974   Northeastern United States

SEARCH TERMS

United States history, 1600-1750
Colonial Period
Thirteen Colonies
Colonialism
Frontier life
Pioneer life
America discovery and exploration

NONFICTION/REFERENCE BOOKS

Colonial Life by Bobbie Kalman. Crabtree Pub. Co., c1992.

Life in the Thirteen Colonies, 1650-1750 by Stuart Kallen. Abdo & Daughters, c1990.

If You Lived in Colonial Times by Ann McGovern. Scholastic, 1992.

African-Americans in the Thirteen Colonies (Cornerstones of Freedom) by Deborah Kent. Children's Press, 1996.

Colonial American Home Life (Colonial America) by John F. Warner. Franklin Watts, 1993.

Growing Up in Colonial America (American Children) by Tracy Barrett. Millbrook Press, 1995.

If You Grew Up With George Washington by Ruth Belov Gross. Scholastic Professional, 1993.

If You Lived in Colonial Times by Ann McGovern. Scholastic, 1992.

Making Thirteen Colonies by Joy Hakim. Oxford University Press, c1993.

A Nation Is Born: Rebellion and Independence in America, 1700-1820 by Richard Steins. Twenty First Century Books, 1993.

FICTION

Ben and Me: A New and Astonishing Life of Benjamin Franklin As Written by His Good Mouse Amos by Robert Lawson. Little, Brown & Co., 1988.

The Courage of Sarah Noble by Alice Dagliesh. Aladdin Books, 1954.

People of the Breaking Day by Marcia Sewall. Atheneum, 1990.

The Printer's Apprentice by Stephen Krensky. Bantam Books Doubleday Dell, 1996.

The Serpent Never Sleeps: A Novel of Jamestown by Scott O'Dell. Houghton Mifflin Co., 1980.

Witch of Blackbird Pond by Elizabeth Speare. Houghton Mifflin Co., 1958.

Witches' Children: A Story of Salem by Patricia Clapp. Puffin Books, 1987.

MULTIMEDIA

CD-ROMS:

American Heritage History of the United States for Young People. Simon & Schuster, 1996.

Colonial America Interactive Multimedia. National Geographic Society, 1997.

Colony Quest. Decision Development Corp., 1996.

Life in Colonial America. Queue, 1995.

PilgrimQuest II. Decision Development Corp., 1997.

VIDEOS:

American History for Children (Video series for K-4). Schlessinger, 1996.

Colonial Life for Children Video (series). Schlessinger, 1998.

Colonizing North America: Early Settlements. Encyclopedia Britannica, 1990.

Colonial and Founding Period. Encyclopaedia Britannica, 1990.

Lost Colony of Roanoke. A&E Entertainment, 1998.

Johnny Tremain. Walt Disney, 1994.

A&E Biography (series). **Benedict Arnold** (1998); **Biography: Thomas Jefferson— Philosopher of Freedom** (1996); **George Washington** (1995); **Patrick Henry** (1998); **Paul Revere** (1996). A&E Entertainment.

Where America Began: Jamestown, Colonial Williamsburg, Yorktown (History in America) American Heritage. Holiday Films, 1988.

WEB SITES

Archiving Early America (Historic Documents from colonial America including Ben Franklin's autobiography and newspapers from the 1750s. Great for primary source materials) www.earlyamerica.com/

Life of Washington (Information about his slaves, tour of Mt. Vernon, images of Washington—a little wordy, but very informative) www.mountvernon.org/education/

Internet resources about Colonial America from the Madison Metropolitan School District www.danenet.wicip.org/mmsd-it/ colonialamerica.html

On-Line Guide and Resources for the PBS Series: Liberty—The American Revolution. (Includes time lines, historic documents, and illustrations) www.pbs.org/ktca/liberty/

> ## ➤ SEE ALSO THESE RELATED PATHFINDERS
Pilgrims; Revolutionary War, American; Thirteen Colonies

Color

How we see color is determined by how the human eye perceives different lengths of light waves. The primary colors of the light spectrum are red, orange, yellow, green, blue, indigo, and violet. In painting, the primary colors are red, yellow, and blue. These three colors are mixed to create the secondary colors, orange, green, and violet. Black, white, and gray are called achromatic colors.

DEWEY DECIMAL CALL NUMBERS

535 Visible light
701 Fine art, Philosophy and theory, Color

SEARCH TERMS

Color
Color theory
Color experiments
Light

NONFICTION/REFERENCE BOOKS

Of Colors and Things by Tana Hoban. Greenwillow Books, 1989.

Chidi Only Likes Blue: An African Book of Colors by Ifeoma Onyefula. Cobblehill Books, 1997.

A Color Sampler by Kathleen Westray. Ticknor & Fields, 1993.

Naming Colors by Ariane Dewey. HarperCollins, 1995.

The Science Book of Color by Neil Ardley. Harcourt Brace Jovanovich, 1991.

The Nature and Science of Colors by Jane Burton. Gareth Stevens Pub., 1998.

Color (Scholastic Discovery Box) Scholastic Trade, 1997.

The Art of Colors: For Children and Adults by Margaret Steele. Museum of Contemporary Art, 1998.

FICTION

Cat's Colors by Jane Cabrera. Dial Books for Young Readers, 1997.

Color Zoo by Lois Ehlert. Lippincott, 1989.

Frieght Train by Donald Crews. Greenwillow Books, 1978.

Hailstones and Halibut Bones: Adventures in Color by Mary O'Neill. Doubleday, 1989.

I Went Walking by Sue Williams. Harcourt Brace & Co., 1990.

Lunch by Denise Fleming. Henry Holt & Co., 1992.

Mouse Paint by Ellen Stoll Walsh. Harcourt Brace Jovanovich, 1989.

Who Said Red? by Mary Serfozo. Aladdin Books, 1992.

The Magic School Bus Makes a Rainbow: A Book About Color adapted by George Bloom and Jocelyn Stevenson. Scholastic, 1997.

MULTIMEDIA

 ### CD-ROMS:

ArtRageous! Interactive Multimedia: The Amazing World of Art. SoftKey, 1995.

Make a Masterpiece (Crayola). EDMARK, 1998

 ### VIDEOS:

Color and Light (Science in Action). TMW Media Group, 1990.

Color Concepts by Stephan Quiller. Crystal Press., 1998.

Color: Light Fantastic. National Geographic Film & TV, 1988.

Exploring Light and Color. United Learning, 1993.

How Light Changes Colors (Way Things Work). Films for the Humanities, 1988.

 ## WEB SITES

How Light Works
www.curry.edschool.virginia.edu/murray/Light/How_Light_Works.html

Color Perception
www.insteam.com/LauraFunderburk/

Comanche Indians

The Comanche Indians are a North American Indian tribe that lived on the Great Plains from western Kansas to northern Texas. The Comanche Indians are related to the Shoshoni Indians of Wyoming. They were a nomadic tribe who hunted buffalo. Food, clothing, and shelter all came from buffalo. Today, some Comanche live on the Kiowa Reservation in Oklahoma.

DEWEY DECIMAL CALL NUMBERS

970.1 Indians of North America
970.004 History, North America (1800-1900)
973 History, United States
398.2 Folk literature

SEARCH TERMS

Comanche Indians
Indians of North America
Plains Indians
Quanah Parker

NONFICTION/REFERENCE BOOKS

The Comanche by Sally Lodge. Rourke, 1992.

The Comanche Indians by Bill Lund. Bridgestone Books, 1997.

The Comanche Indians by Martin Mooney. Chelsea House, 1993.

The Comanches by Judy Alter. Franklin Watts, 1994.

Encyclopedia of Native American Tribes by Carl Waldman. Facts on File, 1988.

The Encyclopedia of North American Indians. Marshall Cavendish, 1997.

Plains Warrior: Chief Quanah Parker and the Comanches by Albert Marrin. Atheneum Books for Young Readers, 1996.

Quanah Parker, Comanche Warrior by William R. Sanford. Enslow Publishers, 1994.

FICTION

Buffalo Moon by G. Clifton Wisler. Dutton, 1984.

The Legend of the Bluebonnet: An Old Tale of Texas by Tomie dePaola. G. P. Putnam's Sons, 1983.

New Medicine by Jeanne Williams. Hendrick-Long, 1994.

Wait for Me, Watch for Me, Eula Bee by Patricia Beatty. William Morrow & Co., 1978.

Where the Broken Heart Still Beats: The Story of Cynthia Ann Parker by Carolyn Meyer. Harcourt Brace Jovanovich, 1992.

Winter of the Wolf by G. Clifton Wisler. Dutton, 1981.

MULTIMEDIA

VIDEO:

Comanche (Indians of North America). Schlessinger, 1993.

➤ *SEE ALSO THIS RELATED PATHFINDER*
Native Americans

Computers

The first computers, called mainframe computers, were made just over 50 years ago and were so large that one computer would fill an entire room. Today, significant technological developments have produced faster and smaller computers. The electronic digital computers we use now are made with tiny microchips and can fit on a desk or even in the palm of your hand. Computers have transformed society. They influence nearly every aspect of our lives, including how we live, work, play, learn and communicate. There are now more than 50 million personal computers in use all of the world.

200s 300s 400s DEWEY DECIMAL CALL NUMBERS

004.16 Personal computers
004   Computer science
510   Mathematics
519   Probabilities and applied mathematics
629   Branches of engineering
651   Office services

SEARCH TERMS

Computers
Artificial intelligence
Internet
Computer chips

Software
Microsoft
Apple
Virtual reality

NONFICTION/REFERENCE BOOKS

300 Incredible Things for Kids on the Internet by Ken Leebow. Vip Pub., 1998.

The Age of Computers (Young Scientist Series). World Book, 1996.

Alan Turing: The Architect of the Computer Age (Impact Biography) by Ted Gottfried. Franklin Watts, 1996.

The Big Machines (Kids & Computers) by Charles A. Jortberg. Abdo & Daughters, 1997.

Bill Gates: Helping People Use Computers (Community Builders) by Charnan Simon. Children's Press, 1998.

Careers for Computer Buffs (Choices) by Andrew Kaplan. Millbrook Press Trade, 1994.

Communication (Yesterday's Science, Today's Technology) by Robert Gardner. Twenty First Century Books, 1995.

A Computer Dictionary for Kids and Their Parents by Jami Lynne Borman. Barron's Juveniles, 1995.

Computers (20th Century Inventions) by Steve Parker. Raintree/Steck Vaughn, 1997.

Exploring Information Technology (Exploring Science) by John Hill. Raintree/Steck Vaughn, 1993.

The Internet (First Books) by Kerry Cochrane. Franklin Watts, 1995.

The Internet for Kids by Charnan and Tom Kazunas. Children's Press, 1997.

Personal Computers by Charnan and Tom Kazunas. Children's Press, 1997.

The Super Computers (Kids & Computers) by Charles A. Jortberg. Abdo & Daughters, 1997.

The Usborne Computer Dictionary for Beginners (Computer Guides Series) by Anna Claybourne. E D C Pub., 1996.

FICTION

The A.I. Gang: Operation Sherlock by Bruce Coville. Minstrel Books, 1995.

Blackout in the Amazon (Cyber.Kdz, No 4) by Bruce Balan. Camelot, 1997.

The Bumblebee and the Ram by Barry Rudner. Tiny Thought Press, 1990.

Caught in the Net (Ghostwriter) by Nancy Butcher . Bantam Books, 1997.

Computer Club by Debra Schepp, Brad Schepp. Windcrest, 1993.

The Computer Nut by Betsy Cromer Byars. Viking, 1986.

Grandpa's Amazing Computer by Ursel Scheffler. North-South Books, 1997.

A Very Personal Computer by Justine Rendal. HarperCollins Juvenile Books, 1995.

MULTIMEDIA

 ### CD-ROM:

The Way Things Work 2.0. DK Multimedia, 1996.

 ### VIDEOS:

Artificial Intelligence: Mankind's Mind-Child (Great Minds of Science).Unapix Entertainment, 1996.

Beyond the Looking Glass. PBS, 1993.

Computer Specialist (Harriet's Magic Hats). Ivn, 1985.

Computers for Kids. Musa Business Systems, 1991.

Smithsonian World—From Information to Wisdom? Unapix Entertainment, 1996.

 ## WEB SITES

3-D Computer Dictionary
207.136.90.76/dictionary/

Computer Virus Myth
www.kumite.com/myths/

History of Computers (1960-1996)
www.dg.com//about/html/generations.html

Scientific American Bio of Thad Starner (Wearable computers)
www.pbs.org/plweb-cgi/fastweb?getdoc+saf+saf+54+29+wAAA+computers
lcs.www.media.mit.edu/Projects/wearables/

Smithsonian Institute Information Age Exhibit
www.si.edu/resource/tours/comphist/computer.htm#toc1

 **SEE ALSO THIS RELATED PATHFINDER**
Technology

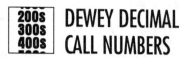

Conflict

Conflict results when two or more people, groups, or nations disagree. Conflict often results in some sort of struggle or fight. When a conflict is between nations or groups of people within a nation, a conflict can result in war. Conflict can be emotional, and anger is a significant element of conflict. The best way to resolve conflict is through talking, negotiating, and constructive problem solving.

DEWEY DECIMAL CALL NUMBERS

200s 300s 400s

152.4 Emotions and feelings
301- 308 Sociology

SEARCH TERMS

Conflict
Conflict management
Conflict resolution
Anger
Bullies
Mediation

NONFICTION/REFERENCE BOOKS

Anger by Laurie Beckelman. Maxwell Macmillan International, 1994.

Dealing with Anger by Marianne Johnston. PowerKids Press, 1996.

Dealing with Bullying by Marianne Johnston. PowerKids Press, 1996.

Everything You Need to Know About Peer Mediation. by Nancy N. Rue. Rosen Pub. Group, 1997.

Make Someone Smile: And 40 More Ways to be a Peaceful Person by Judy Lalli. Free Spirit Pub., 1996.

Peace on the Playground: Nonviolent Ways of Problem-solving by Eileen Lucas. Franklin Watts, 1991.

Why is Everybody Always Picking on Me?: A Guide to Handling Bullies for Young People by Terrence Webster-Doyle. Atrium, 1991.

FICTION

Arthur's April Fool by Marc Brown. Little, Brown & Co., 1995.

The Berenstain Bears and the Bully by Stan and Jan Berenstain. Random House, 1993.

The Berenstain Bears and the Trouble with Friends by Stan & Jan Berenstain. Random House, 1986.

The Bully of Barkham Street by Mary Stolz. Harper & Row, 1985.

I'm Mad by Elizabeth Crary (Dealing With Feelings). Parenting Press, 1992.

It's Great to be Me by Marcia A. Neese. Baker Street Prod., 1984.

Joshua T. Bates in Trouble Again by Susan Shreve. Knopf, 1997.

Monster Boy by Christine Winn. Fairview Press, 1996.

Monster Mama by Liz Rosenberg. Putnam & Grosset Group, 1997.

Painting the Fire by Liz Farrington. Enchante, 1993.

Peace Tales: World Folktales to Talk About by Margaret Read MacDonald. Linnet Books, 1992.

The Rat and the Tiger by Keiko Kasza. Paperstar, 1997.

Smoky Night by Eve Bunting. Harcourt Brace Jovanovich, 1994.

Third Grade Bullies by Elizabeth Levy. Hyperion Books for Children, 1998.

The Three Little Wolves and the Big Bad Pig by Eugene Trivizas. Aladdin Paperbacks, 1993.

The Truth about Cousin Ernie's Head by Matthew McElligott. Simon & Schuster, 1996.

MULTIMEDIA
 ### CD-ROM:
The Berenstain Bears Get in a Fight. Living Books, 1995.

 ### VIDEOS:
The Berenstain Bears and the Trouble with Friends. Goldstar Video Corp., 1992.

Bootsie Barker Bites: Ruby the Copycat (Shelley Duvall's Bedtime Stories). MCA Universal Home Video, 1993.

We Can Work it Out! Conflict Resolution. Sunburst Comm., 1994.

Working it Out. Sunburst Comm., 1992.

 ## WEB SITES

Kid Mediators by Mike Maday
www.context.org/ICLIB/IC38/Maday.htm
Kids Keeping the Peace
www.benjerry.com/esr/kidsindex.html
The People for Peace Conflict Resolution Center
www.members.aol.com/pforpeace/cr/

➤ *SEE ALSO THESE RELATED PATHFINDERS*
Diversity; War

Constellations

A constellation is a group of stars. With the help of your imagination, these groups of stars seem to form pictures. The traditional pictures and names of the constellations were chosen by early astronomers. By naming groups of stars, early astronomers organized and remembered the positions of the stars in the night sky. Perhaps the most well known pair of constellations is the Big Dipper and the Little Dipper, which help us locate the North Star.

 200s 300s 400s DEWEY DECIMAL CALL NUMBERS

523.8 Constellations

520 Astronomy

522 Practical astronomy (observation techniques, telescopes, observatories, etc.)

523 Descriptive astronomy

 SEARCH TERMS

Constellations
Astronomy
Night sky
Stars
Zodiac
Celestial bodies

 NONFICTION/REFERENCE BOOKS

Astronomy by Philip Steele. Crestwood House, 1991.

Astronomy by Graham Peacock and Dennis Ashton. Thomson Learning, 1994.

The Big Dipper by Franklyn M. Branley. HarperCollins, 1991.

Constellations by Diane M. Sipiera. Children's Press, 1997.

Crafts for Kids Who are Wild about Outer Space by Kathy Ross. Millbrook Press, 1997.

Find the Constellations by H. A. Rey. Houghton Mifflin Co., 1976.

The Night Sky (One Small Square) by Donald M Silver. Learning Triangle Press, 1998.

Night Sky by Carole Stott. Dorling Kindersley, 1993.

Orion, the Hunter by Necia H. Apful. Clarion Books, 1995.

Sky: All about Planets, Stars, Galaxies, Eclipses and More by David Allen. Firefly Books, 1993.

A Stargazer's Guide by Isaac Asimov. Gareth Stevens Pub., 1995.

The Starry Sky by Patrick Moore. Copper Beech Books, 1995.

Zoo in the Sky: A Book of Animal Constellations by Jacqueline Mitton. National Geographic Society, 1998.

FICTION

Coyote Places the Stars by Harriet Peck Taylor. Aladdin Books, 1997.

The Heavenly Zoo: Legends and Tales of the Stars by Alison Lurie. Farrar Straus Giroux, 1996.

The Lost Children by Paul Goble. Bradbury Press, 1993.

The Shining Stars: Greek Legends of the Zodiac by Kenneth McLeish. Cambridge University Press, 1989.

Star Shapes by Peter Malone. Chronicle Books, 1997.

MULTIMEDIA

CD-ROMS:

Eyewitness Encyclopedia of Space and the Universe. Dorling Kindersley, 1996.
Vacation to Planet X (Science Sleuths Third Grade Series). MECC, 1997.

VIDEOS:

Astronomy 101 (Children's Science Adventure). Tapeworm, 1994.
Night Sky. Encyclopedia Britannica, 1990.
Stars and Constellations. National Geographic Society, 1993.

WEB SITES

Athena: Space and Astronomy
www.athena.ivv.nasa.gov/curric/space/index.html

Eric's Treasure Trove of Astronomy
www.astro.virginia.edu/%7Eeww6n/astro/astro0.html

Expanding Universe (Search tool for amateur astronomy)
www.mtrl.toronto.on.ca/centres/bsd/astronomy/520.HTM

Izzy's Skylog
www.darkstar.swsc.k12.ar.us/~kwhite/skylog.html

Star Gazer Home Page (From the nationally syndicated PBS program)
www.jackstargazer.com/

➤ **SEE ALSO THESE RELATED PATHFINDERS**
Solar System; Space Travel and Outer Space

Coral Reef

Coral reefs are often called underwater gardens. Corals are tiny, tentacled animals which live in huge groups, or colonies. Millions of corals are grouped together to make a coral reef. Within the caves, cliffs, and valleys of the reef, a variety of sea creatures make their home.

 DEWEY DECIMAL CALL NUMBERS

593.6 Coral

574.5 Biology, Ecology (organisms and their environments)

574.92 Biology, Marine and freshwater

577 General nature of life (conditions needed for life)

578.7789 Microscopy in biology (looking at microscopic organisms)

 SEARCH TERMS

Coral
Coral reef
Ocean ecology
Great Astrolabe Reef (Fiji)
Great Barrier Reef (Australia)
Marine animals
Marine biology

 NONFICTION/REFERENCE BOOKS

A City Under the Sea: Life in a Coral Reef by Norbert Wu. Atheneum Books for Young Readers, 1996.

Coral Reef: A City That Never Sleeps by Mary M. Cerullo. Cobblehill Books, 1996.

Coral Reef (Look Closer) by Barbara Taylor. Dorling Kindersley, 1992.

Coral Reefs (Close Up) by Dwight Holings. Silver Burdett Press, 1995.

The Great Astrolabe Reef (Circle of Life) by Alexandra Siy. Maxwell Macmillan International, 1992.

The Great Barrier Reef (A Vision Book) by Maura Gouck. Child's World, 1993.

A Walk on the Great Barrier Reef (Carolrhoda Books Nature Watch Books) by Caroline Arnold. Carolrhoda Books, 1998.

FICTION

The Sign of the Seahorse: A Tale of Greed and High Adventure in Two Acts by Graeme Base. Harry N. Abrams, 1992.

Baru Bay by Bob Weir and Wendy Weir. Hyperion for Children, 1994.

Coral Reef Hideaway: The Story of a Clown Anemonefish by Doc Boyle. SoundPrints, 1995.

MULTIMEDIA

 CD-ROMS:

Coral Kingdom Interactive Multimedia. Sunburst Communications, 1995.
U*X*L Science. Gale, 1997.

 VIDEOS:

At Home in the Coral Reef. Spoken Arts, 1994.
Living Reef. Bennett Marine Video, 1994.
Reefs. Rainbow Educational Video, 1991.

 WEB SITES

Coral Forest—The Value of Coral Reefs
www.blacktop.com/coralforest/bts.html
Hawai'i Coral Reef Network
www.coralreefs.hawaii.edu/ReefNetwork/frmain.htm
National Oceanic and Atmospheric Administration—International Year of the Coral Reef 1997
www.noaa.gov/public-affairs/coral-reef.html

➤ SEE ALSO THESE RELATED PATHFINDERS

Biomes; Ecology; Sea Animals

Countries

The entire territory of a nation or state is called a country. The word "country" may also refer to all the people who live within this region, especially those people who are native to the area. There are many different counties, each with its own history, form of government, and customs.

DEWEY DECIMAL CALL NUMBERS

200s 300s 400s

910 Geography and travel
930 Ancient history
940 Europe
950 Asia, Far East
960 Africa
970 North America
980 South America
990 Other areas

SEARCH TERMS

Countries
Nations
Geographic regions
Search by names of countries, for example: Ireland

NONFICTION/REFERENCE BOOKS

Canada: The Culture (Lands, Peoples, and Cultures Series) by Bobbie Kalman. Crabtree Pub. Co., 1993. See additional titles in this series **Lands, Peoples, and Culture Series** by Bobbie Kalman, [dates vary].

Children Just Like Me by Barnabas and Anabel Kindersley. Dorling Kindersley, 1995.

The Children of Bolivia (The World's Children) by Jules Hermes. Carolrhoda Books, 1996. See additional titles in this series, authors and dates vary.

Circling the Globe (10-volume set). Raintree/Steck Vaughn, 1995.

Count Your Way Through Africa by Jim Haskins. Carolrhoda Books, 1990. See additional titles in this **Count Your Way Through** series, dates vary.

The DK Geography of the World. Dorling Kindersley, 1996.

I Remember India (Why We Left...) by Anita Ganeri. Raintree/Steck Vaughn, 1995.

Korea by Karen Jacobsen. Children's Press, 1989.

Poland: A Troubled Past, A New Start (Exploring Cultures of the World) by Eleanor Ayer. Benchmark Books, 1996.

FICTION

The Burnt Stick by Anthony Hill. Houghton Mifflin Co., 1995.

From Far Away by Robert Munsch. Annick Press, 1995.

Nine O'clock Lullaby by Marilyn Singer. HarperCollins, 1991.

Sea Maidens of Japan by Lili Bell. Ideals Children's Books, 1996.

Somewhere in the World Right Now by Stacey Schuett. Knopf, 1995.

MULTIMEDIA

CD-ROMS:

Compton's Interactive World Atlas. Compton, 1997.

Encarta '97 World Atlas. Microsoft, 1996.

Global Explorer. Delorme Mapping, 1993.

Nigel's World Adventures. Lawrence Prod., 1996.

Where in the World is Carmen Sandiego? Broderbund, 1996.

VIDEOS:

Exploring the World... (series, 20-volume set). Questar, 1992.

Introducing East Asia. Educational Video Network, 1993.

Mexico and Central America (Hello! From Around the World). Ernst Interactive Media, 1993.

United Nations. Disney Educational, 1989.

WEB SITES

ArabNet (Both current and historical information about individual Arab countries) www.arab.net

China Today (A comprehensive database on contemporary China) www.chinatoday.com

The CIA World Factbook (Geographic and population information) www.odci.gov/cia/publications/factbook/

Encyclopedia of the Orient (Good on the Middle East) www.i-cias.com/e.o/lexles.htm

The Greatest Places www.greatestplaces.org

United Nations Country at a Glance (Maps and vital statistics) www.un.org/Pubs/CyberSchoolBus/information/e_glance.htm

➤ *SEE ALSO THESE RELATED PATHFINDERS*
Ancient Egypt; China

Crow Indians

The Crow Indians were Native Americans who lived on the Great Plains in Wyoming and Montana. They were a war-like, nomadic tribe who hunted bison. Some Crow Indians now live on reservations in Montana.

 DEWEY DECIMAL CALL NUMBERS

970.1 Indians of North America
398.2 Folk literature
970.004 History, North America (1800-1900)

 SEARCH TERMS

Crow Indians
Dakota Indians
Indians of North America
Great Plains Indians

 NONFICTION/REFERENCE BOOKS

Buffalo Days by Diane Hoyt-Goldsmith. Holiday House, 1997.

The Crow by Ruth Hagman. Children's Press, 1990.

The Crow by Frederick E. Hoxie. Chelsea House, 1989.

The Crow Indians by Leigh Hope Wood. Chelsea House, 1993.

Encyclopedia of Native American Tribes by Carl Waldman. Facts on File, 1988.

The Encyclopedia of North American Indians. Marshall Cavendish, 1997.

Plenty Coups by Michael P. Doss. Raintree, 1990.

Powwow by George Ancona. Harcourt Brace Jovanovich, 1993.

FICTION

Crow Chief: A Plains Indians Story by Paul Goble. Orchard Books, 1992.

Little Bear and the White Horse by Neil and Ting Morris. Silver Burdett Press, 1984.

Woman Chief by Rose Sobol. Dial Books, 1976.

MULTIMEDIA
 ## VIDEOS:

Crow (Indians of North America, Two). Schlessinger, 1994.

The Gift of the Sacred Dog (Reading Rainbow). Lancit Media Productions, 1983.

➤ SEE ALSO THESE RELATED PATHFINDERS

Native Americans; Plains Indians

Desert

Deserts are the driest and hottest places on earth. They have little rainfall. Some deserts may go several years without any rainfall. The regions are often sandy with very little vegetation. Compared to other biomes, there are relatively few species of plants and animals that can live in the desert.

 ## DEWEY DECIMAL CALL NUMBERS

574.973 Biology, Deserts

577 General nature of life (conditions needed for life)

591.5 Zoology, Ecology (relationships between organisms and their environment)

 ## SEARCH TERMS

Desert	Desert ecology
Cactus	Desert plants
Desert plants	Ecology
Desert animals	Sahara
Desert biology	Sonoran Desert

 ## NONFICTION/REFERENCE BOOKS

America's Deserts: Guide to Plants and Animals by Marianne D. Wallace. Fulcrum Kids, 1996.

Animals and Nature: Scholastic Reference. Scholastic, 1995.

Animals of the Desert by Stephen Savage. Raintree/Steck Vaughn, 1997.

Cactus Cafe: A Story of the Sonoran Desert by Kathleen Weidner Zoehfeld. SoundPrints, 1997.

Cactus Hotel by Brenda Z. Guiberson. Henry Holt & Co., 1991.

The Desert Alphabet Book by Jerry Pallotta. Charlesbridge Pub., 1994.

The Desert Fox Family Book by Hans Gerold Laukel. North-South Books, 1996.

Desert Giant: The World of the Saguaro by Barbara Bash. Sierra Club, 1989.

The Desert is Theirs by Byrd Baylor. Aladdin Books, 1987.

Desert Life by Barbara Taylor. Dorling Kindersley, 1992.

A Desert Scrapbook: Dawn to Dusk in the Sonoran Desert by Virginia Wright-Frierson. Simon & Schuster, 1996.

Desert Trip by Barbara A. Steiner. Sierra Club Books for Children, 1996.

One Day in the Desert by Jean Craighead George. HarperTrophy, 1996.

Storm on the Desert by Carolyn Lesser. Harcourt Brace & Co. 1997.

Watching Desert Wildlife by Caroline Arnold. Carolrhoda Books, 1994.

Wonders of the Desert by Louis Sabin. Troll Assoc., 1982.

FICTION

Alejandro's Gift by Richard E. Albert. Chronicle Books, 1994.

Ali, Child of the Desert by Jonothan London. Lothrop, Lee & Shepard, 1997.

An Anasazi Welcome by Kay Matthews. Red Crane Books, 1992.

Cleo and the Coyote by Elizabeth Levy. HarperCollins, 1996.

Desert Voices by Byrd Baylor. Scribner, 1981.

Hidden in Sand by Margaret Hodges. Scribner, 1994.

I'm in Charge of Celebrations by Byrd Baylor. Aladdin Books, 1995.

Lost by Paul Brett Johnson. Orchard Books, 1996.

The Tortoise and the Jackrabbit by Susan Lowell. Northland Pub., 1994.

What Good is a Cactus by Peter Marchand. Roberts Rinehart, 1994.

MULTIMEDIA

 ## CD-ROMS:

Life in the Desert (Zoo Guides). REMedia, 1995.

Living Deserts & Rainforests. Bytes of Learning, 1997.

 ## VIDEOS:

Creatures of the Namib Desert. National Geographic Society, 1977.

Desert Animals (Amazing Animals). Dorling-Kindersley, 1997.

Desert Animals (See How They Grow). Sony Music, 1995.

Eyewitness Desert. Dorling Kindersley, 1996.

Guide to Survival in the Desert Southwest (Stay Alive). Westmoreland, 1992.

 ## WEB SITES

Desert Life In the American Southwest (Environment, animals, plants, and people) www.desertusa.com/life.html

National Wildlife Federation's Website (Search articles, not many photos) www.nwf.org/nwf/search.html

➤ SEE ALSO THIS RELATED PATHFINDER

Biomes

Dinosaurs

The word dinosaur comes from Greek, and it means "terrible lizard." Though dinosaurs may not have actually been lizards, judging by their fossils they certainly appeared to be "terrible." Scientists called paleontologists believe that dinosaurs first walked the earth around 220 million years ago and died out mysteriously about 63 million years ago. Paleontologists continue to discover dinosaur fossils and learn more about these prehistoric creatures.

DEWEY DECIMAL CALL NUMBERS

567.9 Dinosaurs
568 Fossil, dinosaurs
560 Prehistoric animals
569 Fossil, mammals

SEARCH TERMS

Dinosaurs
Paleontology
Prehistoric life
Prehistoric animals
Fossils
Search by names of specific dinosaurs, for example: Tyrannosaurus

NONFICTION/REFERENCE BOOKS

An Alphabet of Dinosaurs by Peter Dodson. Scholastic, 1995.

The Big Book of Dinosaurs by Angela Wilkes. Dorling Kindersley, 1994.

Bigger than T-Rex: The Discovery of Giganotosaurus by Don Lessem. Crown, 1997.

Bone Poems by Jeff Moss. Workman Pub., 1997.

Crafts for Kids Who are Wild About Dinosaurs by Kathy Ross. Millbrook Press, 1997.

Digging Up Dinosaurs by Aliki. Crowell, 1988.

Dinosaur (Eyewitness Books) by David Norman and Angela Milner. Knopf, 1989.

Dinosaur Discoveries: How To Create Your Own Prehistoric World by Robin West. Carolrhoda Books, 1989.

The Dinosaur Encyclopedia by Michael Benton. Simon & Schuster Books for Young Readers, 1992.

Dinosaur Ghosts: The Mystery of Coelophysis by J. Lynette Gillette. Dial Books, 1997.

Dinosaur Mountain: Graveyard of the Past by Caroline Arnold. Clarion Books, 1989.

The Dinosaur Society's Dinosaur Encyclopedia by Don Lessem & Donald F. Glut. Random House, 1993.

Dinosaur Tree by Douglas Henderson. Bradbury Press, 1994.

Dinosaurs Walked Here, and Other Stories Fossils Tell by Patricia Lauber. Bradbury Press, 1987.

How Dinosaurs Came to Be by Patricia Lauber. Simon & Schuster, 1996.

Living with Dinosaurs by Patricia Lauber. Bradbury Press, 1991.

The New Illustrated Dinosaur Dictionary by Helen Roney Sattler. Lothrop, Lee & Shepard, 1990.

NONFICTION/REFERENCE BOOKS CONTINUED

The News About Dinosaurs by Patricia Lauber. Macmillan, 1994.
Simon & Schuster Children's Guide to Dinosaurs and other Prehistoric Animals
by Phillip Whitfield. Simon & Schuster, 1992.
The Visual Dictionary of Dinosaurs. Houghton Mifflin Co., 1993.

FICTION

Albert Goes Hollywood by Henry Schwartz. Orchard Books, 1992.
Bones, Bones, Dinosaur Bones by Byron Barton. Crowell, 1990.
Danny and the Dinosaur by Syd Hoff. Harper & Row, 1958.
Dinosaur Dream by Dennis Nolan. Aladdin Books, 1994.
Dinosaurs, Dinosaurs by Byron Barton. HarperCollins, 1989.
How I Captured a Dinosaur by Henry Schwartz. Orchard Books, 1993.
The Magic School Bus in the Time of the Dinosaur by Joanna Cole. Scholastic, 1994.
What Happened to Patrick's Dinosaurs? by Carol Carrick. Clarion Books, 1986.

MULTIMEDIA

CD-ROMS:

Dinosaur Explorers. N-TK Entertainment, 1996.
Dinosaur Hunter. Dorling Kindersley, 1996.
Magic School Bus in the Age of Dinosaurs. Microsoft, 1996.
Message in a Fossil. Edunetics, 1996.

VIDEOS:

Danny and the Dinosaur. Weston Woods, 1990.
Dinosaur! A&E Entertainment, 1991.
Eyewitness Dinosaur. Dorling Kindersley, 1995.
How to Build a Dinosaur. Mazon Productions, 1990.
Where Did They Go? Rainbow Educational Video, 1987.

WEB SITES

Archosauria: Systematics
www.ucmp.berkeley.edu/diapsids/archosy.html
Dino Don.com (Pictures, dictionary, scientist profile)
www.dinodon.com
Dinosauria On-Line
www.dinosauria.com/

➤ *SEE ALSO THESE RELATED PATHFINDERS*
Animals; Reptiles; Birds

Diversity

Diversity means to have a variety in form; cultural diversity means to have a variety of cultures living within one area (city, state, or country). The United States of America has a very diverse culture because its citizens come from so many different countries.

 DEWEY DECIMAL CALL NUMBERS

200s
300s
400s

305 Social groups (multiculturalism)
306 Culture (multiculturalism)
392 Costume and appearance
394 Customs
641 Food and drink
973 History, United States

 SEARCH TERMS

Diversity
Cultures
Customs
Manners and customs
Minorities
Multiculturalism
Ethnic food and dress

 NONFICTION/REFERENCE BOOKS

A is for Asia by Cynthia Chin-Lee. Orchard Books, 1997.

Birthdays!: A Celebrating Life Around the World by Eve B. Feldman. Bridgewater Books, 1996.

Children Just Like Me by Barnabas and Anabel Kindersley. Dorling Kindersley, 1995.

Everybody Cooks Rice by Norah Dooley. Carolrhoda Books, 1991.

Families: A Celebration of Diversity, Commitment, and Love by Aylette Jenness. Houghton Mifflin Co., 1990.

Hands Around the World: 365 Ways to Build Cultural Awareness & Global Respect by Susan Milord. Williamson, 1992.

How My Family Lives in America by Susan Kuklin. Bradbury Press, 1992.

One Earth, One Spirit: A Child's Books of Prayers from Many Faiths and Cultures. Sierra Club Books for Children, 1997.

Painting Faces by Suzanne Haldane. Puffin Unicorn, 1995.

Pass the Bread by Karin Luisa Badt. Children's Press, 1995.

A Ride on Mother's Back: A Day of Babycarrying Around the World by Emery Bernhard. Harcourt Brace & Co., 1996.

FICTION

The Berenstain Bears' New Neighbors by Stan and Jan Berenstain. Random House, 1994.

The Burnt Stick by Anthony Hill. Houghton Mifflin Co., 1995.

City Night by Eve Rice. Greenwillow Books, 1987.

Colors Come From God—Just Like Me! by Carolyn Forche. Abingdon Press, 1995.

The Courage Seed by Jean Richardson. Eakin Press, 1993.

Elijah's Angel: A Story for Chanukah and Christmas by Michael J. Rosen. Harcourt Brace Jovanovich, 1992.

Families: Poems Celebrating the African American Experience. Wordsong/Boyds Mills Press, 1994.

In God's Name by Sandy Eisenberg Sasso. Jewish Lights Pub., 1994.

Jalapeno Bagels by Natasha Wing. Atheneum Books for Young Readers, 1996.

We Sing the City by Mary Beth Lundgren. Clarion Books, 1997.

MULTIMEDIA

 ## CD-ROMS:

Discovering Nations, States, and Cultures. Gale, 1997.

Eyewitness History of the World. DK Multimedia, 1995.

UXL Multicultural CD Interactive: A Comprehensive Resource on African Americans, Hispanic Americans and Native North Americans. Gale, 1997.

 ## VIDEOS:

American Cultures for Children Video Series. Schlessinger, 1997.

Celebrating Cultural Diversity (Book Connections). Cheshire Book Companions, 1992.

Multicultural Peoples of North America. Schlessinger, 1993.

World Cultures: Similarities and Differences. United Learning, 1989.

 # WEB SITES

Celebrating Cultural Diversity (Links to cultural ethnicity sites)
www.webdev.sbis.net/cultural/

Celebrating Our Nation's Diversity (Lesson plans, activities, and information for educators)
www.census.gov/ftp/pub/edu/diversity/

KidLink (Set up e-mail contact with kids from all over the world)
www.kidlink.org/

The United Nations CyberSchoolBus
www.un.org/Pubs/CyberSchoolBus/

> **SEE ALSO THIS RELATED PATHFINDER**
Black History in America

Dolphins

Dolphins are mammals that live in the ocean. They have long noses and smooth skin, which is usually black or grey on top and white underneath. They swim the ocean in family groups called herds, and they are thought to communicate with one another. Dolphins are small whales. A Killer Whale is the largest dolphin in the Dolphin Family.

 DEWEY DECIMAL CALL NUMBERS

597.53 Dolphins
574.92 Hydrographic biology (marine and freshwater biology)
591 Zoology
599.53 Mammals

 SEARCH TERMS

Dolphins
Porpoise
Marine mammals
Cetacean
Search by name of dolphin species, for example: Bottlenose dolphin

 NONFICTION/REFERENCE BOOKS

Dolphin (An I Can Read Book) by Robert A. Morris. HarperTrophy, 1983.

Dolphins! (Step Into Reading. Book 2 Book) by Sharon Bokoske and Margaret Davidson. Random House 1993.

Dolphins! by June Behrens. Children's Press, 1990.

Dolphins and Porpoises by Janelle Hatherly and Delia Nicholls. Facts On File, 1990.

The Friendly Dolphins by Patricia Lauber. Scholastic, 1995.

The Playful Dolphins by Lina McCarter Bridge. National Geographic Society, 1976.

Whales, Dolphins, and Porpoises by Mark Carwardine. Dorling Kindersley, 1992.

Whales and Dolphins in Action by Tanner Ottley Gay. Aladdin Books, 1991.

Zoobooks: Dolphins and Porpoises by Beth Wagner Brust. Wildlife Education Ltd., 1990.

FICTION

Danger, Dolphins, and Ginger Beer by John Vigor. Atheneum, 1993.

A Dolphin Named Bob by Twig C. George. HarperCollins, 1996.

Dolphin Treasure (Beech Tree Chapter Books) by Wayne Grover. Beech Tree Books, 1997.

The Girl Who Danced with Dolphins by Frank DeSaix. Farrar Straus Giroux, 1991.

Island of the Blue Dolphins by Scott O'Dell. Houghton Mifflin Co., 1960.

Story of a Dolphin by Katherine Orr. Carolrhoda Books, 1995.

MULTIMEDIA

CD-ROMS:

Eyewitness Children's Encyclopedia. Dorling Kindersley, 1996.
Amazing Animals Interactive Multimedia. DK Multimedia, 1997.

VIDEOS:

Deep Sea Dive (Really Wild Animals). National Geographic Home Video, 1994.

Dolphin (Seahouse Two). Rainbow Educational Video, 1992.

Dolphins (Animal Profile). Rainbow Educational Video, 1991.

Dolphin. National Geographic Film & TV, 1983.

Dolphins (In the Wild). PBS/Turner Home Video, 1995.

Dolphins and Porpoises (Now I Know). Troll Assoc., 1993.

Island of the Blue Dolphins. MCA Home Video, 1985.

WEB SITES

The Electronic Zoo—Marine Mammals (Links to sites) www.netvet.wustl.edu/marine.htm

Sea World Busch Gardens—Bottlenose Dolphins www.seaworld.org/bottlenose_dolphin/ bottlenose_dolphins.html

David's Whale and Dolphin Watch (Photos and sounds of dolphins sorted by species) www.neptune.atlantis-intl.com/dolphins/

The Dolphin Circle—Especially for Children (Cetacean links, stories, bibliography) www.Pressemier1.net/~iamdavid/ children.html

➤ SEE ALSO THESE RELATED PATHFINDERS

Animals; Ocean; Sea Animals; Whales

Earth

Of all the planets that have been discovered, Earth is the only one that contains life. The Earth is composed of four layers, and the outer layers are different kinds of rock. With the nine other planets of our solar system, Earth orbits the Sun. It takes the Earth one year to make a complete orbit. The Earth also revolves on its axis. It makes one complete revolution every day.

DEWEY DECIMAL CALL NUMBERS

525 Earth, Astronomical geography

550 Geology

551 Physical geology (atmosphere)

577.5 General nature of life (conditions needed for life)

508 Geographic description, travels and surveys

SEARCH TERMS

Earth
Earth science
Earth history
Ecology
Geology
Earth, internal structure
Natural history

NONFICTION/REFERENCE BOOKS

Dictionary of the Earth by John Farndon and Neil Ardley. Dorling Kindersley, 1995.

Earth: the Elements by Ken Robbins. Henry Holt & Co., 1995.

Earth (Eyewitness Visual Dictionary) by Martyn Bramwell. Dorling Kindersley, 1993.

Earth (Picturpedia). Dorling Kindersley, 1993.

Earth Words: A Dictionary of the Environment by Seymour Simon. HarperCollins, 1995.

The Living Earth by Eleonore Schmid. North-South Books, 1994.

This Is Our Earth by Laura Lee Benson. Charlesbridge Pub., 1994.

You're Aboard Spaceship Earth by Patricia Lauber. HarperCollins, 1996.

The Pebble in My Pocket: A History of Our Earth by Meredith Hooper. Viking, 1996.

The Third Planet: Exploring the Earth from Space by Sally Ride and Tam O'Shaughnessy. Crown, 1994.

FICTION

Here in Space by David Milgrim. Bridgewater Books, 1997.

How to Dig a Hole to the Other Side of the World by Raith McNulty. Harper & Row, 1990.

Journey to the Center of the Earth by Jules Verne. New American Library, 1995.

The Magic School Bus Inside the Earth by Joanna Cole. Scholastic, 1987.

MULTIMEDIA

CD-ROMS:

Changing Earth. Discoveryworks, 1996.

Earth's Water. Discoveryworks, 1996

Earth Quest. Dorling Kindersley Multimedia, 1996.

Eyewitness Children's Encyclopedia. Dorling Kindersley Multimedia, 1997.

U*X*L Science. Gale, 1997.

VIDEOS:

Rock & Mineral (Eyewitness). Dorling Kindersley, 1996. See these additional videos in the series: **Island** (1997); **Mountain** (1997); **Ocean** (1997); **Planets** (1997); **Volcano** (1996); **Weather** (1996).

Journey to the Center of the Earth. Twentieth Century Fox, 1959.

Life in the Balance. Vestron Video, 1990.

Magic School Bus Blows Its Top. Scholastic, 1997.

WEB SITES

Athena: Earth Science Resources www.athena.ivv.nasa.gov/curric/land/index.html

Pointers to Earth System Science Educational Resources www.ems.psu.edu/RelatedWebSites.html

View the Earth www.fourmilab.ch/earthview/vplanet.html

➤ SEE ALSO THESE RELATED PATHFINDERS

Planets; Seasons; Solar System

Eastern Woodland Indians

There are many different tribes of Native American Indians who lived in the Eastern Woodland regions. Peoples who lived from the Atlantic coast to the Mississippi River included the Delaware, Huron, Iroquois Confederacy, Mohican, Creek, Seminole, Cherokee, Chickasaw, and Choctaw tribes. They were deer hunters, and they grew corn, squash, and beans. Their houses included the dome-shaped wigwam and the longhouse.

 DEWEY DECIMAL CALL NUMBERS

970.1 Indians of North America
970.004 History, North America (1800-1900)
973 History, United States
974 Northeastern United States
398.2 Folk literature

 SEARCH TERMS

Eastern Woodland Indians
Woodland Indians
Eastern United States Indians
Northeastern Woodland Indians
Mississippian culture
Native Americans
Search by names of tribes, for example:
Oneida

 NONFICTION/REFERENCE BOOKS

The Abenaki (First Books-Indians of the Americas Series) by Elaine Landua. Franklin Watts, 1996.

The Algonquians (First Book) by Patricia Ryon Quiri. Franklin Watts, 1992.

The Cherokees (A First Americans Book) by Virginia Driving Hawk Sneve. Holiday House, 1996.

Encyclopedia of Native American Tribes by Carl Waldman. Facts on File, 1988.

The Encyclopedia of North American Indians. Marshall Cavendish, 1997.

Houses of Bark: Tipi, Wigwam, and Longhouse: Native Dwellings, Woodland Indians by Bonnie Shemie. Tundra Books, 1990.

Indians of the Northeast (First Americans Series) by Colin G. Calloway. Facts on File, 1991.

Indians of the Tidewater Country of Maryland, Virginia, Delaware and North Carolina (3rd ed.) by Thelma Ruskin. Maryland Historical Press, 1996.

The Iroquois: People of the Northeast by Evelyn Wolfson. Millbrook Press, 1992.

The Ojibwas, People of the Northern Forests by Eileen Lucas. Millbrook Press, 1994.

The Seminoles (A First Americans Book) by Virginia Driving Hawk Sneve. Holiday House, 1994.

FICTION

The Boy Who Lived with the Bears and Other Iroquois Stories by Joseph Bruchac. HarperCrest, 1995.

The Children of the Morning Light: Wampanoag Tales by Manitongquat. Simon & Schuster, 1994.

Dog People: Native Dog Stories by Joseph Bruchac. Fulcrum Kids, 1995.

Dove Dream by Hendle Rumbaut. Houghton Mifflin Co., 1994.

Legend of the Windigo: A Tale from Native America by Gayle Ross. Dial Books for Young Readers, 1996.

Little Firefly: An Algonquian Legend (Native American Legends) by Terri Cohlene. Troll Assoc., 1991.

The Star Maiden: An Ojibway Tale by Barbara Esbensen. Little, Brown & Co., 1988.

The Woman Who Fell from the Sky: The Iroquois Story of Creation by John Bierhorst. William Morrow & Co., 1993.

MULTIMEDIA

VIDEOS:

Indians of Early America. Encyclopaedia Britannica, 1990.

Iroquois (Indians of North America). Schlessinger, 1993. Also see additional titles in this series: **The Cherokee; The Creek; The Huron; The Seminole.**

People of the Forest (Native Americans). Rainbow Educational Video, 1994.

 ## WEB SITE

Multicultural Bibliography (Eastern Woodland Indians: Northeastern Indians Bibliography) falcon.jmu.edu/schoollibrary/indnorth.htm

➤ SEE ALSO THESE RELATED PATHFINDERS

Cherokee Indians; Iroquois Confederacy; Native Americans

Ecology

Our world is built on complex relationships among plants, animals, and the places they live. Ecology is the study of these living things and their environment. By studying these relationships, ecologists are able to understand how living things depend on each other for survival.

 DEWEY DECIMAL CALL NUMBERS

574.5 Biology, Ecology

577.5 General nature of life

363.73 Social issues (pollution, recycling, etc.)

508 Geographical descriptions, Travel and surveys

550 Earth and other worlds

 SEARCH TERMS

Ecology
Urban ecology
Soil ecology
Fire ecology
Nature study
Acid Rain
Pollution

 NONFICTION/REFERENCE BOOKS

Acid Rain (Closer Look At...) by Alex Edmonds and David Burroughs. Copper Beech Books, 1997.

Air Alert: Rescuing the Earth's Atmosphere by Christina G. Miller and Louise A. Berry. Atheneum, 1996.

Backyard by Donald M. Silver. Learning Triangle Press, 1997.

The City (The Junior Library of Ecology) by Rosa Costa-Pace and Rosa Costa-Pau. Chelsea House, 1994.

Earth Words: A Dictionary of the Environment by Seymour Simon. HarperCollins, 1995.

Forest Fire by Christopher Lampton. Millbrook Press, 1991.

Global Cities by Phillip Parker. Thomson Learning, 1995.

I am a Part of Nature by Bobbie Kalman and Janine Schaub. Crabtree Pub. Co., 1992.

Lilly Pad Pond by Bianca Lavies. Puffin Books, 1993.

The Living Earth by Eleonore Schmid. North-South Books, 1994.

Rachel Carson: Caring for the Earth by Elizabeth Ring. Millbrook Press, 1992.

Town Life by Philip Parker. Thomas Learning, 1995.

FICTION

The Berenstain Bear Scouts and the Coughing Catfish by Stan & Jan Berenstain. Scholastic, 1995.

The Case of Missing Cutthroats: An Ecological Mystery by Jean Craighead George. HarperCollins, 1996.

Dawn Saves the Planet (Babysitters Club) by Ann Martin. Scholastic, 1992.

Giving Thanks: A Native American Good Morning Message by Chief Jake Swamp. Lee & Low Books, 1995.

My Grandpa and the Sea by Catherine Orr. Carolrhoda Books, 1990.

The Old Ladies Who Liked Cats by Carol Greene. HarperCollins, 1991.

MULTIMEDIA

 CD-ROMS:

Amazon Trail. MECC, 1995.
Kids and the Environment. Tom Snyder, 1996.
Magic School Bus Explores the Rainforest. Microsoft, 1997.
U*X*L Science. Gale, 1997.

 VIDEOS:

Environmental S.W.A.T. Team (New Explorers). PBS Video, 1995.
Island (Eyewitness). Dorling Kindersley, 1996. See these additional titles in the series: **Ocean** (1997); **Pond & River** (1996); **Seashore** (1996); **Arctic & Antarctic** (1996); **Desert** (1996).
Life in the Balance. Vestron, 1990.
The Nature Connection (series). Discovery Channel, 1991.
Save the Earth. International Video Pub., 1990.

 WEB SITES

Ecology Overview
www.efn.org/~dharmika/overview.htm
To Be An Ecologist
www.nceas.ucsb.edu/nceasweb/kids/lab/ecologist/ecologist.html

➤ SEE ALSO THESE RELATED PATHFINDERS

Biomes; Food Chains

Ellis Island

Ellis Island is a small, 27-acre island in Upper New York Bay, in New Jersey waters. From 1892 to 1943, Ellis Island was the primary entry station for immigrants coming into the United States. It is now part of the Statue of Liberty National Monument, with a tourist center and immigration museum.

 ## DEWEY DECIMAL CALL NUMBERS

304 Immigration
325 Ellis Island
973 American History

 ## SEARCH TERMS

Ellis Island
Immigration
Emigration
United States History
New York and immigration

 ## NONFICTION/REFERENCE BOOKS

Ellis Island (Cornerstones of Freedom) by Richard Conrad Stein. Children's Press, 1992.

Ellis Island (Places in American History) by Catherine Reef. Dillon Press, 1991.

Ellis Island: A True Book. Patricia Ryon Quiri. Children's Press, 1998.

Ellis Island: Doorway to Freedom by Steven Kroll. Holiday House, 1995.

Ellis Island: New Hope in a New Land by William Jay Jacobs. Scribner, 1990.

I Was Dreaming to Come to America: Memories from the Ellis Island Oral History Project selected and illustrated by Veronica Lawlor. Viking, 1995.

If Your Name Was Changed at Ellis Island by Ellen Levine. Scholastic, 1994.

FICTION

The Orphan of Ellis Island: A Time-Travel Adventure by Elvira Woodruff. Scholastic, 1997.

An Ellis Island Christmas by Maxine Rhea Leighton. Viking, 1992.

Journey to the Golden Land by Richard Rosenblum. Jewish Pub. Society, 1992.

MULTIMEDIA

 ### CD-ROMS:

Multimedia U.S. History: The Story of a Nation. Bureau of Electronic Pub., [nd].

History of the United States for Young People. American Heritage, 1997.

 ### VIDEOS:

Ellis Island. A&E Entertainment, 1997.

Fiddler on the Roof. MGM/UA Home Video, 1971.

Immigration to the U.S. (American History for Children). Schlessinger, 1996.

Out of Ireland. Shanachie, 1995.

Statue of Liberty (Ken Burns's America) PBS Video/Turner Home Entertainment, 1996.

U.S. History Video Collection: Immigration and Cultural Change. Schlessinger, 1997.

 ## WEB SITES

The American Immigration Homepage (Created by high school students, but a good resource)
www.bergen.org/AAST/Projects/Immigration/index.html

Ellis Island, The New World (Time line, statistics, and audio clips of immigrants telling their stories)
www.historychannel.com/community/ellisisle/newworld.html

➤ SEE ALSO THIS RELATED PATHFINDER
Immigration

Endangered Species

Any species of animal or plant whose ability to survive is seriously in question is an endangered species. Most species are endangered by human misuse of land and destruction of natural habitats, and by unrestricted hunting of animals. In recent years, environmentalists have worked to establish wildlife refuges and other programs to replenish the population of plants and animals that are near extinction.

 DEWEY DECIMAL CALL NUMBERS

574.529 Biology, Ecology
591.52 Zoology, Ecology
591.92 Zoology, Hydrographic (marine and freshwater)

 SEARCH TERMS

Endangered species
Rare animals
Wildlife conservation
Extinct animals
Wildlife rescue

 NONFICTION/REFERENCE BOOKS

And Then There Was One: The Mysteries of Extinction by Margery Facklam. Sierra Club Books/Little, Brown & Co., 1990.

Any Bear Can Wear Glasses: The Spectacled Bear & Other Curious Creatures by Matthew Long and Thomas Long. Chronicle Books, 1995.

Can We Save Them?: Endangered Species of North America by David Dobson. Charlesbridge Pub., 1997.

Endangered Desert Animals (Endangered Animals Series) by Dave Taylor. Crabtree Pub. Co., 1993. See also these additional titles in the series: **Endangered Ocean Animals; Endangered Island Animals; Endangered Savannah Animals; Endangered Mountain Animals; Endangered Grassland Animals; Endangered Forest Animals; Endangered Wetland Animals.**

Ocean Animals in Danger (Survivors Series for Children) by Gary Turbak. Northland Pub., 1994.

Mountain Animals in Danger (Survivors Series for Children) by Gary Turbak. Northland Pub., 1994.

Will We Miss Them?: Endangered Species (Reading Rainbow Book) by Alexandria Wright. Charlesbridge Pub., 1992.

World Water Watch by Michelle Koch. Greenwillow Books, 1993.

FICTION

Hey! Get Off Our Train by John Burningham. Crown, 1994.

There's an Owl in the Shower by Jean Craighead George. HarperCollins, 1995.

Three at Sea by Timothy Bush. Crown, 1994.

V for Vanishing: An Alphabet of Endangered Animals by Patricia Mullins. HarperCollins, 1994.

The Year of the Panda by Miriam Schlein. HarperTrophy, 1992.

MULTIMEDIA

CD-ROMS:

Amazon Trail. MECC, 1997.
Animals in Danger. REM Media, 1996.
Discovering Endangered Wildlife Interactive Multimedia. Sunburst Comm., 1996.
Ozzie's World. Digital Impact, 1994.
U*X*L Science. Gale, 1997.

VIDEOS:

American Discovery: Protecting Our Endangered Species. New Castle Comm., 1996.
Beyond the Bars: Zoos and Zoo Animals. Rainbow Educational Video, 1987.
Endangered Animals: Survivors on the Brink. National Geographic Educational, 1997.
In the Footsteps of Crusoe. National Geographic Educational, 1993.
Protecting Endangered Animals. National Geographic Educational, 1984.
What Is an Endangered Species? New Castle Comm., 1996.

WEB SITES

Endangered Species.com—The Rarest Information Around
www.endangeredspecie.com
Endangered Species Home Page
www.nceet.snre.umich.edu/EndSpp/Endangered.html
Science/Nature for Kids
www.kidscience.miningco.com/library/weekly/aa100697.htm
U.S. Fish & Wildlife Service (Information center for students and teachers)
www.fws.gov/r9endspp/kid_cor/kid_cor.htm
National Wildlife Federation—Endangered Species and Habitats
www.igc.org/nwf/endangered/index.html

➤ SEE ALSO THESE RELATED PATHFINDERS

Animals; Biomes; Ecology; Zoo Animals

Energy

Anything that is living and anything that moves uses energy. Energy never goes away, it changes into other forms of energy. There are many different kinds of energy. Some forms of energy will one day run out, such as natural gas and fossil fuels. These are called "nonrenewable resources." Other forms of energy come in an endless supply, such as the heat from the sun and the power from the wind and naturally flowing water. Each year, Americans consume more nonrenewable energy than any other people in the world.

DEWEY DECIMAL CALL NUMBERS

531 Motion (forces effecting motion)
333.79 Resources (land, oil, coal, trees)
523.7 Solar energy
621.47 Solar energy engineering
622 Mining engineering
662 Technology of fuels

SEARCH TERMS

Energy	Tidal power
Sun	Hydroelectric power
Solar energy	Geothermal energy
Fossil fuels	Wave power
Chemical energy	Biomass energy
Heat	Nuclear energy
Renewable energy	Oil
Petroleum	Coal
Gas	Electricity
Wind power	Power resources
Solar power	Force and energy

NONFICTION/REFERENCE BOOKS

The Sun by Seymour Simon. William Morrow & Co., 1986.

Bioenergy (Alternative Energy) by Graham Houghton. Gareth Stevens Children's Books, 1991. See also these additional titles in the series: **Geothermal Energy; Solar Energy; Water Energy; Wind Energy** all by Graham Rickard.

Done in the Sun: Solar Projects for Children by Mina Yamashita. Sunstone Press, 1983.

Electricity (Resources) by Graham Peacock. Thomson Learning, 1993.

Energy (Cycles in Science) by Peter D. Riley. Heinemann Interactive Library, 1998.

Energy by Larry White. Millbrook Press, 1995.

Energy All Around Us (Facts About) by Donna Bailey. Steck Vaughn, 1991.

Energy From Oil and Gas (Facts About) by Donna Bailey. Steck Vaughn, 1991.

Energy from the Sun (Rookie Read-about Science) by Allan Fowler. Children's Press, 1997.

Exploring Energy (Scholastic Voyages of Discovery). Scholastic, 1995.

Full of Energy (It's Science!) by Sally Hewitt. Children's Press, 1997.

Molecules and Atoms by Rae Bains. Troll Assoc., 1985.

Nuclear Power (20th Century Inventions) by Nina Morgan. Raintree/Steck Vaughn, 1998.

Renewable Energy (What About?) by Jacqueline Dineen. Raintree/Steck Vaughn, 1995.

Saving Energy (What About?) Raintree/Steck Vaughn, 1995.

FICTION

The Green Musketeers and the Incredible Energy Escapade by Sara St. Antoine. Bantam Books, 1994.

Blackout! (Ghostwriter) by Eric Weiner. Bantam Books, 1993.

MULTIMEDIA

CD-ROMS:

Science and the Environment Interactive Multimedia. Voyage Pub., 1996.
The Cartoon Guide to Physics Interactive Multimedia. HarperCollins Interactive, 1995.

VIDEOS:

Elementary Science (Elementary Science). National Geographic Film & TV, 1993.

Energy (Understanding Science). TMW Media Group, 1992.

Exploring Energy. United Learning, 1995.

Future Energy Resources (Think About It). Learning Matters Inc., 1995.

Heat, Temperature and Energy. Rainbow Educational Video, 1995.

Earth at Risk. Nuclear Energy, Nuclear Waste. Schlessinger, 1993.

Power Up: Energy in Our Environment. Rainbow Educational Video, 1992.

Simple Things You Can Do to Save Energy: The Power Is in Your Hands. Noodlehead Network, 1993.

Solar Energy. Science in Action. TMW Media Group, 1994.

What Energy Means. National Geographic Film & TV, 1982.

WEB SITES

Bill Nye the Science Guy
www.nyelabs.kcts.org/
Energy Quest
www.energy.ca.gov/education/index2.html

➤ SEE ALSO THESE RELATED PATHFINDERS
Earth; Ecology

Eskimos

Eskimos, or Inuits, are the native people who live in the cold Arctic coastal regions of North America, parts of Greenland and northeast Siberia. In Alaska and Canada, Eskimos are considered Native Americans. The Eskimo are especially known for their artistic carvings and engravings in wood, bone, horn, and ivory.

DEWEY DECIMAL CALL NUMBERS

305.897 Inuit social life and customs
970.1 Indians of North America
979.8 Pacific Coast states
398.2 Folk literature
970.004 History, North America (1800-1900)
973 History, United States

SEARCH TERMS

Eskimo
Inuit
Inupiat
Native Americans

NONFICTION/REFERENCE BOOKS

Arctic Hunter by Diane Hoyt-Goldsmith. Holiday House, 1992.

Building an Igloo by Ulli Steltzer. Henry Holt & Co., 1995.

A Child's Alaska by Claire Rudolf Murphy. Alaska Northwest Books, 1994.

The Eskimo: The Inuit and Yupik People by Alice Osinski. Children's Press, 1985.

Eskimo Boy: Life in an Inupiaq Eskimo Village by Russ Kendall. Scholastic, 1992.

Frozen Land: Vanishing Cultures by Jan Reynolds. Harcourt Brace Jovanovich, 1993.

The Inuits: People of the Arctic by Jennifer Fleischner. Millbrook Press, 1995.

FICTION

Baseball Bats for Christmas by Michael Kusugak. Annick Press, 1990.

Dance on a Sealskin by Barbara Winslow. Alaska Northwest Books, 1995.

The Eye of the Needle by Teri Sloat. Puffin Books, 1993.

Nessa's Fish by Nancy Luenn. Atheneum, 1990.

Northern Lights: A Hanukkah Story by Diane Cohen Conway. Kar-Ben Copies, 1994.

The Seasons and Someone by Virginia Kroll. Harcourt Brace Jovanovich, 1994.

A Sled Dog for Moshi by Jeanne Bushey. Hyperion for Children, 1994.

Titkala by Margaret Shaw-MacKinnon. Holiday House, 1996.

Very Last First Time by Jan Andrews. Atheneum, 1986.

MULTIMEDIA
VIDEOS:

Beauty and the Beast and other Animated Fables. 3G Home Video, 1990. (Includes Inuit folk tales)

Julie of the Wolves (Newbery Collection). SRA School Group, 1985.

Kids Explore Alaska. Learning Media, 1990.

Tundra Books Tails. Alaska Video Postcards, 1997.

 ## WEB SITE

Native American Website for Children (Tribe—Inuit)
www.nhusd.k12.ca.us/ALVE/
NativeAmerhome.html/
nativeopeningage.html

 ## SEE ALSO THIS RELATED PATHFINDER

Native Americans

Etiquette

Etiquette refers to the practices, customs, and traditions of a society. Using good manners is part of following good etiquette. Etiquette can be considered the rules of society, the right way to do things. Every culture has its own rules of etiquette. What may be good manners in one country could well be considered bad manners in another.

DEWEY DECIMAL CALL NUMBERS

395 Etiquette
390 Customs and folklore

SEARCH TERMS

Etiquette
Manners
Table etiquette
Social life and customs
United States, social life and customs
Traditions
Customs
Behavior
Courtesy

NONFICTION/REFERENCE BOOKS

The Bad Good Manners Book by Babette Cole. Dial Books for Young Readers, 1996.

Don't Do That!: A Child's Guide to Bad Manners, Ridiculous Rules, and Inadequate Etiquette by Barry Louis Polisar. Rainbow Morning Music, 1994.

Eating the Plates: A Pilgrim Book of Food and Manners by Lucille Recht Penner. Macmillan, 1991.

Feelings & Manners (A Child's First Library of Learning). Time-Life Books, 1997.

It's a Spoon, Not a Shovel by Caralyn Beuhner. Dial Books for Young Readers, 1995.

Manners by Aliki. Greenwillow Books, 1990.

Mind Your Manners! (Greenwillow Books Read-alone Guide) by Peggy Parish. Greenwillow Books, 1978.

Oops!: The Manners Guide for Girls by Nancy Holyoke. Pleasant Company Pub., 1997.

What Do You Say, Dear? by Sesyle Joslin. HarperCollins, 1986.

Why Do We Do That? (Why Do We) by Mark Kirtland. Franklin Watts, 1996.

FICTION

Big Black Bear by Wong Herbert Yee. Houghton Mifflin Co., 1993.

A Country Far Away by Nigel Gray. Orchard Books, 1991.

Chicken Chicken (Goosebumps; #53) by R. L. Stine. Scholastic, 1997.

Clifford's Manners (Clifford the Big Red Dog) by Norman Bridwell. Scholastic, 1987.

How My Parents Learned to Eat by Ina R. Friedman. Houghton Mifflin Co., 1984.

I Want My Dinner by Tony Ross. Harcourt Brace Jovanovich, 1996.

Mice Twice: Story & Pictures by Joseph Low. Aladdin Books, 1986.

No More Nice by Amy McDonald. Orchard Books, 1996.

Poem Stew poems selected by William Cole. Lippincott, 1983.

Richard Scarry's Please and Thank You Book by Richard Scarry. Random House, 1973.

MULTIMEDIA

 ### CD-ROM:

Mieko Interactive Multimedia: A Story of Japanese Culture based on the children's story by Leo Politi. Digital Productions, 1996.

 ### VIDEOS:

Customs and Superstitions (Tell Me Why). TMW Media Group, 1990.

Minding Your Manners at School. United Learning, 1996.

Paper Plates to Silver Spoons. Cambridge Career Products, 1994.

Table Manners for Kids. Public Media, 1993.

Amazing Advantage for Kids. Amazing Advantage for Kids, 1996.

Manners Monster: Rudy Goes to Dinner. Tapeworm Video, 1995.

Say Please! Sunburst Comm., 1996.

Everglades

An everglade is a marshy, low-lying tropical area. It is an area of solidly packed muck, saw grass, and marsh hammocks. It is also rich in wildlife. The Everglades, an extensive wetlands wilderness area, is located in South Florida, much of it within the Everglades National Park and Big Cypress National Preserve. The Everglades have been adversely affected by agricultural and urban development, but steps have been made in recent years to correct the damage done to this ecosystem.

DEWEY DECIMAL CALL NUMBERS

333.91 Land use (Wildlife refuge, habitats)

508.759 Geographical descriptions, Travels and surveys

917.59 Geography of and travel in North America, Florida

975.5 Southeastern United States, Florida

SEARCH TERMS

Everglades
Everglades National Park
Florida
Wetlands

NONFICTION/REFERENCE BOOKS

The Alligator and the Everglades by J. David Taylor. Crabtree Pub. Co., 1990.

Everglades by Jason Cooper. Rourke Press, 1995.

Everglades by Jean Craighead George. HarperCollins, 1995.

Everglades by Eileen Lucas. Raintree/Steck Vaughn, 1995.

The Everglades by Cheryl Koenig Morgan. Troll Assoc., 1989.

Everglades: Buffalo Tiger and the River of Grass by Peter Lourie. Boyds Mills Press, 1994.

The Everglades: Exploring the Unknown by Christopher Linn. Troll Assoc., 1976.

Marjory Stoneman Douglas, Friend of the Everglades by Tricia Andryszewski. Millbrook Press, 1994.

Marjory Stoneman Douglas, Voice of the Everglades by Jennifer Bryant. Twenty-first Century Books, 1992.

FICTION

Lost Man's River by Cynthia DeFelice. Macmillan, 1994.

Nine Man Tree by Robert Newton Peck. Random House, 1998.

Sawgrass Poems: A View of the Everglades: Poems by Frank Asch. Harcourt Brace Jovanovich, 1996.

Trouble Dolls by Jimmy Buffet. Harcourt Brace Jovanovich, 1991.

MULTIMEDIA

CD-ROMS:

Eyewitness Children's Encyclopedia. Dorling Kindersley, 1997.
National Parks 3.0. Cambrix, 1997.

VIDEOS:

The Everglades (Parts 1 & 2). Madacy Entertainment, 1994.
Joe Panther. Warner Studios, 1996. (Story of young Seminole looking for work in Everglades)
The Wetlands. View Video, 1988.

WEB SITE

American Park Network—Everglades
www.americanparknetwork.com/
parkinfo/ev/index.html#top

➤ SEE ALSO THIS RELATED PATHFINDER

Biomes

RETA E. KING LIBRARY
CHADRON STATE COLLEGE
CHADRON, NE 69337

Explorers and Exploration

Explorers are people who travel to newly found lands or through little known areas to study the land or to search for something new. Historically, exploration was often done to discover new lands and gain control over them. The great "age of exploration" began with Christopher Columbus searching for a new route to the Orient, and Ferdinand Magellan sailing around the tip of South America, and continued almost 300 years. Some other famous explorers were John Cabot (the first man from England to reach North America), James Cook (who discovered Hawaiian islands), and Neil Armstrong (who landed on the Moon).

 DEWEY DECIMAL CALL NUMBERS

910 Geography & travel
917.04 Geography & travel, North America
919.8 Geography & travel, other areas
920 Collective biographies
921 Individual biographies
970.01 General history of North America
998 Arctic islands & Antarctica

 SEARCH TERMS

Explorers
Exploration
Discovery
Expedition
Search by names of explorers, for example: Christopher Columbus

 NONFICTION/REFERENCE BOOKS

Black Whiteness: Admiral Byrd Alone in the Antarctic by Robert Burleigh. Atheneum, 1998.

Brendan the Navigator: A History Mystery about the Discovery of America by Jean Fritz. Coward, McCann & Geoghegan, 1979.

The Children's Atlas of Exploration by Antony Mason. Millbrook Press, 1993.

Christopher Columbus—How He Did It by Charlotte Yue. Houghton Mifflin Co., 1992.

Coronado's Golden Quest by Barbara Weisberg. Raintree/Steck Vaughn, 1993.

The Discovery of the Americas by Betsy and Giuliu Maestro. Lothrop, Lee & Shepard, 1991.

A Dog Came Too by Ainslie Manson. Margaret K. McElderry Books, 1993.

Exploration and Conquest: The Americas After Columbus, 1500-1620 by Betsy Maestro. Lothrop, Lee & Shepard, 1994.

Explorations: Facts, Things to Make, Activities by Nicola Baxter. Franklin Watts, 1994.

Explorers by Dennis Fradin. Children's Press, 1984.

Follow the Dream by Peter Sis. Knopf, 1996.

How We Crossed the West: The Adventures of Lewis & Clark by Rosalyn Schanzer. National Geographic Society, 1997.

If You Were There in 1492 by Barbara Brenner. Bradbury Press, 1991.

In 1492 by Jean Marzollo. Scholastic, 1991.

In Search of the Grand Canyon by Mary Ann Fraser. Henry Holt & Co., 1995.

Into the Ice: The Story of Arctic Exploration by Lynn Curlee. Houghton Mifflin Co., 1997.

Journey into Space: The Missions of Neil Armstrong by Andrew Langley. Chelsea House, 1994.

Over the Top of the World by Will Steger. Scholastic, 1997.

NONFICTION/REFERENCE BOOKS CONTINUED

Sir Francis Drake: His Daring Deeds by Farrar Straus Giroux, 1988.

Three Ships for Columbus by Eve Spencer. Raintree/Steck Vaughn, 1993.

Trapped by the Ice by Michael McCurdy. Walker & Co., 1997.

Where Do You Think You're Going, Christopher Columbus? by Jean Fritz. G. P. Putnam's Sons, 1980.

Who Really Discovered America? by Stephen Krensky. Hastings House, 1987.

FICTION

Grandpa Takes Me to the Moon by Timothy R. Gaffney. Tambourine Books, 1996.

The Island Below the Stars by James Rumford. Houghton Mifflin Co., 1998.

Lewis & Clark and Davy Hutchins by Nolan Carlson. Hearth Pub., 1994.

My Name is York by Elizabeth Van Steenwyk. Rising Moon Books, 1997.

The Three Astronauts by Umberto Eco. Harcourt Brace & Co., 1989.

Zoom! Zoom! Zoom! I'm Off to the Moon by Dan Yaccarino. Scholastic, 1997.

MULTIMEDIA

CD-ROMS:

Age of Exploration 1 & 2. National Geographic Society, 1996.

Amazon Trail. MECC, 1997.

Explorers of the New World. Softkey, 1995.

Eyewitness Encyclopedia of Space. DK Multimedia, 1996.

Eyewitness History of the World. DK Multimedia, 1998.

WEB SITES

Biography.com (Good, brief biographies of many explorers)
www.biography.com/find/find.html

Christopher Columbus, His Gastronomic Persona (What did Columbus eat?)
www.castellobanfi.com/features/story_3.html

The Columbus Navigation Page
www1.minn.net/~keithp/

Discoverers Web (Lots of good links)
www.win.tue.nl/cs/fm/engels/discovery/

Explorers of the World (Some biographies)
www.bham.wednet.edu/explore.htm

VIDEOS:

A&E Explorers Series: Christopher Columbus (1998); **Leif Ericson** (1998); **Lewis & Clark** (1998); **Marco Polo** (1998); & **Ponce de Leon** (1998). A&E Entertainment.

Christopher Columbus. Warner Studios, 1985.

Explorers: A Century of Discovery. National Geographic Film & TV, 1988.

Exploring Our Universe (NASA Space Flight). A&E Entertainment, 1993.

Ponce de Leon (American Tall Tales and Legends). Lyons Group, 1998.

Survival on the Ice. PBS Video, 1996.

Three Worlds Meet. Schlessinger, 1996.

United States Expansion (History for Children). Schlessinger, 1996.

Where None has Gone Before (Smithsonian World). Unapix Entertainment, 1991.

> ➤ *SEE ALSO THESE RELATED PATHFINDERS*
> *Adventure; Biographies*

Fairy Tales

A fairy tale is a fanciful, fictitious story of legendary deeds and creatures, and not all fairy tales are about fairies. Although today fairy tales are usually intended for children, many fairy tales were originally written to entertain adults. Every culture has some type of fairy tales, and many of these tales are hundreds of years old. Fairy tales are considered to be timeless, and so often begin with the phrase, "Once upon a time . . . ."

200s 300s 400s **DEWEY DECIMAL CALL NUMBERS**

398.2 Folk literature

SEARCH TERMS

Fairy tales   Brothers Grimm
Legends   Hans Christian Anderson
Folklore   Charles Perrault
Fantasy

NONFICTION/REFERENCE BOOKS

The Illustrated Book of Fairy Tales: Spellbinding Stories from Around the World by Neil Philip. Dorling Kindersley, 1998.
The Complete Fairy Tales of the Brothers Grimm translated by Jack Zipes. Bantam Books, 1992.
Hans Christian Andersen the Complete Fairy Tales and Stories by Virginia Haviland, Hans Christian Andersen and Erik C. Haugaard. Anchor, 1983.
The Complete Fairy Tales of Charles Perrault by Charles Perrault. Clarion Books, 1993.
The People Could Fly: American Black Folktales by Virginia Hamilton. Demco Media, 1993.
American Fairy Tales: From Rip Van Winkle to the Rootabaga Stories compiled by Neil Philip. Hyperion, 1996.

FICTION

Baba Yaga and Vasilisa the Brave as told by Marianna Mayer. Morrow Junior Books, 1994.
Beauty and the Beast by Nancy Willard. Harcourt Brace Jovanovich, 1992.
Cinderella, or, The Little Glass Slipper a free translation from the French of Charles Perrault. Aladdin Books, 1988.
Hansel and Gretel retold and illustrated by Jane Ray. Candlewick Press, 1997.
The Happy Prince: From the Fairy Tale by Oscar Wilde. Dutton Children's Books, 1995.
Harold's Fairy Tale: Further Adventures with the Purple Crayon by Crockett Johnson. HarperCollins, 1984.
I-Know-Not-What, I-Know-Not-Where: A Russian Tale adapted by Robert Sauber. Holiday House, 1994.
The Little Humpbacked Horse: A Russian Tale adapted by Elizabeth Winthrop. Clarion Books, 1997.
Little Long-Nose (Candlewick Treasures) by Wilhelm Hauff. Candlewick Press, 1997.
Mufaro's Beautiful Daughters: An African Tale by John Steptoe. Lothrop, Lee & Shepard Books, 1987.

FICTION CONTINUED

The Musicians of Bremen: A Tale from Germany retold by Jane Yolen. Simon & Schuster Books for Young Readers, 1996.

Papa Gatto: An Italian Fairy Tale retold and illustrated by Ruth Sanderson. Little, Brown & Co., 1995.

Puss in Boots by Charles Perrault, translated by Malcolm Arther. Farrar Straus Giroux, 1990.

Puss in Boots retold by Lincoln Kirstein. Little, Brown & Co., 1992.

Rapunzel from the Brothers Grimm; retold by Barbara Rogasky. Holiday House, 1982.

The Steadfast Tin Soldier retold and illustrated by Rachel Isadora. G. P. Putnam's Sons, 1996.

Swan Lake as told by Margot Fonteyn. Harcourt Brace Jovanovich, 1989.

The Tale of the Mandarin Ducks by Katherine Paterson. Penguin Books, 1995.

The Tale of Tsar Saltan by Alexander Pushkin. Dial Books, 1996.

The Three Princes: A Tale from the Middle East retold by Eric A. Kimmel. Holiday House, 1994.

Tim O'Toole and the Wee Folk: An Irish Tale told and illustrated by Gerald McDermott. Puffin Books, 1992.

The Twelve Dancing Princesses retold and illustrated by Jane Ray. Dutton Children's Books, 1996.

The Water of Life: A Tale From the Brothers Grimm retold by Barbara Rogasky. Holiday House, 1986.

MULTIMEDIA

CD-ROMS:

The Adventures of Pinocchio Interactive Multimedia. New Media Schoolhouse, 1992.

Kids Can Read! Interactive Multimedia. Discis, 1995.

Beauty and the Beast Interactive Multimedia. (Talking Storybook Series) New Media Schoolhouse, 1993.

Magic Tales Collection Interactive Multimedia (Magic Tales). Davidson & Assoc., 1995.

Magic Tales Collection #2 Interactive Multimedia (Magic Tales). Davidson & Assoc., 1996.

➤ *SEE ALSO THIS RELATED PATHFINDER*

Mythology

VIDEOS:

Ashpet: An American Cinderella. Davenport Films, 1984.

Fairy Tales From Around the World. 3G Home Video, 1991.

Red Riding Hood and Goldilocks. Rabbit Ears, 1990.

Shoemaker and the Elves. Time-Life, 1997.

Treasury of Fairy Tales (10 VHS tapes, 12 min. each). Spoken Arts, 1967.

WEB SITES

Fairy Tales Origins and Evolutions
www.darkgoddess.com/fairy/

Grimm's Fairy Tales (Text to 209 tales collected by the Brothers Grimm)
www.ul.cs.cmu.edu/books/GrimmFairy/index.html

Hans Christian Andersen Fairy Tales and Stories
www.math.technion.ac.il/~rl/Andersen/

Charles Perrault's Mother Goose Tales
www.pitt.edu/~dash/perrault.html

Folklore and Mythology Electronic Texts
www.pitt.edu/~dash/folktexts.html

Famous Landmarks

A landmark is a prominent feature of a landscape. Some famous landmarks are created by nature and may be part of a National Park. They are notable because of their extraordinary beauty or unusual character. Famous landmarks may also be buildings or sites that have historical significance and are preserved so that these places and events can be remembered.

DEWEY DECIMAL CALL NUMBERS

910 Geography & travel
624 Civil Engineering
932 Ancient history

SEARCH TERMS

Landmark
Monuments
National Monuments
National Historic Sites
National Park

NONFICTION/REFERENCE BOOKS

The Brooklyn Bridge by Elizabeth Mann. Mikaya Press, 1996.

Famous Places. Time-Life Books, 1990.

The Great Pyramid by Elizabeth Mann. Mikaya Press, 1996.

Historical American Landmarks: From the Old North Church to the Santa Fe Trail by C. B. Colby. Coward-McCann, 1968.

Kidding Around... (series). John Muir, 1998.

Landmarks: 18 Wonders of the New York World by Barbaralee Diamonstein. Harry N. Abrams, 1992.

Mount Rushmore by Craig Doherty. Blackbirch Press, 1995.

Our Great Rivers and Waterways by Eleanor Ayer. Millbrook Press, 1994.

Photo Archive of Famous Places of the World (Dover Pictorial Archive Series) by Donald M. Witte. Dover, 1993.

Wonders of the World by Giovanni Caselli. Dorling Kindersley, 1992.

Wonders of the World by Paul Humphrey. Steck Vaughn, 1995.

FICTION

The Armadillo from Amarillo by Lynne Cherry. Harcourt Brace Jovanovich, 1994.

Mr. Potato Head Across America by Nancy Shayne. Playskool Books, 1996.

Riddle City, USA!: A Book of Geography Riddles by Marco and Giulio Maestro. HarperCollins, 1994.

The Three Golden Keys by Peter Sis. Doubleday, 1994.

The Town that Got Out of Town by Robert Priest. D. R. Godine, 1989.

MULTIMEDIA

 CD-ROMS:

My First Amazing World Explorer. DK Multimedia, 1996.
Trudy's Time & Place House. Edmark, 1995.
Rand McNally Children's Atlas of the United States. GameTek, 1995.
Where in the USA is Carmen Sandiego? Broderbund, 1996.
Where in the World is Carmen Sandiego? Broderbund, 1996.

 VIDEOS:

Americana (Tell Me Why). TMW Media, 1987.
Video Visits Travels the USA (series). IVN Entertainment, 1994.

 WEB SITES

Unofficial Guides to the National Parks and Monuments of the Pacific Northwest (Many links to sites for specific parks and monuments in this region) www.halcyon.com/rdpayne/
History in the National Park Service: Meet the Presidents (Links to historic presidential monuments and memorials; American history resources) www.cr.nps.gov/history/Presses.htm
Seven Wonders of the World—National Geographic Society www.mountain.nationalgeographic.com/ resources/knowledge/phenomena/ wonders.html
Geographic superlatives - National Geographic Society (The biggest and best of our world's geography; with links to maps and additional information within this National Geographic Society site) www.mountain.nationalgeographic.com/ resources/knowledge/ geography/superlatives.html

➤ *SEE ALSO THESE RELATED PATHFINDERS*
Countries; States

Famous People

People who are well known and respected are considered famous. They may become famous for doing something important, like discovering a cure for a disease, or being the leader of a country, or creating a great work of art. Some people also become famous simply for playing a sport, starring in a movie, or appearing on a television program.

DEWEY DECIMAL CALL NUMBERS

920   Collective biographies
921   Biographies of individuals

SEARCH TERMS

Biography
Search by the activity a person is famous for, for example: Poet
Search by names of famous people, for example: Gracie Allen

NONFICTION/REFERENCE BOOKS

Ann Frank, Beyond the Diary: A Photographic Remembrance by Rian Verhoeven. Viking, 1993.

Bard of Avon: The Story of William Shakespeare by Diane Stanley and Peter Vennema. Morrow Junior Books, 1992.

Baseball's Greatest Hitters by Sydelle Kramer. Random House, 1995.

Biographies for Beginners. Omnigraphics, 1996.

Frank Lloyd Wright for Kids by Kathleen Thorne-Thomsen. Chicago Review Press, 1994.

Helen Keller: Crusader for the Blind and Deaf by Stewart and Polly Anne Graff. Bantam/Doubleday, 1991.

The Heroine of the Titanic: A Tale Both True and Otherwise of the Life of Molly Brown by Joan W. Blos. Morrow Junior Books, 1991.

Laura Ingalls Wilder: Author of the Little House Books by Carol Greene. Children's Press, 1990.

Lives of the Artists: Masterpieces, Messes (and What the Neighbors Thought) by Kathleen Krull. Harcourt Brace Jovanovich, 1995.

Margaret, Frank, and Andy: Three Writers' Stories by Cynthia Rylant. Harcourt Brace Jovanovich, 1996.

Minty: A Story of Young Harriet Tubman by Alan Schroeder. Dial Books, 1996.

Mother Teresa by John Barraclough. Heinemann Interactive Library, 1998.

The Oxford Children's Book of Famous People. Oxford University Press, 1994.

Starry Messenger: A Book Depicting the Life of a Famous Scientist, Mathematician, Astronomer, Philosopher, Physicist, Galileo Galilei by Peter Sis. Farrar Straus Giroux, 1996.

The Play's the Thing: A Story About William Shakespeare by Ruth Turk. Carolrhoda Books, 1997.

Who Said That?: Famous Americans Speak by Robert Burleigh. Henry Holt & Co., 1997.

Young Martin's Promise by Walter Dean Myers. Raintree/Steck Vaughn, 1993.

FICTION

Beethoven Lives Upstairs by Barbara Nichol. Orchard Books, 1994.

Bonjour, Mr. Satie by Tomie De Paola. G. P. Putnam's Sons, 1991.

Brighty of the Grand Canyon by Marguerite Henry. Aladdin Books, 1991.

Broadway Chicken by Jean-Luc Fromental. Hyperion, 1995.

Camille and the Sunflowers by Laurence Anholt. Barron's, 1994.

Dear Napolean, I Know You're Dead, But... by Elvira Woodruff. Bantam Books, 1992.

Dinner at Magritte's by Michael Garland. Dutton Children's Books, 1995.

Hear, Hear, Mr. Shakespeare by Bruce Koscielniak. Houghton Mifflin Co., 1998.

Tchaikovsky Discovers America by Esther Kalman. Orchard Books, 1995.

MULTIMEDIA

CD-ROMS:

Biographies Interactive Multimedia. UXL, 1996.

Encarta Multimedia Encyclopedia. Microsoft, 1997.

Events That Changed the World. ICE Integrated Comm. Entertainment, 1995.

Genius of Edison. Compton's, 1996.

Great Artists Interactive Multimedia. Attica Cybernautics, 1994.

The Guide to Classical Music. Cambrix, 1996.

His Name Was Lincoln Interactive. Sunburst Comm., 1996.

Infopedia Interactive (Includes *Webster's New Biographical Dictionary*). Softkey, 1996.

Leonardo The Inventor 2.0. Softkey, 1994.

People Behind the Holidays. National Geographic Society, 1994.

VIDEOS:

A&E Biography (series). A&E Entertainment, [dates vary].

American Women of Achievement (series). Schlessinger, 1995.

Black Americans of Achievement (series). Schlessinger, 1992.

Famous Americans of the 20th Century (series). Questar, 1991.

Hispanic and Latin American Heritage (series). Schlessinger, 1995.

WEB SITES

A&E Biography Series (Searchable database with brief biographical entries) www.biography.com

Biographical Dictionary (25,000 brief entries of important people from ancient times to present) www.s9.com/biography/

Biographies of the Saints www.hillsdale.edu/Dept/Phil&Rel/Biographies.html

Distinguished Women of the Past and Present www.netsrq.com/~dbois/

NASA Astronaut Biographies www.jsc.nasa.gov/Bios/astrobio.html

Presidents of the United States www.ipl.org/ref/POTUS/

➤ SEE ALSO THESE RELATED PATHFINDERS

Adventure; Artists; Biographies; Black History in America; Explorers and Exploration; Famous Women; Heroes; Inventors; Sports; U.S. Presidents

Famous Women

Women who are well known and respected are considered famous. They may become famous for doing something important, like discovering a cure for a disease, or being the leader of a country, or creating a great work of art. They may also become famous simply for playing a sport or starring in a movie.

 DEWEY DECIMAL CALL NUMBERS

301.41	Sociology (study of women)
331.4	Women and labor (workforce)
376	Education of women
398	Folklore
920	Collective biographies
921	Individual biographies

 SEARCH TERMS

Women
First Lady
Women, social conditions
Search by the activity a person is famous for, for example: Politician
Search by names of famous women, for example: Barbara Jordan

 NONFICTION/REFERENCE BOOKS

Author: A True Story by Helen Lester. Houghton Mifflin Co., 1997.

Babe Didrikson Zaharias by William R. Sanford. Crestwood House, 1993.

Clara Barton: Soldier of Mercy by Mary Catherine Rose. Chelsea Juniors, 1991.

Cleopatra by Diane Stanley. Morrow Junior Books, 1994.

Good Queen Bess: The Story of Elizabeth I of England by Diane Stanley. Four Winds Press, 1990.

Inspirations: Stories about Women Artists: Georgia O'Keeffe, Frida Kahlo, Alice Neel, Faith Ringgold by Leslie Sills. Albert Whitman & Co., 1989.

Margaret Bourke-White by Catherine Welch. Carolrhoda Books, 1997.

Painting Dreams: Minnie Evans, Visionary Artist by Mary Lyons. Houghton Mifflin Co., 1996.

Scholastic Encyclopedia of Women in the United States by Sheila Keenan. Scholastic, 1996.

Shooting Star: Annie Oakley, the Legend by Debbie Dadey. Walker & Co., 1997.

Wilma Unlimited: How Wilma Rudolph Became the World's Fastest Woman by Kathleen Krull. Harcourt Brace Jovanovich, 1996.

FICTION

The Ballad of the Pirate Queen by Jane Yolen. Harcourt Brace Jovanovich, 1995.

The Boston Coffee Party by Doreen Rappaport. HarperTrophy, 1990.

Cut from the Same Cloth: American Women of Myth, Legend, and Tall Tale by Robert D. San Souci. Philomel Books, 1993.

Dinner at Aunt Connie's House by Faith Ringgold. Hyperion, 1993.

Just Us Women by Jeanette Franklin Caines. Harper & Row, 1982.

Seven Brave Women by Betsy Hearne. Greenwillow Books, 1997.

Three Strong Women: A Tall Tale from Japan by Claus Stamm. Viking, 1990.

Two Mrs. Gibsons by Toyomi Igus. Children's Press, 1996.

MULTIMEDIA

 ### CD-ROMS:

American Journey, History in Your Hands: Women in America. Research Pub. International, 1995.

Her Heritage. Pilgrim New Media, 1994.

Infopedia Interactive (Includes *Webster's New Biographical Dictionary*). Softkey, 1996.

Telling Our Stories: Women in Science. McLean Media, 1997.

 ### VIDEOS:

American Women of Achievement. Schlessinger, 1995.

Hidden Army: Women in World War II. OnDeck Home Entertainment, 1995.

Little Women. Columbia/Tri-Star, 1995.

Sojourner Truth: Anti-Slavery Activist. Schlessinger, 1992.

Women of the West. United Learning, 1994.

 ## WEB SITES

All American Girls Professional Baseball League 1943-1954
www.dlcwest.com/~Smudge/Index.html

National Women's History Project (Information, links, and promotional materials) www.Nwhp.org/

Www Women's Sports Page
www.Fiat.gslis.utexas.edu/~Lewisa/Womsprst.html

➤ SEE ALSO THESE RELATED PATHFINDERS

Adventure; Artists; Black History in America; Explorers and Exploration; Famous People; Inventors; Sports

Flowers

The blossom of any seed-bearing plant is called a flower. There are many different flowers of many shapes, designs, and colors, but they characteristically contain the same basic parts: petals, stamen, and pistil. There are more than 250,000 species of flowers in the world.

DEWEY DECIMAL CALL NUMBERS

582.13 Flowers
580 Flowering plants
582 Seed-bearing plants
635.9 Gardening
574 Biology

SEARCH TERMS

Flowers
Gardens
Pollination
Search by names of individual flowers, for example: Sunflower

NONFICTION/REFERENCE BOOKS

Alphabet Garden by Laura Jane Coats. Maxwell Macmillan International, 1993.

Counting Wildflowers by Bruce McMillan. Mulberry Books, 1995.

Dandelion by Barrie Watts. Silver Burdett Press, 1987.

Flowers: A Guide to Familiar American Wildflowers (Golden Guides) by Alexander C. Martin, Herbert S. Zim, and Rudolf Freund. Golden Books, 1987.

Flowers for You: Blooms for Every Month by Anita Holmes. Bradbury Press, 1993.

Plants (DK Picturepedia). Dorling Kindersley, 1993.

Pollinating a Flower by Paul Bennett. Thomson Learning, 1994.

State Flowers by Elaine Landau. Franklin Watts, 1992.

Wildflowers (National Audubon Society First Field Guide) by Susan Hood. Scholastic, 1998.

FICTION

Alison's Zinnia by Anita Lobel. Greenwillow Books, 1990.

Flower Garden by Eve Bunting. Harcourt Brace Jovanovich, 1994.

Planting a Rainbow by Lois Ehlert. Harcourt Brace Jovanovich, 1988.

The Rose in My Garden by Arnold Lobel. Greenwillow Books, 1984.

Sunflower by Miela Ford. Greenwillow Books, 1995.

MULTIMEDIA

 ### CD-ROM:

A World of Plants. National Geographic Society, 1994.

 ### VIDEOS:

Eyewitness Plants. Dorling Kindersley, 1997.

Magic School Bus Goes to Seed. Kid Vision, 1995.

Reason for a Flower. Spoken Arts, 1989.

What is a Flower? National Geographic Educational, 1991.

 ## WEB SITES

Gardening for Kids
www.geocities.com/EnchantedForest/Glade/3313/

The Time-Life Complete Gardener Encyclopedia
www.cgi.pathfinder.com/cgi-bin/VG/vg

➤ SEE ALSO THESE RELATED PATHFINDERS

Bees & Beekeeping; Plants

Food Chain

The food chain refers to the series of organisms, plants, and animals that create a continuation of food from one plant or animal to the next. Each member of the food chain consumes a lower member and in turn is preyed upon and eaten by a higher member. The food chain links different species into a community. Aquatic animals form the longest food chains, but most food chains are no larger than six species.

DEWEY DECIMAL CALL NUMBERS

577   Food chain, Ecology
574.5 Biology, Ecology
577.69 General nature of life
591.5 Zoology, Ecology

SEARCH TERMS

Food chains
Ecology
Pond ecology
Tide pool ecology
Ocean ecology
Island ecology

NONFICTION/REFERENCE BOOKS

Barnacles Eat with Their Feet: Delicious Facts about the Tide Pool Food Chain by Sherry Shahan. Millbrook Press, 1996.

Beneath the Oceans by Penny Clarke. Franklin Watts, 1997.

Hungry Animals: My First Look at a Food Chain by Pamela Hickman. Kids Can Press, 1997.

Over the Steamy Swamp by Paul Geraghty. Harcourt Brace Jovanovich, 1989.

Predator by Bruce Brooks. Farrar Straus Giroux, 1991.

Who Eats What?: Food Chains and Food Webs (Let's-Read-And-Find-Out Science. Stage 2) by Patricia Lauber. HarperCollins, 1995.

World Food by Sally Morgan. Franklin Watts, 1998.

FICTION

The Magic School Bus Gets Eaten: A Book about Food Chains by Patricia Relf. Scholastic, 1996.

A Most Unusual Lunch by Robert Bender. Dial Books for Young Readers, 1994.

The Peach Tree by Norman Pike. Stemmer House, 1983.

Pond Life: The Fishing Trip (Discovery World) by Donna Koren. Child's World, 1990.

Wolf Island by Celia Godkin. Scientific American Books for Young Readers, 1993.

Yum-Yum! by Mick Manning. Franklin Watts, 1997.

MULTIMEDIA

CD-ROMS:

Frog File. Videodiscovery, 1997.
Great Ocean Rescue. Tom Snyder, 1996.
Rainforests. World Book, 1997.
U*X*L Science. Gale, 1997.
Zurk's Learning Safari. Soleil, 1995.

VIDEOS:

Food Chain. AIMS Media, 1994.
Food Chain (On Nature's Trail). National Geographic Educational, 1995.
Little Wanderers (Seahouse Two). Rainbow Educational Video, 1992.
Magic School Bus Gets Eaten. Kid Vision, 1995.
What Is a Food Chain? (Understanding Ecology). Coronet/MTI/Centron, 1992.

WEB SITES

The Food Chain (Let the Sun Shine In) (Classroom activity)
www.avocado.dade.k12.fl.us/Projects/food-chain/
The Food Chain (Classroom activity)
www.flash.lakeheadu.ca/~dlkosowi/animal1.html

➤ SEE ALSO THESE RELATED PATHFINDERS
Animals; Biomes; Ecology

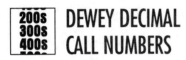
Food Groups

The four food groups are grains and grain products; fruits and vegetables; meat and dairy; and sugars, fats, and oils. It is considered nutritious to eat a proper balance of food from each of these four groups.

200s 300s 400s **DEWEY DECIMAL CALL NUMBERS**

613.2 Dietetics
641.3 Foods and foodstuffs

SEARCH TERMS

Nutrition
Food
Food groups
Four food groups
Diet
Health

NONFICTION/REFERENCE BOOKS

Eat the Right Stuff by Catherine Reef. Twenty First Century Books, 1995.

The Edible Pyramid: Good Eating Every Day by Loreen Leedy. Holiday House, 1994.

The Food Pyramid (A True Book) by Joan Kalbacken. Children's Press, 1998.

Harvest Year by Cris Peterson. Boyd Mills Press, 1996.

The Kids Multicultural Cookbook: Food & Fun Around the World by Deanna Cook. Williamson, 1995.

Nutrition and Exercise (Five Kids & A Monkey, Series One) by Nina Riccio. Creative Attic, 1997.

Peas and Honey: Recipes for Kids (with a Pinch of Poetry) by Kimberly Colen. Boyds Mills Press, 1995.

Pretend Soup and Other Real Recipes by Mollie Katzen and Ann Henderson. Tricycle Press, 1994.

The Vegetable Show by Laurie Krasny Brown. Little, Brown & Co., 1995.

What Food is This? by Rosemarie Hausherr. Scholastic, 1994.

What We Eat (Play & Discover) by Sara Lynn and Diane James. Thomson Learning, 1994.

FICTION

ABC Yummy by Lisa Jahn-Clough. Houghton Mifflin Co., 1997.

The Boy Who Ate Around by Henrik Drescher. Hyperion, 1994.

Bread and Jam for Frances by Russell Hoban. HarperCollins, 1992.

Chato's Kitchen by Gary Soto. Putnam & Grosset Group, 1997.

Cloudy With a Chance of Meatballs by Judith Barrett. Atheneum, 1978.

Dinosaurs Alive and Well: A Guide to Good Health by Laurie Krasny Brown. Little, Brown & Co., 1990.

D.W., the Picky Eater by Marc Brown. Little, Brown & Co., 1995.

Five Kids & A Monkey Solve the Great Cupcake Caper: A Learning Adventure About Gregory, the Terrible Eater by Mitchell Sharmat. Scholastic Trade, 1989.

Heckedy Peg by Audrey Wood. Harcourt Brace Jovanovich, 1987.

Now I Will Never Leave the Dinner Table by Jane Read Martin. HarperCollins, 1996.

MULTIMEDIA

 ### CD-ROM:

The Human Body Interactive Multimedia. National Geographic Society, 1994.

 ### VIDEOS:

Daily Food Choices for Healthy Living. United Learning, 1994.

Eat Well, Grow Well (Our Wonderful Body). Coronet/MTI/Centron, 1993.

Food Guide Pyramid: Contemporary Nutrition. Cambridge Career Products, 1993.

Healthy Food (My Body, My Buddy). Rainbow Educational Video, 1993.

Nutrition: Keep Your Balance. United Learning, 1993.

 ## WEB SITES

Kids Food Cyber Club!
www.kidsfood.org/kf_cyber.html

ADA Information—American Dietetic Association/Food Guide Pyramid
204.149.104.173/fgp.html

American Heath Foundation Presents: National Child Health Day
www.ahf.org/chd98/kids/

Food Guide Pyramid
www.mealformation.com/fdpyram.htm

Vegetarian Awareness Network—The Four New Food Groups
204.192.121.201/page_5.html

You Are What You Eat—A Guide to Good Nutrition
www.hyperion.advanced.org/11163/gather/cgi-bin/wookie.cgi/?id=1kQm

Forest (Temperate Forest)

Forests cover large areas of land and are made up of a dense growth of tree, plants, underbrush, and wildlife. Temperate Forests are found in regions of North America and Europe which have a mild climate, but distinct seasons. They are home to a wide variety of plant and animal life.

DEWEY DECIMAL CALL NUMBERS

200s 300s 400s

333.75 Forest lands
508.747 Geography, descriptions, Travels and surveys
585 Naked seed plants, Gymnosperms
574.5 Biology, Ecology
577.3 General nature of life
591.73 Zoology

SEARCH TERMS

Forest	Forest fires
Forest ecology	Wildfires
Old-growth forest	Forest animals
Ecology	Forest plants
Trees	Forest birds
Forestry	Natural history

NONFICTION/REFERENCE BOOKS

Ancient Ones: The World of the Old-Growth Douglas Fir (Tree Tales) by Barbara Bash. Sierra Club Books for Children, 1994.

Crinkleroot's Guide to Knowing the Trees by Jim Arnosky. Maxwell Macmillan Canada, 1991.

How the Forest Grew by William Jaspersohn. Mulberry Books, 1992.

Fire in the Forest: A Cycle of Growth and Renewal by Laurence Pringle. Atheneum Books for Young Readers, 1995.

Forest Life (Look Closer) by Barbara Taylor. Dorling Kindersley, 1993.

The Gift of the Tree by Alvin Tresselt. Lothrop, Lee & Shepard, 1992.

In the Forest (Wild Wonders) by Ann Cooper. Denver Museum of Natural History Press, 1996.

A Tree in a Forest by Jan Thornhill. Simon & Schuster Books for Young Readers, 1992.

The Tree in the Ancient Forest by Carol Reed-Jones. Dawn Pub., 1995.

Wildfire (Nature in Action) by Patrick Cone. Carolrhoda Books, 1997.

FICTION

In the Forest: Story and Pictures by Marie Hall Ets. Puffin Books, 1978, c1944.

One Day in the Woods (Trophy Chapter Book) by Jean Craighead George. HarperTrophy, 1995.

The Big Snow by Berta and Elmer Hader. Macmillan, 1976.

The First Forest by John Gile. John Gile Comm., 1989.

In the Woods: Who's Been Here? By Lindsay Barrett George. Greenwillow Books, 1995.

My First Spring by Matthew Lambert. Raintree/Steck Vaughn, 1994.

My Night Forest by Roy Owen. Maxwell Macmillan International, 1994.

Song for the Ancient Forest by Nancy Lucnn. Maxwell Macmillan International, 1993.

Whisper from the Woods by Victoria Wirth. Green Tiger Press, 1991.

The Year of Fire by Teddy Jam. McElderry/Macmillan, 1993.

MULTIMEDIA

 ### CD-ROMS:

Eyewitness Encyclopedia of Nature 2.0. DK Multimedia, 1996.
U*X*L Science. Gale, 1997.

 ### VIDEOS:

Babes in the Woods (Mother Nature Tales of Discovery). Discovery Channel, 1992.
Forest Habitats (Mother Nature Tales of Discovery). Discovery Channel, 1991.
In Celebration of Trees. Discovery Channel, 1991.
Let's Explore a Forest (Let's Explore). National Geographic Educational, 1994.
Life of a Forest. United Learning, 1993.
Old-Growth Forest (Life Science: Nature). Natural History Educational, 1995.

 ## WEB SITES

Explore the Fantastic Forest—National Geographic
www.nationalgeographic.com/features/96/forest/html/enter.html
Ecosystems of Our World—Temperate Forests
tqd.advanced.org/2988/tempforest.htm
Ecosystems of Our World—Cold Climate Forests (The Taiga)
tqd.advanced.org/2988/ccforest.htm

➤ SEE ALSO THESE RELATED PATHFINDERS

Biomes; Ecology; Rainforest

Friends

A friend is a person whom you know well and like. Friends enjoy spending time together and depend upon each other for companionship and support. Some friends may see each other often, while other friends may live far apart and know each other only by telephone conversations and letter writing.

 DEWEY DECIMAL CALL NUMBERS

177 Ethics of social relations (friendship)
152.4 Emotions and feelings
158 Applied psychology
398.2 Folk literature

 SEARCH TERMS

Friendship
Friends
Relationships
Pen pals

 NONFICTION/REFERENCE BOOKS

The Best Friends Book: True Stories About Real Best Friends, Fun Things To Do With Your Best Friend, Solving Best Friend Problems, Long-Distant Friends, Finding New Friends, and More! by Arlene Erlback. Free Spirit, 1995.

Dinosaurs Alive and Well! A Guide to Good Health by Laurie Krasny Brown. Little, Brown & Co., 1990.

Friendly (Feelings) by Janine Amos. Raintree/Steck Vaughn, 1994.

Friendship Bracelets by Camilla Gryski. Morrow Junior Books, 1993.

How Humans Make Friends by Loreen Leedy. Holiday House, 1996.

Together by George Ella Lyon. Orchard Books, 1994.

FICTION

Amber Brown Goes Fourth by Paula Danziger. G. P. Putnam's Sons, 1995.

Amos & Boris by William Steig. Farrar Straus Giroux, 1971.

Andy and the Lion: A Tale of Kindness Remembered or the Power of Gratitude (Picture Puffins) by James Daugherty. Puffin Books, 1989.

Arthur's Great Big Valentine by Lillian Hoban. Harper & Row, 1989.

Backyard Rescue by Hope Ryden. Beech Tree Paperback, 1997.

A Bargain for Frances by Russell Hoban. HarperTrophy, 1992.

Best Friends by Steven Kellogg. Dial Books for Young Readers, 1990.

Best Friends Think Alike by Lynn Reiser. Greenwillow Books, 1997.

Blow Me a Kiss, Miss Lilly by Nancy White Carlstrom. Harper & Row, 1990.

Charlotte's Web by E. B. White. HarperCollins, 1980.

Chester's Way by Kevin Henkes. Greenwillow Books, 1988.

The Cybil War by Betsy Byars. Puffin Books, 1990.

Frog and Toad All Year (An I Can Read Book) by Arnold Lobel. Harper & Row, 1976.

Frog and Toad Together (An I Can Read Book) by Arnold Lobel. Harper & Row, 1972.

Josie's Troubles by Phyllis Reynolds Naylor. Maxwell Macmillan International, 1992.

Lily's Crossing by Patricia Reilly Giff. Delacorte Press, 1997.

You and Me: Poems of Friendship selected and illustrated by Salley Mavor. Orchard Books, 1997.

MULTIMEDIA

 ### CD-ROM:

Playground of Friends. Comfy, 1997.

VIDEOS:

Caring and Sharing (My Body, My Buddy). Rainbow Educational Video, 1995.

Casey's Revenge: A Story About Fighting and Disagreements (Human Race Club). Rainbow Educational Video, 1989.

Caught in the Middle: The Peer Pressure Squeeze. Rainbow Educational Video, 1993.

Exploring Friendships (Book Connections). Cheshire Book Companions, 1992.

Fair Weather Friend: A Story About Making Friends (Human Race Club). Rainbow Educational Video, 1989.

 ### WEB SITES

Dino Pals!
www.members.aol.com/kidz4peace/
dinopals/index.htm
Friendship
www.ucs.mun.ca/~sherryw/friend.htm
Making Friends —Computer Crafts for Kids www.makingfriends.com/

➤ *SEE ALSO THIS RELATED PATHFINDER*
Conflict

Heroism

Heroism is the act of doing something very brave, such as risking your life to protect or save another person. Heroism may also be shown by people who stand up for what they believe is right. For instance, Martin Luther King Jr. was a hero when he stood up for civil rights.

 DEWEY DECIMAL CALL NUMBERS

920 Collective biography
921 Biography
398 Folklore

 SEARCH TERMS

Folklore
Heroes
Heroines
Heroism

 NONFICTION/REFERENCE BOOKS

A Boy Called Slow: The True Story of Sitting Bull by Joseph Bruchac. Philomel Books, 1994.

Afro-bets Book of Black Heroes from A to Z by Wade Hudson. Just Us Books, 1988.

Animals Who Have Won Our Hearts by Jean Craighead George. HarperCollins, 1994.

Benito Juarez: Hero of Modern Mexico by Rae Bains. Troll Assoc., 1993.

Black Frontiers: A History of African American Heroes in the Old West by Lillian Schlissel. Simon & Schuster Books for Young Readers, 1995.

Charles Lindbergh, Hero Pilot by David Collins. Chelsea House, 1991.

Clara Barton and the American Red Cross by Eve Marko. Baronet Books, 1996.

Daniel Boone: Taming the Wilds by Katherine Wilkie. Chelsea Juniors, 1991.

Davy Crockett: An American Hero by Tom Townsend. Eakin Press, 1987.

Dog to the Rescue: Seventeen True Tales of Dog Heroism by Jeanatte Sanders. Scholastic, 1993.

Dorothy Day: Friend to the Forgotten by Deborah Kent. William B. Eerdmans, 1996.

Girls Who Rocked the World: Heroines from Sacajawea to Sheryl Swoopes by Amelie Weldon. Beyond Words Pub., 1998.

John Paul Jones, Hero of the Seas by Keith Brandt. Troll Assoc., 1983.

Jose de San Martin: Latin America's Quiet Hero by Jose Fernandez. Millbrook Press, 1994.

Kate Shelley: Bound for Legend by Robert D. San Souci. Dial Books for Young Readers, 1995.

Kid Heroes by Neal Shusterman. TOR Books, 1991.

The Real Johnny Appleseed by Laurie Lawler. Albert Whitman & Co., 1995.

Robert E. Lee, Hero of the South by Charles Parlin Graves. Chelsea House, 1991.

Sam Houston, American Hero by Ann Fears Crawford. Hendrick-Long, 1993.

FICTION

The Adventures of Isabel by Ogden Nash. Joy Street Books, 1991.

The Adventures of Odysseus by Neil Philip. Orchard Books, 1997.

American Tall Tales by Mary Pope Osborne. Knopf, 1991.

Be Not Far From Me: The Oldest Love Story: Legends From the Bible by Eric Kimmel. Simon & Schuster, 1998.

By the Great Horn Spoon! by Sid Fleischman. Little, Brown & Co., 1988.

Children's Book of Heroes. Simon & Schuster, 1997.

Defenders of the Universe by D. V. Kelleher. Houghton Mifflin Co., 1993.

Hercules: Hero of the Night Sky by Robin Moore. Simon & Schuster, 1997.

Hero of Bremen by Margaret Hodges. Holiday House, 1993.

Hero of the Land of Snow by Sylvia Gretchen. Dharma Pub., 1990.

John Jeremy Colton by Bryan Jeffrey Leech. Hyperion for Children, 1994.

Larger than Life: The Adventures of American Legendary Heroes by Robert D. San Souci. Doubleday Books for Young Readers, 1995.

The Little Ships: The Heroic Rescue at Dunkirk in World War II by Louise Borden. Margaret K. McElderry Books, 1997.

The Macmillan Book of Greek Gods and Heroes by Alice Low. Macmillan, 1985.

Robin Hood in the Greenwood by Jane Louise Curry. Margaret K. McElderry Books, 1995.

The Truth about Mary Rose by Marilyn Sachs. Puffin Books, 1995.

The Wainscott Weasel by Tor Seidler. HarperCollins, 1993.

William Tell by Margaret Early. Harry N. Abrams, 1991.

MULTIMEDIA

CD-ROMS:

Biographies Interactive Multimedia. UXL, 1996.

Encarta (Multimedia Encyclopedia). Microsoft, 1998.

Infopedia Interactive (Includes *Webster's New Biographical Dictionary*). Softkey, 1996.

People Behind the Holidays. National Geographic Society, 1994

WEB SITES

Biography.Com (Bios of historic figures) www.biography.com/bio_main.html

Unsung Heroes and Heroines www.home.on.rogers.wave.ca/eliza/cyber/Project.htm

VIDEOS:

Animated Hero Classics (series). Schlessinger, 1997.

Davy Crockett. Rabbit Ears, 1992.

Finn McCoul. Rabbit Ears, 1991.

Happily Ever After. Time-Life, 1997.

Homer Price Stories (Children's Circle Series). Weston Woods, 1993.

Horton Hears a Who. Sony Wonder, 1966.

Little Tim and the Brave Sea Captain. Weston Woods, 1980.

Secret of NIMH (Based on *Mrs. Frisby and the Rats of NIMH*). MGM/UA, 1982.

➤ SEE ALSO THESE RELATED PATHFINDERS

Explorers and Exploration; Famous People; Famous Women; Mythology

Holidays Around the World

Holidays are special days set aside to remember and recognize important events, people, or times of the year. Many holidays and festivals have special food, costumes, and events associated with them. People all over the world celebrate holidays, but not all people celebrate the same holidays. Many celebrations are unique to a particular country, culture, or religion. And some holidays, such as Christmas, are celebrated by many people all over the world, but the celebrations differ depending of the customs and traditions of that part of the world.

 DEWEY DECIMAL CALL NUMBERS

394.2 Holidays
290's Religion and comparative religions
(holy days)

 SEARCH TERMS

Holidays
Social life and customs
Festivals
Fasts and feasts

 NONFICTION/REFERENCE BOOKS

Celebrate! in South Asia by Joe Viesti and Diane Hall. Lothrop, Lee & Shepard, 1996.

Celebrating Independence Day by Shelly Neilsen. Abdo & Daughters, 1992.

Celebrating Thanksgiving by Shelly Nielsen. Abdo & Daughters, 1992.

Children Just Like Me: Celebrations by Barnabas and Anabel Kindersley. Dorling Kindersley, 1997.

Chinese New Year by Catherine Chambers. Raintree/Steck Vaughn, 1997.

Customs and Traditions by Bobbie Kalman. Crabtree Pub. Co., 1994.

Fiesta U.S.A. by George Ancona. Lodestar Books, 1995.

Festival Crafts by Chris Deshpande. Gareth Stevens Pub., 1994.

The First Thanksgiving by Linda Hayward. Random House, 1990.

Holidays & Festivals Activities by Debbie Smith. Crabtree Pub. Co., 1994.

How to Make Holiday Pop-Ups by Joan Irvine. Beech Tree Books, 1996.

Id-ul-Filtr by Rosalind Kerven. Raintree/Steck Vaughn, 1997.

A Jewish Holiday ABC by Malka Drucker. Harcourt Brace Jovanovich, 1992.

A Kwanzaa Celebration Pop-Up Book by Nancy Williams. Little Simon, 1995.

Labor Day by Geoffrey Scott. Carolrhoda Books, 1982.

Light the Candle, Bang the Drum: A Book of Holidays Around the World by Ann Morris. Dutton Children's Books, 1997.

Martin Luther King Day by Linda Lowery. Carolrhoda Books, 1987.

A Picture Book of Jewish Holidays by David Adler. Holiday House, 1981.

Presidents Day by Diane MacMillan. Enslow, 1997.

Tet: Vietnamese New Year by Dianne MacMillan. Enslow, 1994.

The World Holiday Book: Celebrations for Every Day of the Year by Anneli S. Rufus. HarperSanFrancisco, 1994.

A World of Holidays by Louisa Campbell. Silver Moon/August House, 1993.

FICTION

Celebrations (A collection of holiday poetry) by Myra Cohn Livingston. Holiday House, 1985.

A Great Miracle Happened There by Karla Kuskin. Willa Perlman Books, 1993.

Elijah's Tears: Stories for the Jewish Holidays by Sydelle Pearl. Henry Holt & Co., 1996.

First Plays for Children: A Collection of Little Plays for the Youngest Players by Helen Gotwalt. Plays, 1995.

Happy Holidaysaurus! by Bernard Most. Harcourt Brace Jovanovich, 1992.

Here Comes Zelda Claus, and Other Holiday Disasters by Lynn Hall. Harcourt Brace Jovanovich, 1989.

How Many Days to America?: A Thanksgiving Story by Eve Bunting. Clarion Books, 1988.

It's Thanksgiving by Jack Prelutsky. Greenwillow Books, 1982.

An Old-Fashioned Thanksgiving by Louisa May Alcott. Holiday House, 1989.

Over and Over by Charlotte Zolotow. HarperCollins, 1987.

Small Plays for Special Days by Sue Alexander. Seabury Press, 1977.

The Three Bears Holiday Rhyme Book by Jane Yolen. Harcourt Brace Jovanovich 1996.

The Truth about Cousin Ernie's Head by Matthew McElligott. Simon & Schuster, 1996.

The Uninvited Guest: And Other Jewish Holiday Tales by Nina Jaffe. Scholastic, 1993.

MULTIMEDIA

CD-ROMS:

Mieko Interactive: A Story of Japanese Culture (Based on the book by Leo Politi). Digital, 1996.

Ozzie's Travels Tour Mexico, Japan and India. Digital Impact, 1996.

People Behind the Holidays. National Geographic Society, 1994.

World Book Multimedia Encyclopedia. World Book, 1998.

VIDEOS:

Holiday Songs Around the World. Educational Activities, 1994.

Holidays for Children (16-volume series, from Arbor day to Valentine's Day). Schlessinger, 1994.

Maccabees: The Story of Hanukkah (Animated Hero Classics Video Series). Schlessinger, 1995.

Sesame Street Celebrates Around the World. CTW, 1994.

WEB SITES

Chinese Holidays and Festivals
www.indiana.edu/~chasso/holiday.html

Holidays on the Net (Good, brief information) www.holidays.net/index2.htm

Holidays Around the World (Links to resources)
www.rialto.k12.ca.us/school/frisbie/holiday.html

The World Wide Holiday and Festival Site (List of holiday dates by country. Not a lot of information)
194.30.129.38/bdecie/Countries.html

Multicultural Calendar
www.kidlink.org/KIDPROJ/MCC/

➤ *SEE ALSO THIS RELATED PATHFINDER*
Christmas Around the World

Human Body

The human body is an amazing machine. It has many different parts that all work together. Each group of parts is called a system. The digestive system, nervous system, skeletal system, circulatory system, and muscular system all work together to keep the body alive.

DEWEY DECIMAL CALL NUMBERS

200s 300s 400s

612 Human body (how it works)
611 Anatomy, Humans

SEARCH TERMS

Human physiology	Digestive system
Human anatomy	Muscular system
Circulatory system	Skeleton
Blood	Skin
Heart	Pregnancy
Ear	Childbirth
Hearing	Sense and sensation
Nervous system	*Search by names of*
Respiratory system	*the parts of the body,*
Digestion	*for example:* Stomach

NONFICTION/REFERENCE BOOKS

Grossology by Sylvia Branzei. Planet Dexter, 1995.

The Heart: Our Circulatory System by Seymour Simon. Morrow Junior Books, 1996.

How You Were Born by Joanna Cole. Morrow Junior Books, 1993.

My Five Senses by Margaret Miller. Simon & Schuster Books for Young Readers, 1994.

Blood (Body Books) by Anna Sandeman. Copper Beech Books, 1996.

The Body Atlas by Mark Crocker. Oxford, Award Pub., 1991.

The Brain: Our Nervous System by Seymour Simon. Morrow Junior Books, 1997.

Breathing (Body Books) by Anne Sandeman. Copper Beech Books, 1995.

Cuts, Breaks, Bruises, and Burns: How Your Body Heals by Joanna Cole. Crowell, 1985.

Human Body (Eyewitness Explorers) by Steve Parker. Dorling Kindersley, 1994.

Moving (First Starts) by Anita Ganeri. Raintree/Steck Vaughn, 1994.

My Body (What's Inside) by Angela Royston. Dorling Kindersley, 1991.

My First Body Book by Melanie and Chris Rice. Dorling Kindersley, 1995.

FICTION

The Magic School Bus Inside the Human Body by Joanna Cole. Scholastic, 1989.

Here Are My Hands by Bill Martin, Jr. and John Archambault. Henry Holt & Co., 1989.

Parts by Tedd Arnold. Dial Books for Young Readers, 1997.

MULTIMEDIA

 CD-ROMS:

Scholastic's The Magic School Bus Explores the Human Body Interactive Multimedia. Microsoft Home, 1995.

The Ultimate Human Body Interactive Multimedia. Dorling Kindersley Multimedia, 1996.

What is a Bellybutton? Interactive Multimedia: First Questions and Answers About the Human Body. IVI Pub., 1994.

VIDEOS:

Breath of Life: Our Respiratory System. Rainbow Educational Video, 1992.

Circulatory and Respiratory Systems (Your Body). National Geographic Film & TV, 1994.

Digestive System (Your Body). National Geographic Film & TV, 1994.

Food Into Fuel: Our Digestive System. Rainbow Educational Video, 1992.

Human Body: The Inside Scoop (Bill Nye, the Science Guy). Disney Home Video, 1995.

In Control: Our Brain and Nervous System. Rainbow Educational Video, 1993.

Magic School Bus Flexes Its Muscles. Kid Vision, 1996.

Magic School Bus for Lunch. Kid Vision, 1995.

Nervous System (Your Body). National Geographic Film & TV, 1994.

Pumping Life: The Heart and Circulatory System. Rainbow Educational Video, 1989.

You and Your Ears (2nd Ed., This is You). Disney Educational, 1993.

 WEB SITES

Atlas of the Human Body (Contains good graphics, clearly labeled)
www.amaassn.org/insight/gen_hlth/atlas/atlas.htm

Human Anatomy On-Line
www.innerbody.com/

Virtual Body
www.medtropolis.com/vbody/

Hurricanes

A hurricane is a severe tropical storm with winds of at least 75 miles per hour. The winds of a hurricane spiral inward, toward the eye, or center of the storm. Hurricanes originate in the ocean near the equator. Many of these storms remain over the ocean and last only a few days, but some hurricanes travel toward islands and coastal regions. These storms, with their high winds, rain, and huge waves, can have devastating results.

 DEWEY DECIMAL CALL NUMBERS

551.55   Hurricanes
363.3   Public safety
551.5   Meteorology

 SEARCH TERMS

Hurricanes
Meteorology
Natural disaster
Storms
Weather

 NONFICTION/REFERENCE BOOKS

Eye of the Storm: Chasing Storms with Warren Faidley by Stephen P. Kramer. G. P. Putnam's Sons, 1997.

Hurricane by Christopher Lampton. Millbrook Press, 1991.

Hurricanes by Peter Murray. Child's World, 1996.

Hurricanes: Earth's Mightiest Storms by Patricia Lauber. Scholastic, 1996.

It's Raining Cats and Dogs: All Kinds of Weather and Why We Have It by Franklyn Mansfield Branley. Houghton Mifflin Co., 1987.

Storms by Seymour Simon. Morrow Junior Books, 1989.

FICTION

Django by John Cech. Four Winds Press, 1994.

Hurricane by David Wiesner. Clarion Books, 1990.

The Magic School Bus Inside a Hurricane by Joanna Cole. Scholastic, 1995.

Time of Wonder by Robert McCloskey. Puffin Books, 1977.

MULTIMEDIA

CD-ROMS:

Radar Rooster Cooping with Natural Disasters. Meridian, 1996.
Weather and Climate. Discoveryworks, 1996.
Weather Science Explorer. New Media Schoolhouse, 1996.

VIDEOS:

Hurricanes and Tornadoes (Weather Fundamentals). Schlessinger, 1998.
Hurricane. NOVA, 1989.
Monsters of the Deep. PBS Video, 1996.

WEB SITES

Personal AccuWeather Hurricane Center—Facts
www.accuweather.com/hurr98f/facts_qx01
Hurricane History in the Atlantic
www.sunsentinel.com/storm/history/tim_1979.htm
USA Today—Hurricane Information Guide
www.usatoday.com/weather/whur0.htm

➤ SEE ALSO THESE RELATED PATHFINDERS

Clouds; Natural Disasters; Weather

Immigration

When a person or group of people chooses to move from one country to the other in order to resettle and live in the new country, it is called immigration. Most people immigrate to a new land in search of a better life with greater opportunity. The United States of America was formed by people who chose to immigrate to America. The earliest immigrants were from England, but they were soon followed by people from other European countries. Asian immigration into the United States began in the late 1800s. People from all over the world continue to immigrate to America and become American citizens.

DEWEY DECIMAL CALL NUMBERS

304 Immigration
325 Ellis Island
973 American History

SEARCH TERMS

Immigration
Emigration
Ellis Island

NONFICTION/REFERENCE BOOKS

Coming to America: The Story of Immigration by Betsy Maestro. Scholastic Trade, 1996.

Immigrants by Martin Sandler. HarperCollins, 1995.

My Two Worlds by Ginger Gordon. Clarion, 1996.

We Came From Vietnam by Muriel Stanek. Albert Whitman & Co., 1985.

Where Did Your Family Come From by Melvin Berger. Ideals Children's Books, 1993.

FICTION

All the Lights in the Night by Arthur A. Levine, James E. Ransome. William Morrow & Co., 1991.

The American Wei by Marion Hess Pomeranc. Albert Whitman & Co, 1998.

Dancing with Dziadziu by Susan Bartoletti. Harcourt Brace Jovanovich, 1997.

The Long Way to a New Land by Joan Sandin. HarperTrophy, 1986.

MULTIMEDIA

CD-ROMS:

American Journey: The Immigrant Experience. Primary Source Media, 1997.

Decisions, Decisions 5.0: Immigration. Tom Snyder, 1997.

VIDEOS:

America's Westward Expansion. Knowledge Unlimited, 1996.

Immigration to the U.S. (American History for Children) Schlessinger, 1996.

Multicultural People of North America Video Series Schlessinger, 1997. (Looks at 15 different cultural groups, reasons for their emigration to North America, their contributions, and their cultures)

One World, Many Worlds: Hispanic Diversity in the United States. Rainbow Educational Video 1993. (Covers reasons for Hispanic immigration to U.S.)

WEB SITES

The American Immigration Homepage (Created by high school students, but a good resource) www.bergen.org/AAST/Projects/Immigration/index.html

Ellis Island, The New World (Time line, statistics, and audio clips of immigrants telling their stories) www.historychannel.com/community/ellisisle/newworld.html

➤ SEE ALSO THESE RELATED PATHFINDERS
Diversity; Ellis Island

Insects

There are more than a million known types of insects in the world. They are identified by the way their body is divided into three parts: a head, a thorax, and an abdomen. All adult insects have six legs, attached to the thorax. Some of the more well-known insects are the butterfly, the beetle, the dragonfly, the wasp, and the grasshopper.

DEWEY DECIMAL CALL NUMBERS

200s
300s
400s

595.7 Insects
595 Invertebrates
638 Insect culture

SEARCH TERMS

Insects
Bugs
Invertebrates
Search by names of particular insects, for example: Centipede

NONFICTION/REFERENCE BOOKS

Amazing Bugs (Inside Guides) by Miranda MacQuitty. Dorling Kindersley, 1996.

Amazing Insects by L. A. Mound. Knopf, 1993.

Animals and Nature: Scholastic Reference. Scholastic, 1995.

Backyard Hunter by Bianca Lavies. Puffin Unicorn Books, 1995.

Backyard Insects by Millicent Ellis Selsam. Scholastic, 1981.

The Big Bug Book by Margery Facklam. Little, Brown & Co., 1994.

Blood-feeding Bugs and Beasts by Patricia Kite. Millbrook Press, 1996.

Creepy, Crawly Baby Bugs by Sandra Markle. Walker & Co., 1996.

Insect Attack by Christopher Lampton. Millbrook Press, 1992.

Insect Metamorphosis: From Egg to Adult by Ron and Nancy Goor. Atheneum, 1990.

Insects by Sue Hadden. Thomson Learning, 1993.

Insects by Joni Phelps Hunt. Silver Burdett Press, 1995.

Insects and Spiders (Picturepedia) by Paul Hillyard. Dorling Kindersley, 1993.

Insects are My Life by Megan McDonald. Orchard Books, 1995.

Pet Bugs: A Kid's Guide to Catching and Keeping Touchable Insects by Sally Stenhouse Kneidel. Wiley, 1994.

Those Amazing Ants by Patricia Demuth. Macmillan, 1994.

What is an Insect? (Sierra Club Book) by Robert Snedden. Sierra Club, 1993.

FICTION

Buggy Riddles by Katy Hall and Lisa Eisenberg. Puffin Books, 1993.

Buz by Richard Egielski. HarperCollins, 1995.

Fireflies! by Julie Brinckloe. Aladdin Books, 1986.

In the Tall, Tall Grass by Denise Fleming. Henry Holt & Co., 1991.

Miss Spider's Tea Party by David Kirk. Callaway, 1994.

MULTIMEDIA
CD-ROMS:

Bug Explorers Interactive Multimedia (Memorex Children's Series). Entertainment Technology, 1996.

Insects: Little Creature in a Big World. The Learning Team, 1997.

Insects Interactive Multimedia (Junior Nature Guides Series). ICE Integrated Communications & Entertainment, 1996.

Multimedia Bugs Interactive Multimedia: The Complete Interactive Guide to Insects. Inroads Interactive, 1996.

 VIDEOS:

Backyard Bugs. National Geographic Educational, 1990.

Benefits of Insects. National Geographic Educational, 1990.

Bugs Don't Bug Us. Bo-Peep Productions, 1991.

Camouflage, Cuttlefish, and Chameleons Changing Color (Geo Kids). National Geographic Home Video, 1994.

Insects (Tell Me Why). TMW Media Group, 1987.

Insects (Animal Classes). National Geographic Educational, 1997.

Insects: Little Things that Run the World. Unapix Entertainment, 1989.

Little Creatures Who Run the World. NOVA, 1995.

WEB SITES

Electronic Zoo (Entomology links) netvet.wustl.edu/invert.htm

Amazing Insects Project (Third grade school project) www.minnetonka.k12.mn.us/SCHOOLS/groveland/insect.Proj/insects.html

The AES Bug Club for young Entomologists www.ex.ac.uk/bugclub/main.html

Fun Insect Facts ham.spa.umn.edu/kris/science.html

➤ SEE ALSO THESE RELATED PATHFINDERS
Animals; Bees and Beekeeping

Inventions

An invention is anything thought up, planned, and made for the first time. An inventor's imagination, skill, and sometimes, good luck, work together to create an invention. Sometimes people work for years and years to turn an idea into a working invention. Inventions can be machines, products, or processes.

 DEWEY DECIMAL CALL NUMBERS

608 Inventions

609.2 Historical, geographic, persons treatment

621.32 Illumination and lighting (gas lighting, lightbulb)

629.2 Other branches of engineering

686.2 Printing and related activities

 SEARCH TERMS

Inventions
Inventors
Technology
Engineering
Search by names of invention, for example: Printing press

 NONFICTION/REFERENCE BOOKS

Click! A Story about George Eastman by Barbara Mitchell. Carolrhoda Books, 1986.

Eureka! It's an Automobile by Jeanne Bendick. Millbrook Press, 1992.

Great Inventions. Time-Life Books, 1995.

Great Inventions (What's Inside?). Dorling Kindersley, 1993.

Light: A Bright Idea by Siegfried Aust. Lerner Pub. Co., 1992.

Mistakes that Worked by Charlotte Foltz Jones. Doubleday, 1991.

The Renaissance: The Invention of Perspective by Lillo Canta. Chelsea House, 1995.

Steven Caney's Invention Book by Steven Caney. Workman Pub., 1985.

Smithsonian Visual Timeline of Inventions by Richard Platt. Dorling Kindersley, 1994.

TV's Forgotten Hero: The Story of Philo Farnsworth by Stephanie Sarmmartino McPherson. Carolrhoda Books, 1996.

Who?: Famous Experiments for the Young by Robert W. Wood. TAB Books, 1995.

Wizard of Sound: A Story about Thomas Edison by Barbara Mitchell. Carolrhoda Books, 1991.

FICTION

Bravo Minski by Arthur Yorinks. Farrar Straus Giroux, 1988.

The Day-Off Machine by John Himmelman. Silver Press, 1990.

Dog for a Day by Dick Gackenbach. Clarion Books, 1987.

Dream Cars by Jack C. Harris. Crestwood House, 1988.

The Gadget War by Betsy Duffey. Puffin Books, 1991.

I Gave Thomas Edison My Sandwich by Floyd C. Moore. Albert Whitman & Co., 1995.

Tiny for a Day by Dick Gackenbach. Clarion Books, 1993.

MULTIMEDIA

CD-ROMS:

Genius of Edison. Compton, 1996.
Invention Studio Interactive. Discovery Channel Multimedia, 1996.
InventorLabs Collection. Houghton Mifflin Co., 1996.
Little Blimp that Couldn't (Science Sleuths). Videodiscovery, 1997.
The Way Things Work 2.0. DK Multimedia, 1996.

VIDEOS:

The Great Inventors. Paramount, 1994. (Peanuts characters salute great inventors)
Inventions. Discovery Channel, 1990.
Rocket Men: Goddard Space Exploration. Fast Forward, 1994.
The Wrong Trousers (Wallace & Gromit). Twentieth Century Fox, 1995.

WEB SITES

Alexander Graham Bell's Path to the Telephone
www.jefferson.village.virginia.edu/albell/homepage.html
American Experience Invention Page
www.pbs.org/wgbh/pages/amex/technology/forgotteninv.html
Concoctions and Inventions
www.members.aol.com/acalendar/February/11th.html
Invention Dimension
www.web.mit.edu/invent/
Learn about What it Takes to be an Inventor
www.mustang.coled.umn.edu/inventing/inventing.html

➤ SEE ALSO THESE RELATED PATHFINDERS
Computors; Inventors; Technology

Inventors

An inventor is someone who thinks up and makes new things that have never been before, often simply by adapting existing ideas and materials. Thomas Edison and Alexander Graham Bell are two famous inventors.

 DEWEY DECIMAL CALL NUMBERS

609.2 History of inventions
621.32 Illumination (Inventions, lightbulb)
629.2 Engineering (Cars, motorcycles, and other motorized vehicles)
686.2 Printing (Invention of the printing press)
920 Collective biographies
921 Biographies

 SEARCH TERMS

Inventors
Inventions
Technology
Engineering
Search by names of particular inventors,
for example: Eli Whitney

 NONFICTION/REFERENCE BOOKS

Benjamin Franklin — Printer, Inventor, Statesman by David Adler. Holiday House, 1992.
Click! A Story about George Eastman by Barbara Mitchell. Carolrhoda Books, 1986.
Eureka! It's an Automobile by Jeanne Bendick. Millbrook Press, 1992.
Fine Print: A Story about Johann Gutenberg by Joann Johansen Burch. Carolrhoda Books, 1991.
First Flight: The Story of Tom Tate and the Wright Brothers by George Shea. HarperCollins, 1997.
Great Inventions. Time-Life Books, 1995.
A Head Full of Notions: A Story about Robert Fulton by Andy Russell Bowen. Carolrhoda Books , 1997.
Inventors by Martin W. Sandler. HarperCollins, 1996.
Leonardo da Vinci by Diane Stanley. Morrow Junior Books, 1996.
Light: A Bright Idea by Siegfried Aust. Lerner Pub. Co., 1992.
Louis Braille: The Blind Boy Who Wanted to Read by Dennis Fradin. Silver Press, 1997.
Made in China: Ideas and Inventions from Ancient China by Suzanne Williams. Pacific View, 1996.
Mistakes that Worked by Charlotte Foltz Jones. Doubleday, 1991.
Monticello by Norman Richards. Children's Press, 1995.
Thomas Alva Edison by David Adler. Holiday House, 1990.
TV's Forgotten Hero: The Story of Philo Farnsworth by Stephanie Sarmmartino McPherson. Carolrhoda Books, 1996.
Who?: Famous Experiments for the Young by Robert W. Wood. TAB Books, 1995.

FICTION

Ben and Me: A New and Astonishing Life of Benjamin Franklin as Written by His Good Mouse Amos by Robert Lawson. Little, Brown & Co., 1988.

Bravo Minski by Arthur Yorinks. Farrar Straus Giroux, 1988.

Chitty Chitty Bang Bang; The Magical Car by Ian Fleming. Random House, 1964.

The Day-Off Machine by John Himmelman. Silver Press, 1990.

The Gadget War by Betsy Duffey. Puffin Books, 1991.

I Gave Thomas Edison My Sandwich by Floyd C. Moore. Albert Whitman & Co., 1995.

MULTIMEDIA

 ### CD-ROMS:

Inventor Labs Collection. Houghton Mifflin Co., 1996.
Invention Studio Interactive. Discovery Channel Multimedia, 1996.
Leonardo the Inventor. Softkey, 1994.
The Way Things Work 2.0. DK Multimedia, 1996.

VIDEOS:

Edison Effect (series includes four parts: **Edison Effect; Electric Light; Motion Picture; Phonograph**). A&E Entertainment, 1998.
George Washington Carver (Influential African Americans). Schlessinger, 1992.
The Great Inventors (Peanuts characters salute great inventors). Paramount, 1994.
Inventions. Discovery Channel, 1990.
Madam C. J. Walker: Entrepreneur (Black Americans of Achievement). Schlessinger, 1992.
Rocket Men: Goddard Space Exploration. Fast Forward, 1994.
What's the Big Idea, Ben Franklin?(Jean Fritz Collection). Weston Woods, 1993.

 ## WEB SITES

Alexander Graham Bell's Path to the Telephone
www.jefferson.village.virginia.edu/albell/homepage.html
Dead Inventors Corner
www.discovery.com/past/stories/moreinventors.html
Eric's Treasure Trove of Scientific Biography
www.astro.virginia.edu/~eww6n/bios/bios0.html
Invention Dimension
www.web.mit.edu/invent/
Learn about What it Takes to be an Inventor
www.mustang.coled.umn.edu/inventing/inventing.html

➤ SEE ALSO THESE RELATED PATHFINDERS

Biographies; Famous People; Famous Women; Inventions

Iroquois Confederacy

The Iroquois Confederacy refers to a group of Native American tribal peoples (Mohawk, Mohican, Oneida, Onondaga, Cayuga, and Seneca Indians) who originally lived in the Woodland regions of western New York from Seneca Lake to Lake Erie. Today people of these tribes live in this same area and in southeast Ontario. The Seneca are the westernmost member of the original Iroquois Confederacy.

DEWEY DECIMAL CALL NUMBERS

970.1 Indians of North America
398.2 Folk literature
970.004 History, North America (1800-1900)

SEARCH TERMS

Iroquois Confederacy
Seneca Indians
Mohican
Mohawk Indians
Oneida Indians
Woodland Indians
Native Americans
North American Indians

NONFICTION/REFERENCE BOOKS

Ely S. Parker, Spokesman for the Senecas by Harold W. Felton. Dodd, Mead, 1973.

Encyclopedia of Native American Tribes by Carl Waldman. Facts on File, 1988.

The Encyclopedia of North American Indians Marshall Cavendish, 1997.

Houses of Bark: Tipi, Wigwam, and Longhouse: Native Dwellings, Woodland Indians by Bonnie Shemie. Tundra Books, 1990.

A Narrative of the Life of Mrs. Mary Jemison... by James E. Seaver. Syracuse University Press, 1990.

The Seneca by Jill Duvall. Children's Press, 1991.

FICTION

Brother Wolf: A Seneca Tale by Harriet Peck Taylor. Farrar Straus Giroux, 1996.

The Great Buffalo Race: How the Buffalo Got Its Hump: A Seneca Tale by Barbara Juster Esbensen. Little, Brown & Co., 1994.

Indian Captive: The Story of Mary Jemison by Lois Lenski. HarperTrophy, 1995.

Maggie Among the Seneca by Robin Moore. Lippincott, 1990.

The Monster from the Swamp by C. J. Taylor. Tundra Books, 1995.

Muskrat Will Be Swimming by Cheryl Savageau. Northland Pub., 1996.

Skunny Wundy: Seneca Indian Tales by Arthur Caswell Parker. Albert Whitman & Co., 1970.

MULTIMEDIA

 **VIDEOS:**

Indians of Early America. Encyclopaedia Britannica, 1990.

Iroquois (Indians of North America). Schlessinger, 1993.

People of the Forest (Native Americans). Rainbow Educational Video, 1994.

➤ *SEE ALSO THESE RELATED PATHFINDERS*
Eastern Woodland Indians; Native Americans

Life Cycles

The birth, growth, reproduction, and death of any living thing are considered a life cycle. Someone studying the life cycle of a species is concerned with the different stages of development of the plant or animal. Some animals, such as insects, have very short life cycles, lasting only a matter of days. Other species have very long life cycles, like some trees, which can live for hundreds of years.

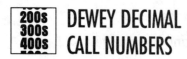 DEWEY DECIMAL CALL NUMBERS

571.8 Life cycle
574.3 Biology, Development and maturation
591.3 Zoology, Development and maturation

 SEARCH TERMS

Life cycles
Animal life cycles
Seasons

 NONFICTION/REFERENCE BOOKS

Ancient Ones: The World of the Old-growth Douglas Fir by Barbara Bash. Sierra Club Books for Children, 1994.

Dragonflies by Molly McLaughlin. Walker & Co., 1989.

An Extraordinary Life: The Story of a Monarch Butterfly by Laurence Pressingle. Orchard Books, 1997.

From Birth to Death (Life's Cycles) by Irene Yates. Millbrook Press., 1997.

From Tadpole to Frog (Let's-read-and-find-out Science. Stage 1) by Wendy Pfeffer. HarperCollins, 1994.

A Gathering of Garter Snakes by Bianca Lavies. Dutton Children's Books, 1993.

The Life and Times of the Honeybee by Charles Micucci. Ticknor & Fields Books for Young Readers, 1995.

Life Circles of a Dozen Diverse Creatures by Paul Fleisher. Millbrook Press, 1996.

Rhinos by Sally M. Walker. Carolrhoda Books, 1996.

Shadows of Night: The Hidden World of the Little Brown Bat by Barbara Bash. Sierra Club Books for Children, 1993.

Tree of Life: the World of the African Baobab (Tree Tales) by Barbara Bash. Sierra Club/Little, Brown & Co., 1989.

Wings Along the Waterway by Mary Barrett Brown. Orchard Books, 1992.

What Is A Life Cycle? (Science of Living Things) by Bobbie Kalman and Jacqueline Langille. Crabtree Pub. Co., 1998.

FICTION

Shag: Last of the Plains Buffalo (The Animal Life Cycle Series) by Robert McClung. Linnet Books, 1991. Additional titles in this series include: **Black Jack: Last of the Big Alligators** (1991); **Samson: Last of the California Grizzlies** (1997).

Minn of the Mississippi by Holling Clancy Holling. Houghton Mifflin Co., 1979.

Whisper From the Woods by Victoria Wirth. Green Tiger Press, 1991.

MULTIMEDIA

CD-ROMS:

Amphibians & Reptiles Interactive Multimedia (Junior Nature Guides Series). ICE Integrated Communications & Entertainment, 1996.
Animal Planet Interactive Multimedia: The Ultimate Wildlife Adventure. Discovery Channel Multimedia, 1996.
Birds Interactive Multimedia (Junior Nature Guides Series). ICE Integrated Communications & Entertainment, 1996.
Changes Around Us Interactive Multimedia. Edunetics Interactive, c1996.
Insects Interactive Multimedia (Junior Nature Guides Series). ICE Integrated Communications & Entertainment, 1996.

VIDEOS:

Autumn (Four Seasons). National Geographic Film & TV, 1983.
Bug City Series. Schlessinger, 1997.
Ox-Cart Man. Live Oak Media, 1988.
What Is A Plant? (Kingdom of Plants). National Geographic Film & TV, 1991.

 WEB SITES

The City Naturalist Guide to Animals
www.nysite.com/nature/fauna.htm
Cecropia Moth—Life Cycle
www.geocities.com/RainForest/5479/page2.htm

➤ *SEE ALSO THESE RELATED PATHFINDERS*
Animals; Biomes; Ecology

Middle Ages

The Middle Ages, also called the Medieval Period, was a period in Western European history from the fall of the West Roman Empire in the fifth century to the 15th century. It was once called the Dark Ages because it was thought of as a time of intellectual decline and incivility. However, historians know that this was not true. During the Middle Ages, Christianity became a predominant and unifying force among the people of Europe. The Holy Roman Empire was very influential, initiating religious crusades and encouraging the development of academic universities. It was an age of great thinkers and writers, such as St. Thomas Aquinas, Dante, and Chaucer, and of daring Gothic Architecture.

 DEWEY DECIMAL CALL NUMBERS

940.1 Europe, Middle Ages, 476-1453 A.D.
909.07 World history, crusades
709.02 Fine arts, 500-1500 A.D.
745.6 Illuminations

 SEARCH TERMS

Middle Ages
Medieval civilization
Medieval
European history
Knights and knighthood
Castles
Medieval illuminations of books and manuscripts
Search by names of countries, for example:
England, Middle Ages

 NONFICTION/REFERENCE BOOKS

Arms and Armor (Eyewitness Books) by Michelle Byam, et al. Knopf, 1988.

Castle (Eyewitness Books) by Christopher Gravett. Knopf, 1994.

Clothes and Crafts in the Middle Ages by Imogen Dawson. Silver Burdett Press., 1998.

The Duke and the Peasant: Life in the Middle Ages by Wendy Beckett. Prestel, 1997.

Exploring the Past: The Middle Ages by Catherine Oakes. Harcourt Brace Jovanovich, 1989.

Illuminations by Jonathan Hunt. Maxwell Macmillan International, 1993.

Knight (Eyewitness Books) by Christopher Gravett, et al. Knopf, 1993.

Knights in Shining Armor by Gail Gibbons. LB, 1995.

Medieval Castle by Fiona Macdonald. Peter Bedrick Books, 1993.

Medieval Cathedral by Fiona Macdonald. Peter Bedrick Books, 1991.

Medieval Feast by Aliki. Harper & Row, 1986.

Medieval Life (Eyewitness Books) by Andrew E. Langley. Knopf, 1996.

Medieval Places by Sarah Howarth. Millbrook Press, 1992.

Medieval People by Sarah Howarth. Millbrook Press, 1992.

Medieval Times by Antony Mason. Simon & Schuster Books for Young Readers, 1996.

Middle Ages by Kate Hayden. World Book, 1998.

Middle Ages by Sarah Howarth. Viking, 1993.

FICTION

Adam of the Road (Puffin Books Newbery Library) by Elizabeth Janet Gray. Viking Press., 1987.

Alvin the Knight by Ulf Lofgren. Carolrhoda Books, 1992.

The Door in the Wall by Marguerite De Angeli. Dell, 1990.

Happily Ever After by Anna Quindlen. Viking, 1997.

Juliet: A Dream Takes Flight, England, 1339 by Anna Kirwan. Aladdin Paperbacks, 1996.

The Minstrel in the Tower (A Stepping Stone Book) by Gloria Skurzynski. Random House, 1988.

Sir Cedric by Roy Gerrard. Farrar Straus Giroux, 1986.

MULTIMEDIA

CD-ROMS:

Castle Explorer. Dorling Kindersley, 1996.

Crayola 3D Castle Creator. IBM Software, 1998.

Eyewitness Children's Encyclopedia. DK Multimedia, 1996.

Eyewitness History of the World. Dorling Kindersley, 1995.

Where in Time is Carmen Sandiego? Broderbund, 1997.

VIDEOS:

Castle (David McCaulay's World of Ancient Engineering). PBS Video, 1988.

Cathedral (David McCaulay's World of Ancient Engineering). PBS Video, 1988.

Crusades (Four-part series). History Channel, 1996.

Medieval Times: Life in the Middle Ages. United Learning, 1992.

The Middle Ages Series (Five-part series on three tapes). Schlessinger, 1997.

Sounds of a Distant Tyme. Ricky Levy, 1995. (Period music performed before a school audience)

 WEB SITES

Castles on the Web
www.castles.org
Journey Through the Middle Ages
www.tqjunior.advanced.org/4051/titlepg.htm

Movies

"Motion pictures," "film," and "cinema" are all words that refer to movies. The motion picture is the most recently developed of all the art forms, and it is perhaps the most influential. Not only is film an art form, it is also an industry. Moviemaking can involve millions of dollars and a wide variety of creative and technical people. Movies are used in several different ways: to entertain, to educate, or to record significant events.

DEWEY DECIMAL CALL NUMBER

791.43 Motion pictures

SEARCH TERMS

Movies
Animated films
Cinema
Cinematography
Film
Motion pictures, history
Motion pictures, production and direction
Musicals
Silent movies
Special effects

NONFICTION/REFERENCE BOOKS

Animated Magic: A Behind-the-Scenes Look at How an Animated Film is Made by Don Hahn. Disney Press, 1996.

Film by Richard Platt. Knopf, 1992.

The History of Moviemaking. Scholastic, 1995.

Make Your Own Animated Movies and Videotapes by Yvonne Andersen. Little, Brown & Co., 1991.

Movie Classics by Marc Perlman. Lerner Pub. Co., 1993.

Movie Magic: Behind the Scenes with Special Effects by Elaine Scott. Morrow Junior Books, 1995.

Movie Monsters by Tom Powers. Lerner Pub. Co., 1989.

Movies by Chris Oxlade. Rigby Interactive Library, 1997.

The Movies of Alfred Hitchcock by Judy Arginteanu. Lerner Pub. Co., 1994.

Special Effects by Jake Hamilton. Dorling Kindersley, 1998.

Toy Story: The Art and Making of the Animated Film by John Lasseter and Steve Daly. Hyperion, 1995.

Walt Disney: His Life in Pictures by Russell Schroeder. Disney Press, 1996.

FICTION

Albert Goes to Hollywood by Henry Schwartz. Orchard Books, 1992.

Cam Jansen and the Mystery of the Monster Movie by David Adler. Puffin Books, 1992.

Karen's Movie (Baby-sitters Little Sister) by Ann M. Martin. Scholastic, 1995.

The Piano Man by Deborah Newton Chocolate. Walker & Co., 1998.

Sabotage on the Set by Joan Lowery Nixon. Disney Press, 1996.

You Must Remember This by Karen L. B. Evans and Pat Dade. Hyperion, 1997.

MULTIMEDIA

CD-ROM:
Microsoft Cinemania '97: Guide to Movies and Moviemakers. Microsoft, 1996.

VIDEOS:
The Golden Age of Comedy. Madacy, 1998.

Hollywood Dinosaur Chronicles. Uni, 1987. (Features movies' most monstrous reptiles)

Race Movies: The Early History of Black Cinema. OnDeck Home Entertainment, 1996.

Singing in the Rain. MGM, 1952.

That's Entertainment. MGM, 1974.

WEB SITES

Animation 101 (From the WB Animation page)
www.wbanimation.warnerbros.com/cmp/ani_04if.htm

The Greatest Films (Lists of great films and links to more, plus trivia, criticism, and dialogue)
www.filmsite.org/home.html

Nightmare Before Christmas Web Page
www.halloweentown.com/mainindex.shtml

Slapstick
www.uno.edu/~drcom/SLAPSTICK

Walt Disney Web Page
www.disney.com/disneypictures/index.html

➤ *SEE ALSO THIS RELATED PATHFINDER*
Famous People

Music

Music is a way of organizing the sounds made by the human voice or by musical instruments. To organize the sounds, composers (people who write music) use rhythm, melody, and harmony. Music has always been a significant part of any culture. Music often is produced or written in response to the cultural ideals of a period.

 DEWEY DECIMAL CALL NUMBERS

780 Music
781 Musical Principles
782 Dramatic music (musical theater)
784 Vocal music (folks songs)
785 Instrumental music
789 Electrical instruments and musical recordings

 SEARCH TERMS

Music
Musicians
Musical instruments
Jazz
Ragtime
Blues
Classical music
Opera
Musical theater

Country Western
Bluegrass
Gospel
Folk music
Rock and Roll
Soul music
Rap

 NONFICTION/REFERENCE BOOKS

American Folk Songs for Children in Home, School and Nursery School by Ruth Crawford Seeger. Doubleday, 1948.

Brass by Alyn Shipton. Raintree/Steck Vaughn, 1994.

Charlie Parker Played Be Bop by Chris Raschka. Orchard Books, 1992.

Duke Ellington by Adam Woog. Lucent Books, 1996.

Elvis Presley: The King by Katherine E. Krohn. Lerner Pub. Co., 1994.

Getting to Know the World's Greatest Composers Series (Featuring individual volumes on famous composers)by Mike Venezia. Children's Press, 1994.

Great Composers by Piero Ventura. G. P. Putnam's Sons, 1989.

Hidden Music: The Life of Fanny Mendelssohn by Gloria Kamen. Atheneum, 1996.

I Wonder Why Flutes Have Holes and other Questions about Music by Josephine Parker. Kingfisher Books, 1995.

If I Only Had a Horn: Young Louis Armstrong by Roxanne Orgill. Houghton Mifflin Co., 1997.

Introducing Mozart by Roland Vernon. Silver Burdett Press, 1996.

Jazz by Richard Carlin. Facts on File, 1991.

Little Louis and the Jazz Band: The Story of Louis "Satchmo" Armstrong by Angela Shelf. Lodestar Books, 1994.

NONFICTION/REFERENCE BOOKS CONTINUED

Lives of the Musicians: Good Times, Bad Times (and What the Neighbors Thought) by Kathleen Krull. Harcourt Brace Jovanovich, 1993.

Long Live Music by Les Chats peles. Harcourt Brace Jovanovich, 1996.

Meet the Orchestra by Ann Hayes. Harcourt Brace Jovanovich, 1991.

Music, an Illustrated Encyclopedia by Neil Ardley. Facts on File, 1986.

My First Music Book by Helen Drew. Dorling Kindersley, 1993.

Mysterious Thelonious by Chris Raschka. Orchard Books, 1997.

The Orchestra: An Introduction to the World of Classical Music by Alan Blackwood. Millbrook Press, 1993.

A Pianist's Debut: Preparing for the Concert Stage by Barbara Beirne. Carolrhoda Books, 1990.

Scott Joplin by Katherine Preston. Chelsea House, 1988.

Singing by Alyn Shipton. Raintree/Steck Vaughn, 1994.

The Usborne First Book of Music by Emma Danes. Usborne, 1994.

 ## FICTION

Barn Dance! by Bill Martin. Henry Holt & Co., 1986.

The Bremen Town Musicians by The Brothers Grimm. Troll Assoc., 1979.

The Cricket in Times Square by George Selden. Dell, 1984.

The Facts and Fictions of Minna Pratt by Patricia MacLachlan. Harper & Row, 1988.

Gabriella's Song by Candace Fleming. Atheneum Books for Young Readers, 1997.

Hip Cat by Jonathan London. Chronicle Books, 1993.

Little Lil and the Swing-Singing Sax by Libbie Gray. Simon & Schuster, 1996.

The Maestro Plays by Bill Martin, Jr. Henry Holt & Co., 1994.

Music, Music for Everyone by Vera B. Williams. Greenwillow Books, 1984.

Musicians of the Sun by Gerald McDermott. Simon & Schuster, 1997.

The Philharmonic Gets Dressed by Karla Kuskin. HarperTrophy, 1986.

The Sea King's Daughter: A Russian Legend by Aaron Shepard. Atheneum, 1997.

The Singing Man: A West African Folk Tale by Angela Medearis. Holiday House, 1994.

Thump, Thump, Rat-a-tat-tat by Gene Baer. HarperTrophy, 1991.

Zin! Zin! Zin!: A Violin by Lloyd Moss. Simon & Schuster, 1995.

MULTIMEDIA

CD-ROMS:

Guide to the Orchestra. Cambrix Pub, 1996.

Morton Subotnick's Making Music Interactive. Voyager, 1995.

Music Ace Interactive Multimedia. Harmonic Vision, 1996.

Music DoodlePad Interactive. Harmonic Vision, 1996.

The Musical World of Professor Piccolo. Opcode Interactive, 1993.

VIDEOS:

Bach's Fight for Freedom. Sony Classical Film & Video, 1995.

Beethoven Lives Upstairs. Children's Group, 1991.

Bizet's Dream. Sony Classical Film & Video, 1995.

How to Read Music. Allied Video, 1995.

JVC Video Anthology of World Music and Dance (30-volume set). JVC, 1991.

Kids Make Music. Bogner Entertainment, 1994.

My First Music Video. Sony Kids Music, 1993.

Peter and the Wolf (Puppets by Jim Gamble). BEI, 1996.

Sounds of a Distant Tyme (Medieval and Renaissance music). Rick Levy, 1995.

WEB SITES

Catalogue of Classical Composers (Very brief bios)
www.thanatos.uoregon.edu/~lincicum/complst.html

Classical Net—Basic Repertoire & Quick Composer Reference
www.classical.net/music/rep/lists/index.html

History of Country Music
www.roughstock.com/history/

Lush Lives—Ladies of Jazz
www.ddg.com/LIS/InfoDesignF96/Ismael/jazz/jzindex.html

Red Hot Jazz (History, bios, and audio clips)
www.technoir.net/jazz

Rock and Roll Hall of Fame
www.rockhall.com/

➤ SEE ALSO THESE RELATED PATHFINDERS

Bibographies; Famous People; Famous Women; Musical Instruments

Musical Instruments

When played, musical instruments make vibrations that the human ear recognizes as musical sounds. Instruments are usually categorized into five families: brass, woodwind, percussion, keyboard, and stringed.

DEWEY DECIMAL CALL NUMBERS

786 Keyboard instruments

787 String instruments (violins, guitars, cellos, etc.)

788 Wind instruments (horns, bagpipes, harmonicas)

789 Percussion instruments (drums, bells, xylophones, etc.)

SEARCH TERMS

Musical instrument   Brass instruments
String instruments   Percussion instruments
Wind instruments   Keyboard instruments
Woodwinds
Search by names of particular instruments, for example: Viola

NONFICTION/REFERENCE BOOKS

Brass by Alyn Shipton. Raintree/Steck Vaughn, 1994.

Great Inventions. Time-Life Books, 1995.

I Wonder Why Flutes Have Holes and other Questions about Music by Josephine Parker. Kingfisher Books, 1995.

If I Only Had a Horn: Young Louis Armstrong by Roxanne Orgill. Houghton Mifflin Co., 1997.

The Living... (series includes **Clarinet, Flute, Violin,** and **Piano)** by Barrie Turner. Knopf, 1996.

Long Live Music by Les Chats Peles. Harcourt Brace Jovanovich, 1996.

Making Music: 6 Instruments You Can Create by Eddie Oates. HarperCollins, 1995.

Meet the Orchestra by Ann Hayes. Harcourt Brace Jovanovich, 1991.

Music, an Illustrated Encyclopedia by Neil Ardley. Facts on File, 1986.

Musical Instruments by Claude Delafosse. Scholastic, 1994.

Musical Instruments from A to Z by Bobbie Kalman. Crabtree Pub. Co., 1998.

My First Music Book by Helen Drew. Dorling Kindersley, 1993.

The Orchestra: An Introduction to the World of Classical Music by Alan Blackwood. Millbrook Press, 1993.

Pluck and Scrape by Sally Hewitt. Children's Press, 1994.

Shake, Rattle, and Strum by Sara Corbett. Children's Press, 1995.

Singing by Alyn Shipton. Raintree/Steck Vaughn, 1994.

World Music by Roger Thomas. Heinemann, 1998.

The World of Music by Nicola Barber and Mary Mure. Silver Burdett Press, 1995.

The Young Person's Guide to the Orchestra by Anita Ganeri. Harcourt Brace Jovanovich, 1996.

FICTION

Little Lil and the Swing-Singing Sax by Libbie Gray. Simon & Schuster, 1996.

The Magic School Bus in the Haunted Museum: A Book About Sound. Scholastic, 1995.

The Philharmonic Gets Dressed by Karla Kuskin. HarperTrophy, 1986.

Play Me a Story: Nine Stories about Musical Instruments by Naomi Adler. Millbrook Press, 1997.

Sebastian's Trumpet by Miko Imai. Candlewick Press, 1995.

Thump, Thump, Rat-a-tat-tat by Gene Baer. HarperTrophy, 1991.

Zin! Zin! Zin!: A Violin by Lloyd Moss. Simon & Schuster, 1995.

MULTIMEDIA

 ### CD-ROMS:

Guide to the Orchestra. Cambrix, 1996.

The Musical World of Professor Piccolo. Opcode Interactive, 1993.

 ### VIDEOS:

Discovering the Music of Africa. AIMS Media, 1967.

Maestro Plays (based on the book by Bill Martin, Jr.). American School Publishers, 1996.

Music Mania. Learning Channel, 1992.

Peter and the Wolf (puppets by Jim Gamble). BEI, 1996.

 ## WEB SITES

Guide to Medieval and Renaissance Instruments
www.shamilton.k12.ia.us/antiqua/
instrumt.html

Music Heritage Network—Instrument Encyclopedia
www.si.umich.edu/CHICO/MHN/
mhnmenu.html

➤ *SEE ALSO THIS RELATED PATHFINDER*
Music

Mythology

Traditional stories about gods, kings and queens, and heroes are called myths or mythology. Myths may tell about the creation of the world, or about heroic people and events, or teach us the right way to live by providing moral guidance. Often myths were created to explain natural events and human emotions. Most myths began as oral tales, being retold from generation to generation until finally they were written down. Ancient myths may reveal a culture's science and religion, or their views of heroism. They often teach a lesson.

 DEWEY DECIMAL CALL NUMBERS

200.4 Religious mythology
292-299 Religion and religious mythology
398 Folklore
883 Classical Greek epic poetry and fiction

 SEARCH TERMS

Mythology, Greek
Mythology, Roman
Mythology, Norse
Mythology, Tibetan
Mythology, Celtic
Mythology, Native American
Mythical Folklore
Folklore

 NONFICTION/REFERENCE BOOKS

Favorite Norse Myths retold by Mary Pope Osborne. Scholastic, 1996.

Mythical Birds & Beasts From Many Lands retold by Margaret Mayo. Dutton Children's Books, 1997.

Celtic Myths by Sam McBratney. Peter Bedrick Books, 1998.

The Gods and Goddesses of Ancient Egypt by Leonard Everett Fisher. Holiday House, 1997.

The Illustrated Book of Myths: Tales & Legends of the World retold by Neil Philip. Dorling Kindersley, 1995.

Ingri and Edgar Parin D'Aulaire's Book of Greek Myths by Ingri D'Aulaire. Dell, 1962.

The Olympians: Great Gods and Goddesses of Ancient Greece by Leonard Everett Fisher. Holiday House, 1984.

FICTION

The Adventures of Odysseus retold by Neil Philip. Orchard Books, 1997.

Atalanta's Race: A Greek Myth retold by Shirley Climo. Clarion Books, 1995.

Cyclops by Leonard Everett Fisher. Holiday House, 1991.

Hero of the Land of Snow (Kind Gesar Series) adapted by Sylvia Gretchen from the Tibetan epic *Tale of Gesar*. Dharma Pub., 1990.

The Trojan Horse by Warwick Hutton. McElderry/Macmillan, 1992.

The Wanderings of Odysseus: The Story of the Odyssey by Rosemary Sutcliff. Delacorte Press, 1996.

The Adventures of Odysseus retold by Neil Philip. Orchard Books, 1997.

MULTIMEDIA

CD-ROM:

Wishbone and the Amazing Odyssey Interactive Multimedia. Palladium Interactive, 1996.

VIDEOS:

Clash of the Titans. MGM/UA, 1981.

Mythology: Gods and Goddesses. Guidance Assoc., 1978.

Pyramid. PBS Video, 1988.

Pegasus (Stories to Remember). Lightyear Entertainment, 1990.

Jason and the Argonauts. Columbia/Tri-Star, 1963.

WEB SITES

Encyclopedia Mythica
www.pantheon.org/mythica/

Beazley Dictionary (From the University of Oxford—Greek myth, art, architecture, maps, and place names)
www.beazley.ox.ac.uk/CGprograms/Dict/Script/DictionaryIndexBody.html

Encyclopedia of Greek Mythology
www.mythweb.com/encyc/

➤ SEE ALSO THIS RELATED PATHFINDER

Adventure; Fairy Tales; Heroes

Native Americans

The people who lived in North America before the European colonists arrived are called Native Americans. Native Americans migrated from Asia, beginning in 35,000 B.C., and they lived in North America for thousands of years before the arrival of European explorers. Native Americans spoke a variety of languages and lived in tribes. They lived in six major cultural areas: Northwest Coast, Plains, Plateau, Eastern Woodlands, Northern, and Southwest. Native Americans are also called Indians.

DEWEY DECIMAL CALL NUMBERS

970.1   Indians of North America
398.2   Folk literature
970.004 History, North America (1800-1900)
973   History, United States

SEARCH TERMS

Native Americans
North American Indians
Search by names of individual tribes, for example: Cherokee
Search by names of regions, for example: Plains Indians

NONFICTION/REFERENCE BOOKS

See titles in these series: **Indians of North America** and **Junior Library of American Indians** (Chelsea House) with volumes on individual tribes.

Eyewitness Anthologies American Peoples. Dorling Kindersley, 1996.

The Apaches and Navajos by Craig A. Doherty and Katherine M. Doherty. Franklin Watts, 1989.

The Cherokees: People of the Southeast by Eileen Lucas. Millbrook Press, 1993.

Children of the Sun: The Pueblos, Navajos, and Apaches of New Mexico by Maudie Robinson. J. Messner, 1983.

Double Life of Pocahontas by Jean Fritz. Viking, 1997.

Encyclopedia of Native American Tribes by Carl Waldman. Facts on File, 1988.

The Encyclopedia of North American Indians. Marshall Cavendish, 1997.

The Great Indian Chiefs: Cochise, Geronimo, Crazy Horse, Sitting Bull by Jean-Robert Masson. Barron's 1994.

Happily May I Walk by Arlene Hirschfelder. Scribner, 1986

Indian Chiefs by Russell Freedman. Holiday House, 1987.

Indians of North America by Daniel Jacobson. Franklin Watts, 1983.

Mounds of Earth and Shell: Native Sites—The Southeast by Bonnie Shemie. Tundra Books, 1993.

Native Americans. Time-Life Books, 1995.

NONFICTION/REFERENCE BOOKS CONTINUED

The Navajos: People of the Southwest by Nancy Bonvillain. Millbrook Press, 1995.

One Nation, Many Tribes: How Kids Live in Milwaukee's Indian Community by Kathleen Krull. Lodestar Books, 1995.

Only the Names Remain: the Cherokees and the Trail of Tears by Alex Bealer. Little, Brown & Co., 1996.

A Picture Book of Sitting Bull by David Adler. Holiday House, 1993.

Sacajawea: The Journey West by Elaine Raphael. Scholastic, 1994.

Stories on Stone: Rock Art, Images from the Ancient Ones by Jennifer Dewey. Little, Brown & Co., 1996.

The Story of Wounded Knee (Cornerstones of Freedom) by R. Conrad Stein. Children's Press, 1983.

 ## FICTION

Annie and the Old One by Miska Miles. Little, Brown & Co., 1971.

Bones in the Basket: Native Stories of the Origin of People by C. J. Taylor. Tundra Books, 1994.

Eagle Song by Joseph Bruchac. Dial Books for Young Readers, 1997.

Full Moon Stories: Thirteen Native American Legends by Eagle Walking Turtle. Hyperion, 1997.

The Girl Who Married a Ghost and Other Tales from the North American Indian by John Bierhorst. Macmillan, 1978.

In the Trail of the Wind: American Indian Poems and Ritual Orations by John Bierhorst. Farrar Straus Giroux, 1971.

The Indian in the Cupboard by Lynne Reid Banks. Avon, 1982.

Less than Half, More than Whole by Kathleen Lacapa. Northland Pub., 1994.

Muskrat will be Swimming by Cheryl Savageau. Northland Pub., 1996.

Sees Behind Trees by Michael Dorris. Hyperion for Children, 1996.

Sing Down the Moon by Scott O'Dell. Dell, 1976.

Small Wolf by Nathaniel Benchley. HarperCollins, 1994.

The Talking Earth by Jean George. Harper, 1987.

Warrior Maiden: A Hopi Legend by Ellen Schecter. Bantam Books, 1992.

Where the Buffaloes Begin by Olaf Baker. Puffin Books, 1985.

Thirteen Moons on Turtle's Back: A Native American Year of Moons by Joseph Bruchac and Jonathan London. Philomel Books, 1992.

MULTIMEDIA

CD-ROMS:

Native Americans 2 Interactive Multimedia: Southwest, Northwest Coast, and Arctic. National Geographic Society, 1995.

Multicultural CD Interactive Multimedia: A Comprehensive Resource on African Americans, Hispanic Americans, and Native North Americans. UXL, 1997.

The Native Americans. Rainbow, 1997.

VIDEOS:

Indians of North America. Schlessinger, 1993.

Indians of Early America (Vol. 1 & 2; 20-video series). Encyclopaedia Britannica, 1990.

Indians of North America Series. January Prod., 1990.

Indian Legacy. January Prod., 1989.

Hawk, I'm Your Brother. Southwest Series, 1988.

Knots on a Counting Rope. Spoken Arts, 1989.

Native American Heritage (American Cultures for Children). Schlessinger, 1997.

Native American Life (American History for Children). Schlessinger, 1996.

People of the Desert (Native Americans). Rainbow Educational Video, 1993.

WEB SITES

First Nations Histories (Capsule histories of tribes)
www.dickshovel.netgate.net/Compacts.html

Native Nations: Official and Unofficial Tribal Sites (Links to lots of sites)
www.indy4.fdl.cc.mn.us/~isk/tribes/tribes.htm

Native American Web site for Children
www.nhusd.k12.ca.us/ALVE/NativeAmerhome.html/nativeopening-page.html

➤ SEE ALSO THESE RELATED PATHFINDERS

Apache Indians; Cherokee Indians; Comanche Indians; Crow Indians; Eastern Woodland Indians; Eskimos; Iroquois Confederacy; Nez Perce Indians; Plains Indians; Shoshoni Indians; Sioux Indians; Southwest Indians

Natural Disasters

Natural disasters occur when the forces of nature act with extreme power and devastating results. Most, but not all natural disasters are a result of severe weather conditions such as drought, floods, hurricanes, or tornadoes, or of disturbances within the earth, such as volcanoes and earthquakes.

 DEWEY DECIMAL CALL NUMBERS

155.9 Natural disasters
363.3 Storms
363.8 Public safety, utilities
551 Physical and dynamic geology

 SEARCH TERMS

Natural disaster
Drought
Earthquake
Famine
Flood
Hurricane
Tornado
Natural disaster
Storm
Volcano

 NONFICTION/REFERENCE BOOKS

The Big Storm by Bruce Hiscock. Atheneum, 1993.

Earthquake (A Disaster!) by Christopher Lampton. Millbrook Press, 1991.

Environmental Disasters by John D. Baines. Thomson Learning, 1993.

Eye of the Storm: Chasing Storms with Warren Faidley by Stephen Kramer. G. P. Putnam's Sons, 1997.

Famine (A Disaster!) by Christopher Lampton. Millbrook Press, 1994.

Forest Fire (A Disaster!) by Christopher Lampton. Millbrook Press, 1991.

I'll Know What to Do by Bonnie S. Mark. Magination Press, 1997.

Natural Disasters by Tim Wood. Thomson Learning, 1993.

One Day in the Prairie by Jean Craighead George. Crowell, 1986.

Tornado by Stephen Kramer. Carolrhoda Books, 1992.

Volcano (A Disaster!) by Christopher Lampton. Millbrook Press, 1991.

FICTION

Earthquake: A Story of Old San Francisco by Kathleen V. Kudlinski. Puffin Books, 1995.

Fountain of Fire by Gill McBarnet. Ruwange Trading, 1987.

I am Lavina Cumming by Susan Lowell. Milkweed, 1993.

Tornado by Betsy Cromer Byars. HarperCollins, 1996.

The Year of Fire by Teddy Jam. McElderry/Macmillan, 1993.

MULTIMEDIA

CD-ROM:

Radar Rooster Cooping with Natural Disasters. Meridian, 1996.

VIDEOS:

Earthquake: The Terrifying Truth. ABC News, 1994.

Natural Disasters (Eyewitness Discovery). Dorling Kinderlsey, 1997.

Volcano. Dorling Kindersley, 1996.

Weather. Dorling Kindersley, 1996.

Wrath of God Series. A&E Entertainment, 1998.

WEB SITES

Fema for Kids (Federal Emergency Management Agency Web site for kids)
www.fema.gov/kids/

National Earthquake Information Center
www.neic.cr.usgs.gov/neis/equlists/10maps.html

Wild Wild Weather Page (Tornado and hurricane information)
www.whnt19.com/kidwx/

Volcano World
www.volcano.und.nodak.edu/

Storm Spotter's Guide—National Oceanic and Atmospheric Administration
www.nssl.noaa.gov/~nws/spotterguide.html

➤ SEE ALSO THESE RELATED PATHFINDERS

Hurricanes; Weather

Newbery Books

Named for 18th-century British bookseller John Newbery, the Newbery Award is given annually, by the Association for Library Service to Children, to the author of the most distinguished contribution to American literature for children. A Newbery Book is a book that has been awarded the Newbery Medal.

200s 300s 400s DEWEY DECIMAL CALL NUMBERS

Fiction (Many Newbery books are novels and will be catalogued as fiction)
028 Reading and reading aids

SEARCH TERMS

Children's literature history and criticism
Authors, American
Newbery Medal

NONFICTION/REFERENCE BOOKS

A History of the Newbery and Caldecott Medals by Irene Smith. Viking, 1957.

The Newbery and Caldecott Awards: a Guide to the Medal and Honor Books. American Library Assoc., 1997.

Newbery and Caldecott Medal Books, 1976-1985: With Acceptance Papers, Biographies, And Related Material Chiefly from the Horn Book Magazine. Horn Book, 1986.

The Newbery Award: These Are Winners by Bertha Woolman. T. S. Denison, 1978.

NEWBERY BOOKS

1998: **Out of the Dust** by Karen Hesse (Scholastic)

1997: **The View from Saturday** by E.L. Konigsburg (Jean Karl/Atheneum)

1996: **The Midwife's Apprentice** by Karen Cushman (Clarion Books)

1995: **Walk Two Moons** by Sharon Creech (HarperCollins)

1994: **The Giver** by Lois Lowry (Houghton Mifflin Co.)

1993: **Missing May** by Cynthia Rylant (Jackson/Orchard)

1992: **Shiloh** by Phyllis Reynolds Naylor (Atheneum)

1991: **Maniac Magee** by Jerry Spinelli (Little, Brown & Co.)

1990: **Number the Stars** by Lois Lowry (Houghton Mifflin Co.)

1989: **Joyful Noise: Poems for Two Voices** by Paul Fleischman (Harper)

1988: **Lincoln: A Photobiography** by Russell Freedman (Clarion)

1987: **The Whipping Boy** by Sid Fleischman (Greenwillow Books)

1986: **Sarah, Plain and Tall** by Patricia MacLachlan (Harper)

1985: **The Hero and the Crown** by Robin McKinley (Greenwillow Books)

1984: **Dear Mr. Henshaw** by Beverly Cleary (William Morrow & Co.)

1983: **Dicey's Song** by Cynthia Voigt (Atheneum)

1982: **A Visit to William Blake's Inn: Poems for Innocent and Experienced Travelers** by Nancy Willard (Harcourt Brace Jovanovich)

NONFICTION/REFERENCE BOOKS CONTINUED

1981: **Jacob Have I Loved** by Katherine Paterson (Crowell)

1980: **A Gathering of Days: A New England Girl's Journal, 1830-1832** by Joan W. Blos (Scribner)

1979: **The Westing Game** by Ellen Raskin (Dutton)

1978: **Bridge to Terabithia** by Katherine Paterson (Crowell)

1977: **Roll of Thunder, Hear My Cry** by Mildred D. Taylor (Dial Books)

1976: **The Grey King** by Susan Cooper (McElderry/Atheneum)

1975: **M. C. Higgins, the Great** by Virginia Hamilton (Macmillan)

1974: **The Slave Dancer** by Paula Fox (Bradbury Press)

1973: **Julie of the Wolves** by Jean Craighead George (Harper)

1972: **Mrs. Frisby and the Rats of NIMH** by Robert C. O'Brien (Atheneum)

1971: **Summer of the Swans** by Betsy Byars (Viking)

1970: **Sounder** by William H. Armstrong (Harper)

1969: **The High King** by Lloyd Alexander (Henry Holt & Co.)

1968: **From the Mixed-Up Files of Mrs. Basil E. Frankweiler** by E. L. Konigsburg (Atheneum)

1967: **Up a Road Slowly** by Irene Hunt (Follett)

1966: **I, Juan de Pareja** by Elizabeth Borton de Trevino (Farrar Straus Giroux)

1930: **Hitty, Her First Hundred Years** by Rachel Field (Macmillan)

1929: **The Trumpeter of Krakow** by Eric P. Kelly (Macmillan)

1928: **Gay Neck, the Story of a Pigeon** by Dhan Gopal Mukerji (Dutton)

1927: **Smoky, the Cowhorse** by Will James (Scribner)

1926: **Shen of the Sea** by Arthur Bowie Chrisman (Dutton)

1925: **Tales from Silver Lands** by Charles Finger (Doubleday)

1924: **The Dark Frigate** by Charles Hawes (Little, Brown & Co.)

1923: **The Voyages of Doctor Dolittle** by Hugh Lofting (Lippincott)

1922: **The Story of Mankind** by Hendrik Willem van Loon (Liveright)

MULTIMEDIA

AUDIO:

(Several Newbery books have been recorded for audio books.)

WEB SITES

Newbery Medal Home Page
www.ala.org/alsc/newbery.html
Children Literature Web Guide Newbery Page
www.acs.ucalgary.ca/~dkbrown/newbery.html

VIDEOS:

From the Mixed-Up Files of Mrs. Basil E. Frankweiler (Stars Lauren Bacall). Hallmark Home Entertainment, 1995.
Good Conversation!. Tim Podell Productions, 1994. (Series of interviews with children's authors—including several Newbery winners or Newbery Honor recipients.)
Island of the Blue Dolphins. MCA, 1985.
Johnny Tremain. Walt Disney, 1957.
Where the Lilies Bloom. MGM/UA, 1973.

➤ SEE ALSO THIS RELATED PATHFINDER
Caldecott Books

Nez Perce Indians

The Nez Perce Indians are a Native American people who originally settled in two separate groups along the lower Snake River. They lived in western Idaho, northeast Oregon, and southeast Washington, where they fished and hunted small animals. They were forced from their lands as white settlers moved westward in the mid-1800s. Today the Nez Perce live on reservations in Washington and Idaho.

DEWEY DECIMAL CALL NUMBERS

970.1 Indians of North America
970   History, North America
973   History, United States
979.5 Pacific Coast states
398.2 Folk literature

SEARCH TERMS

Nez Perce
North American Indians
Native Americans
Indians of the West
Chief Joseph

NONFICTION/REFERENCE BOOKS

Encyclopedia of Native American Tribes by Carl Waldman. Facts on File, 1988.

The Encyclopedia of North American Indians. Marshall Cavendish, 1997.

Chief Joseph, Leader of Destiny by Kate Jassem. Troll Assoc., 1979.

Chief Joseph of the Nez Perce a Photo-Illustrated Biography by Bill Mcauliffe. Bridgestone Books, 1998.

Horsemen of the Western Plateaus: The Nez Perce Indians by Sonia Bleeker. William Morrow & Co., 1957.

The Nez Perce (A First Book) by Madelyn Klein Anderson. Franklin Watts, 1994.

The Nez Perce (New True Books) by Alice Osinski. Children's Press, 1988.

The Nez Perce (A First Americans Book) by Virginia Driving Hawk Sneve. Holiday House, 1994.

The Nez Perce Indians (Junior Library of American Indians) by Mark Rifkin. Chelsea House, 1994.

The Nez Perce: People of the Far West by Victoria Sherrow. Millbrook Press, 1994.

FICTION

Legends of the Great Chiefs compiled by Emerson N. Watson. T. Nelson, 1972.

Thunder Rolling in the Mountains by Scott O'Dell and Elizabeth Hall. Houghton Mifflin Co., 1992.

Best Friends by Loretta Krupinski. Disney Press, 1998.

Soun Tetoken: Nez Perce Boy Tames a Stallion by Ken Thomasma. Grandview Pub. Co., 1984.

Spirit of the West: The Story of an Appaloosa Mare, Her Precious Foal, and the Girl Whose Pride Endangers Them All (Treasured Horses, No. 1) by Jahnna N. Malcolm. Scholastic, 1997.

 WEB SITE

"Nee Mee Poo" The People (Nez Perce Tribe page)
www.uidaho.edu/nezperce/neemepoo.htm

 SEE ALSO THESE RELATED PATHFINDERS

Native Americans; Westward Expansion

Ocean

Oceans are the largest ecosystems of all, covering more then 70 percent of the earth's surface. There are many different habitats in the ocean, from coral reefs to open waters. Only about 20 percent of the earth's species live in the ocean, and most of these live on the ocean floor.

DEWEY DECIMAL CALL NUMBERS

200s
300s
400s

551.46   Oceanography
591.92   Zoology, Marine and freshwater life

SEARCH TERMS

Ocean
Marine biology
Oceanography
Marine animals

NONFICTION/REFERENCE BOOKS

Exploring an Ocean Tide Pool (Redfeather Book) by Jean Bendick. Henry Holt & Co., 1994.

Ocean (Biomes of the World) by Edward R. Ricciuti. Marshall Cavendish, 1996.

Ocean: The Living World. Dorling Kindersley, 1995.

Ocean (Inside Guides). Dorling Kindersley, 1994.

Ocean Animals in Danger (Survivors Series for Children) by Gary Turback. Northland Pub., 1994.

Oceans by Seymour Simon. Morrow Junior Books, 1990.

The Ocean Atlas by Anita Ganeri. Dorling Kindersley, 1994.

Sea Animals (Eye Openers) by Angela Royston. Aladdin Books, 1992.

Under the Sea (Discoveries Library) edited by Frank H. Talbot. Time-Life Books, 1995.

Way Down Deep: Strange Ocean Creatures by Patricia Demuth. Grosset & Dunlap, 1995.

Wonders of the Sea by Louis Sabin. Troll Assoc., 1982.

Sea Life (Picturepedia) edited by Malcolm Macgarvin. Dorling Kindersley, 1992.

FICTION

The Magic School Bus on the Ocean Floor by Joanna Cole. Scholastic, 1992.

In the Palace of the Ocean King by Marilyn Singer.
Atheneum Books for Young Readers, 1995.

The Mermaid and other Sea Poems compiled and illustrated by Sophie Windham.
Scholastic, 1996.

Ocean Day by Shelley Rotner and Ken Kreisler. Maxwell Macmillan International, 1993.

MULTIMEDIA

 ### CD-ROMS:

Destination, Ocean Interactive Multimedia (Imagination Express). Edmark, 1995.
The Magic School Bus Explores the Ocean Interactive Multimedia. Microsoft, 1996.
Undersea Adventure Interactive Multimedia (Adventure Series: Animals & Nature). Knowledge Adventure, 1995.

 ### VIDEOS:

Locomotion in the Ocean (Life in the Sea). National Geographic Educational, 1995.
Magic School Bus Gets Eaten. Kid Vision, 1995.
Ocean Drifters. National Geographic Home Video, 1994.
Oceans: Earth's Last Frontier. Rainbow Educational Video, 1995.
What's Under the Ocean (Now I Know). Troll Assoc, 1993.
Where Did They Go? (Seahouse One). Rainbow Educational Video, 1991.
Blue Planet (Plant Earth). Unapix Entertainment, 1986.
Deep and Dark (Seahouse Two). Rainbow Educational Video, 1992.
Deep Sea Dive (Really Wild Animals). National Geographic Home Video, 1994.
Desert in the Sea (Seahouse Three). Rainbow Educational Video, 1993.

 ## WEB SITES

Ocean Planet—Smithsonian Institution
www.seawifs.gsfc.nasa.gov/
ocean_planet.html
Seaweb
www.seaweb.org/

➤ SEE ALSO THESE RELATED PATHFINDERS
Biomes; Sea Animals

Pattern

A pattern is something that happens over and over again in a predictable fashion. For instance, the sun rising every morning or setting every evening is a pattern. A pattern can also be a model which we might follow, for example: a dressmaker's pattern.

 DEWEY DECIMAL CALL NUMBERS

745.4 Art, Design or decoration
793.7 Games, Puzzles
512 Algebra
516 Geometry

 SEARCH TERMS

Pattern
Pattern perception
Flight patterns
Mathematical patterns
Sewing patterns
Patterns in nature

 NONFICTION/REFERENCE BOOKS

All About Pattern by Irene Yates. Benchmark Books, 1998.

The First Book of Rhythms by Langston Hughes. Oxford University Press, 1995.

Collage by Sue Stocks. Thomson Learning, 1994.

Discovering Patterns by Andrew King. Copper Beech Books, 1998.

Everyday Mysteries by Jerome Wexler. Dutton Children's Books, 1995.

Flip-Flap by Sandra Jenkins. DK Publishing, 1995.

Frank Lloyd Wright for Kids by Kathleen Thorne-Thomsen. Chicago Review Press, 1994.

Games by Ivan Bullock. Thomson Learning, 1994.

Let's Look at Patterns by Nicola Tuxworth. Lorenz Books, 1997.

Look Once, Look Twice by Janet Marshall. Ticknor & Fields, 1995.

On the Move!: Patterns of Change by Sharon Franklin. GoodYearBooks, 1995.

Pattern by Kim Taylor. Wiley, 1992.

Patterns by David Stienecker. Benchmark Books, 1997.

Patterns by Ivan Bullock. Thomson Learning, 1994.

Where Am I: The Story of Maps and Navigation by A. G. Smith. Stoddart Kids, 1997.

FICTION

Echoes for the Eye: Poems to Celebrate Patterns in Nature by Barbara Juster Esbensen. HarperCollins, 1996.

Ten Bright Eyes by Judy Hindley. Peachtree Pub., 1998.

MULTIMEDIA

CD-ROMS:

Exploring Patterns. IntelliTools, 1997.

Eyewitness Virtual Reality. Bird Interactive. DK Multimedia, 1995.

Mighty Math Carnival Countdown. Edmark, 1996.

Millie's Math House Interactive. Edmark, 1995.

VIDEOS:

Animals in Spring and Summer. Encyclopedia Britannica, 1983.

Colors and Patterns. Rainbow Educational Video, 1992.

How Living Things are Classified. United Learning, 1993.

Patterning; Classifying. Educational Activities, 1993.

Yellowstone Magic. Terra Prod., 1994.

WEB SITE

Dance of Chance (Patterns in nature exhibit)
www.polymer.bu.edu/museum/

➤ SEE ALSO THIS RELATED PATHFINDER

Quilts

Penguins

There are several different kinds of penguins all living in the cool regions of the Southern Hemisphere. Penguins cannot fly, but they have wings that work as flippers and webbed feet which make them very good at swimming underwater. They are covered with short feathers and are white in front and black on the back. Penguins are seabirds. Like all seabirds, they gather on the shore in the summer to build their nests and lay their eggs.

 DEWEY DECIMAL CALL NUMBERS

598 Birds

598.3 Specific types of birds

 SEARCH TERMS

Penguins
Sea birds
Birds
Search by names of specific species, for example: Emperor penguin

 NONFICTION/REFERENCE BOOKS

Looking at Penguins by Dorothy Hinshaw Patent. Holiday House, 1993.

Penguin (See How They Grow) by Mary Ling; photographs by Neil Fletcher. Dorling Kindersley, 1993.

Penguin (Life Story) by Clarie Robinson. Troll Assoc., 1994.

Penguins at Home: Gentoos of Antarctica by Bruce McMillan. Houghton Mifflin Co., 1993.

The Penguin (Life Cycles) by Sabrina Crewe. Raintree/Steck Vaughn, 1998.

Puffins Climb, Penguins Rhyme by Bruce McMillan. Harcourt Brace Jovanovich, 1995.

What's a Penguin Doing in a Place Like This? by Miriam Schlein. Millbrook Press, 1997.

FICTION

Antarctica by Helen Cowcher. Farrar Straus Giroux, 1991.

Little Penguin's Tale by Audrey Wood. Harcourt Brace Jovanovich, 1989.

Mr. Popper's Penguins by Richard and Florence Atwater. Little, Brown & Co., 1988.

Penguin Pete and Little Tim by Marcus Pfister. North-South Books, 1997.

MULTIMEDIA

CD-ROMS:

Birds Interactive Multimedia. ICE Integrated Communications & Entertainment, 1996.

Eyewitness Virtual Reality. Bird Interactive Multimedia. DK Multimedia, 1996.

VIDEOS:

Birds of the Sea (Seahouse Three). Rainbow Educational Video, 1993.

Arctic & Antarctic (Eyewitness). Dorling Kindersley Videos, 1996.

WEB SITES

The Penguin Page
www.vni.net/~kwelch/penguins/

Penguins in North Otago New Zealand
www.es.co.nz/~houston/penguins.html

Pete & Barb's Penguin Pages (with bibliography)
www.ourworld.compuserve.com/home-pages/Peter_and_Barbara_Barham/pengies.htm

SeaWorld Busch Garden's Penguin Cam Page (Sea penguins live)
www.seaworld.org/Penguins/penguincam.html

> ➤ SEE ALSO THESE RELATED PATHFINDERS
Animals; Birds

Pets

A pet is an animal that is kept for companionship and is treated with affection. Most common pets are domesticated animals such as cats, dogs, and birds. But other types of animals are also kept as pets in small cages, such as hamsters and guinea pigs. Some exotic animals, such as iguanas and boa constrictors, are also kept as pets.

 DEWEY DECIMAL CALL NUMBERS

636 Animal husbandry (care and training)

 SEARCH TERMS

Pets
Domestic animals
Exotic pets
Search by names of particular pets, for example: Iguana

 NONFICTION/REFERENCE BOOKS

Becoming Best Friends With Your Hamster, Guinea Pig, or Rabbit (Pet Friends) by Bill Gutman. Millbrook Press, 1997.

Becoming Your Bird's Best Friend (Pet Friends) by Bill Gutman. Millbrook Press, 1996.

Becoming Your Cat's Best Friend (Pet Friends) by Bill Gutman. Millbrook Press, 1997.

Becoming Your Dog's Best Friend (Pet Friends) by Bill Gutman. Millbrook Press, 1996.

Let's Get a Pet by Harriet Ziefert. Puffin Books, 1996.

Pets: A Comprehensive Guidebook for Kids by Frances Chrystie. Little, Brown & Co., 1995.

Puppy by Mark Evans. Dorling Kindersley, 1992.

FICTION

Arthur's Pet Business by Marc Brown. Joy Street Books, 1990.

Arthur's New Puppy by Marc Brown, Little, Brown & Co., 1993.

Bonny's Big Day by James Herriot. St. Martin's Press, 1991.

Chuck and Danielle by Peter Dickinson. Bantam Books Doubleday Dell Books for Young People, 1996.

The Day Jimmy's Boa Ate the Wash (Picture Puffin Books) by Trinka Hakes Nobel. Dial Books for Young Readers, 1984.

Eliza's Dog by Betsy Hearne. Margaret K. McElderry Books, 1996.

How Smudge Came by Nan Gregory. Walker & Co., 1997.

Madeline's Rescue by Ludwig Bemelman. Viking, 1953.

Mouse Views: What the Class Pet Saw by Bruce McMillan. Holiday House, 1993.

My Elephant Can Do Almost Anything by Anke de Vries. Front Street/Lemniscaat, 1995.

The Mysterious Tadpole by Steven Kellogg. Dial Books, 1979.

The Nature of the Beast by Jan Carr. Tambourine Books, 1996.

An Octopus Followed Me Home by Dan Taccarino. Viking, 1997.

A Pocketful of Cricket by Rebecca Caudill. Henry Holt & Co., 1964.

MULTIMEDIA

CD-ROMS:

Amazing Animals Interactive Multimedia. DK Multimedia, 1997.

Multimedia Exotic Pets Interactive. Inroads Interactive, 1995.

Who Wants Arthur. Media Vision, 1995.

Zookeeper Interactive. ROMTECH, 1996.

VIDEOS:

Homeward Bound. Walt Disney, 1993.

Paws, Claws, Feathers, and Fins. Kidviz Special Interest, 1993.

Pets. Sony Wonder, 1994.

Pets and Their Wild Relatives. National Geographic Society, 1989.

WEB SITES

Horse Country
www.horse-country.com/

PetStation Kids—Around the World
(Talk about pets with kids from around the world)
www.petstation.com/kids.html

Puppy Place
www.puppyplace.com/

➤ SEE ALSO THIS RELATED PATHFINDER

Animals

Pilgrims

Some of the earliest American colonists were Pilgrims. They came to America from England in 1620 and settled Plymouth colony, which grew to be the town of Plymouth in Massachusetts. These early American colonists were Puritans, a religious group from England that was seeking religious freedom. And it is because they traveled to America for religious reasons that they are called pilgrims.

 200s 300s 400s DEWEY DECIMAL CALL NUMBERS

394.1 Pilgrims (New Plymouth Colony), Social Life and customs
973.2 Colonial period, 1607-1773
974.4 Wampanoag Indians. Indians of North America.
394.2 Thanksgiving Day. Pilgrims (New Plymouth Colony)

 SEARCH TERMS

Pilgrims
Colonial period
Puritans
Plymouth
Thanksgiving
New Plymouth Colony

 NONFICTION/REFERENCE BOOKS

Pilgrim Voices: Our First Year in the New World edited by Connie Roop. Walker & Co., 1997.

Eating the Plates: A Pilgrim Book of Food and Manners by Lucille Recht Penner. Maxwell Macmillan International, 1991.

The First Thanksgiving by Jean Craighead George. Philomel Books, 1993.

On the Mayflower: Voyage of the Ship's Apprentice & a Passenger Girl by Kate Waters. Scholastic, 1996.

Pilgrim Voices: Our First Year in the New World edited by Connie and Peter Roop. Walker & Co., 1995.

The Pilgrims of Plymouth by Marcia Sewall. Aladdin Paperbacks, 1996.

Samuel Eaton's Day: A Day in the Life of a Pilgrim Boy by Kate Waters. Scholastic, 1993.

Sarah Morton's Day: A Day in the Life of a Pilgrim Girl by Kate Waters. Scholastic, 1989.

Stranded at Plymouth Plantation, 1626 by Gary Bowen. HarperCollins, 1994.

Tapenum's Day: A Wampanoag Indian Boy in Pilgrim Times by Kate Waters. Scholastic, 1996.

Thunder from the Clear Sky by Marcia Sewall. Atheneum Books for Young Readers, 1995.

FICTION

The Dangerous Voyage by Gilbert Morris. Bethany House, 1995.

Friendship's First Thanksgiving by William Accorsi. Holiday House, 1992.

The Thanksgiving Story by Alice Dalgiesh. Scribner, 1988.

Three Young Pilgrims by Cheryl Harness. Bradbury Press, 1992.

Pilgrims of Plymouth by Marcia Sewell. Macmillan, 1986

MULTIMEDIA

 ### CD-ROMS:

Life in Colonial America. Queue, 1995.

People Behind the Holidays Interactive Multimedia. National Geographic Society, 1994.

PilgrimQuest II. Decision Development Corp, 1997.

VIDEOS:

Early Settlers (American History for Children). Schlessinger, 1996.

The Mayflower Pilgrims. PA Communications, 1995

Pilgrims of Plimoth. Weston Woods, 1988.

Plymouth Plantation. Video Tours, 1989.

This is America, Charlie Brown. Paramount, 1988.

 ## WEB SITES

Caleb Johnson's Mayflower Web Page (Excellent site for teachers and students with extensive primary sources) wwwmembers.aol.com/mayflo1620/ welcome.html

Plimoth-on-Web:Plimoth Plantation's Web Page! (Site for this living history museum with teacher and student resources) www.plimoth.org

➤ SEE ALSO THESE RELATED PATHFINDERS
Colonial Life, American; Holidays Around the World

Pioneer Life

American pioneers traveled west from the Atlantic coastal states during the 1800s. Individuals and families traveled by covered wagon to unknown or unclaimed territories. They often settled in areas miles from any other people and began building their homesteads. The United States government encouraged this westward development by offering large tracts of land to anyone who would claim it and live on it.

DEWEY DECIMAL CALL NUMBERS

973.5 Early 19th century, 1809-1845
973.6 Middle 19th century, 1845-1861
978 Western United States
970 History of North America

SEARCH TERMS

Pioneer
American West
Western United States
Westward expansion

NONFICTION/REFERENCE BOOKS

Along the Santa Fe Trail by Ginger Wadsworth. Albert Whitman & Co., 1993.

The American West. World Book, 1997.

Black Frontiers: A History of African American Heroes in the Old West by Lillian Schlissel. Simon & Schuster, 1995.

A Child's Day by Bobbie Kalman. Crabtree Pub. Co., 1994.

Daniel Boone by Robert Hogrogian. January Prod., 1981.

Frontier Home by Raymond Bial. Houghton Mifflin Co., 1993.

The Oregon Trail by R. Conrad Stein. Children's Press, 1994.

Pioneer Life from A to Z by Bobbie Kalman. Crabtree Pub. Co., 1997.

Pioneer Projects by Bobbie Kalman. Crabtree Pub. Co., 1997.

FICTION

The Courage of Sarah Noble by Alice Dagliesh. Scribner, 1986.

The Golly Sisters Ride Again by Betsy Byars. HarperCollins, 1994.

Johnny Appleseed: A Poem by Reeve Lindbergh. Joy Street Books, 1990.

Little House in the Big Woods; Little House on the Prairie; By the Shores of Silver Lake; Farmer Boy; On the Banks of Plum Creek; The Long Winter; Little Town on the Prairie; These Happy Golden Years (The Little House Series) by Laura Ingalls Wilder. Harper & Row, 1971.

Nine for California by Sonia Levitin. Orchard Books, 1996.

Sarah, Plain and Tall by Patricia MacLachlan. Harper & Row, 1985.

Swamp Angel by Anne Isaacs. Dutton, 1994.

The Year of the Ranch by Alice McLerren. Viking, 1996.

MULTIMEDIA

CD-ROMS:

America Goes West. Queue, 1996.

American Heritage History of the United States for Young People. Simon & Schuster, 1997.

American History. Multieducator, [nd].

Life in Pioneer America. Queue, 1996.

MultiMedia U.S. History: Story of a Nation. Learning Lane, [nd].

Oregon Trail II (3rd ed.). The Learning Co., 1997.

VIDEOS:

Caddie Woodlawn. Wonder Works, 1989.

Christmas at Plum Creek (Episode from the Little House on the Prairie TV Series). Time-Life, [nd].

Her Own Words: Pioneer Women's Diaries. Her Own Words, 1986.

Little House on the Prairie: Premiere Movie (Made-for-TV movie).Time-Life, 1974.

Seven Alone. Bridgestone, 1974.

United States Expansion (American History for Children). Schlessinger, 1996.

Westward Expansion: The Pioneer Challenge. Rainbow Educational Video, 1992.

 WEB SITES

Daniel Boone (Informative slide show)
www.truman.edu/academics/fa/faculty/jpaulding/menu.html

Black Pioneers of the Oregon Country
www.teleport.com/~eotic/family/black.html

Lewis and Clark Expedition (Taken from the PBS film by Ken Burns, this site covers the history of the expedition, including supplies taken and journal entries. This is a great source for a report.)
www.pbs.org/lewisandclark/

The Oregon Trail
www.isu.edu/~trinmich/Oregontrail.html

Pioneer Life in Ohio
www.rootsweb.com/~ohpickaw/life.html

➤ *SEE ALSO THIS RELATED PATHFINDER*
Westward Expansion

Plains Indians

The Plains Indians refer to the various Native American tribes who lived in the grasslands from the Mississippi River to the Rocky Mountains, and from southern Canada to Texas. Some of these tribes were sedentary tribes who farmed the river valleys and lived in walled villages of domed earth lodges. Others were nomadic tribes who hunted buffalo and lived in tepees. The Plains Indian tribes spoke different languages, but they were able to communicate with a sign language which they all understood. Some Plains tribes are Blackfoot, Cheyenne, Comanche, and Pawnee.

DEWEY DECIMAL CALL NUMBERS

970.1 Indians of North America
973 History, United States
970.004 History, North America (1800-1900)
398.2 Folk literature

SEARCH TERMS

Plains Indians
Native Americans
North American Indians
Search by names of tribes, for example:
Comanche

NONFICTION/REFERENCE BOOKS

American Indian Children of the Past by Victoria Sherrow. Millbrook Press, 1997.

The Blackfeet Indians by Ann-Marie Hendrickson. Chelsea House, 1997.

Encyclopedia of Native American Tribes by Carl Waldman. Facts on File, 1988.

The Encyclopedia of North American Indians. Marshall Cavendish, 1997.

Pawnee by Dennis B. Fradin. Children's Press, 1988.

The Santee Sioux by Nancy Bonvillain. Chelsea House, 1997.

The Sioux by Virginia Driving Hawk Sneve. Holiday House, 1993.

This Land is My Land by George Littlechild. Children's Press, 1993.

Warriors of the Plains by Thomas E. Mails. Council Oak Books, 1997.

The Cheyenne (A New True Book) by Dennis B. Fradin. Children's Press, 1988.

FICTION

Adopted by the Eagle by Paul Goble. Maxwell Macmillan International, 1994.

Beyond the Ridge by Paul Goble. Bradbury Press, 1989.

Crow Chief: A Plains Indian Story by Paul Goble. Orchard Books, 1992.

Doesn't Fall off His Horse by Virginia Stroud. Dial Books for Young People, 1994.

Full Moon Stories: Thirteen Native American Legends by Eagle Walking Turtle. Hyperion, 1997.

The Legend of the Indian Paintbrush by Tomie De Paola. G. P. Putnam's Sons, 1988.

The Mud Pony: A Traditional Skidi Pawnee Tale by Caron Lee Cohen. Scholastic, 1988.

Spotted Eagle & Black Crow: A Lakota Legend by Emery Bernhard. Holiday House, 1993.

The Story of Jumping Mouse by John Steptoe. Lothrop, Lee & Shepard, 1984.

Why Buffalo Roam by L. Michael Kershen. Stemmer House, 1993.

Her Seven Brothers by Paul Goble. Bradbury Press, 1988.

MULTIMEDIA

 ### CD-ROM:

Native Americans: People of the Plains. Rainbow Educational Media, 1998.

 ### VIDEOS:

People of the Plains (Native Americans). Rainbow Educational Video, 1993.

Cheyenne (Indians of North America). Schlessinger, 1993.

 ## WEB SITE

Native American Home Page–Cheyenne—Native Americans of the Plains
www.nhusd.k12.ca.us/ALVE/
NativeAmerhome.html/Cheyenne/
cheyenne.html

➤ *SEE ALSO THESE RELATED PATHFINDERS*

Apache Indians; Comanche Indians; Crow Indians; Native Americans; Pioneer Life; Sioux Indians; Westward Expansion

Plants

Plants are living organisms, such as trees, shrubs, flowers, vegetables, grains, and grass, that use chlorophyll to make food from sunlight. Many important things come from plants—food, paper, clothes—but perhaps the most important of all is oxygen.

DEWEY DECIMAL CALL NUMBERS

580 Plants
575 Specific parts & systems of plants
577 Ecology

SEARCH TERMS

Plants
Botany
Germination
Seeds
Trees
Search by names of plants, for example:
Fern

NONFICTION/REFERENCE BOOKS

Container Gardening for Kids by Ellen Talmage. Sterling Pub. Co., 1996.

Experiments with Plants by Monica Byles. Lerner Pub. Co., 1994.

Growing Things by Ting Morris. Franklin Watts, 1994.

Incredible Plants (Inside Guides). Dorling Kindersley, 1997.

Incredible Plants by Lesley Dow. Time-Life Books, 1997.

Insect-Eating Plants by L. Patricia Kite. Millbrook Press, 1995.

Janice VanCleave's Plants: Mind-Boggling Experiments You Can Turn into Science Fair Projects by Janice VanCleave. Wiley, 1997.

Linnea's Windowsill Garden by Christina Bjork. Farrar Straus Giroux, 1988.

The Magic School Bus Plants Seeds by Patricia Relf. Scholastic, 1995.

My First Book of Nature by Dwight Kuhn. Scholastic, 1993.

Plant Families by Carol Lerner. Morrow Junior Books, 1989.

Plants (DK Picturepedia). Dorling Kindersley, 1993.

Plants That Never Ever Bloom by Ruth Heller. Grosset & Dunlap, 1984.

The Science Book of Things that Grow by Neil Ardley. Harcourt Brace Jovanovich, 1991.

The Story of Rosy Dock by Jeannie Baker. Greenwillow Books, 1995.

The Visual Dictionary of Plants. Dorling Kindersley, 1992.

FICTION

Anna's Garden Songs by Mary Q. Steele. Greenwillow Books, 1989.

Jacob and the Stranger by Sally Derby. Ticknor & Fields, 1994.

Pumpkin, Pumpkin by Jeanne Titherington. Mulberry Books, 1990.

Something is Growing by Walter Krudop. Atheneum Books, 1995.

Vegetable Garden by Douglas Florian. Harcourt Brace Jovanovich, 1996.

MULTIMEDIA

CD-ROMS:

Investigating Plant Science Interactive Multimedia. Attica Cybernetics, 1994.

One Small Square Interactive Multimedia: Backyard. Virgin Sound and Vision, 1996.

Science Blaster Jr. Davidson, 1996.

A World of Plants Interactive Multimedia. National Geographic Society, 1994.

VIDEOS:

All About Seeds. Troll Assoc., 1993.

Debbie Greenthumb. United Learning, 1991.

Flowers, Plants, and Trees. TMW Media Group, 1987.

How Plants are Used. National Geographic Educational, 1991.

How to Recognize Plant Fingerprints. Films for the Humanities, 1988.

The Magic School Bus Goes to Seed. Scholastic, 1995.

Plants: Green, Growing, Giving Life. Rainbow Educational Video, 1991.

World of Plants. United Learning, 1989.

WEB SITES

Gardening.com
www.gardening.com/Encyclopedia/
cgi-bin/Default.asp

Gardening for Kids
www.geocities.com/EnchantedForest/
Glade/3313/

The Time-Life Complete Gardener Encyclopedia
www.cgi.pathfinder.com/cgi-bin/VG/vg

➤ SEE ALSO THESE RELATED PATHFINDERS

Ecology; Flowers; Trees

Poetry

Poetry is the art of writing poems. A poem is created through an arrangement of words, written in a pattern of sounds and rhythm. This structure is called verse. Poetry may or may not rhyme and can express facts, ideas, or emotions. It has the power to engage feelings and imagination and is more powerful than ordinary speech.

DEWEY DECIMAL CALL NUMBERS

811　American poetry in English
821　English poetry
861　Spanish poetry
808　Collections of literature
809　History, description, criticism
810　American literature in English
398　Folklore

SEARCH TERMS

Poetry
Children's literature
Children's poetry
Nursery rhymes

NONFICTION/REFERENCE BOOKS

American Writers for Children. Gale, 1984.

Authors of Books for Young People. Scarecrow Press, 1990.

Childmade: Awakening Children to Creative Writing by Cynde Gregory. Talman Co., 1989.

International Companion Encyclopedia of Children's Literature edited by Peter Hunt and Sheila Ray. Routledge, 1996.

The New Princeton Encyclopedia of Poetry and Poetics. Princeton University Press, 1993.

Stories, Songs and Poetry to Teach Reading and Writing Literacy Through Language by Marlene McCracken. Peguis, 1987.

The Magic Pencil: Teaching Children Creative Writing: Exercises and Activities for Children, Their Parents, and Their Teachers by Eve Shelnutt, Paulette L. Lambert. Peachtree Pub., 1994.

Poem-Making: Ways to Begin Writing Poetry by Myra Cohn Livingston. HarperCollins, 1991.

POETRY COLLECTIONS

A Book of Nonsense (Everyman's Library Children's Classic) by Edward Lear. Everyman's Library, 1992.

A Child's Garden of Verse by Robert Lewis Stevenson. Chronicle Books, 1989.

The Real Mother Goose. Scholastic Trade, 1994.

A Pizza the Size of the Sun: Poems by Jack Prelutsky, illustrated by James Stevenson. Greenwillow Books, 1996.

Insectlopedia: Poems and Paintings by Douglas Florian. Harcourt Brace Jovanovich, 1998.

Stopping by Woods on a Snowy Evening by Robert Frost. Dutton, 1985.

A Book of Americans by Rosemary and Stephen Vincent Benet. Henry Holt & Co., 1987.

MULTIMEDIA

CD-ROMS:

American Poetry: The 19th Century Lab Pack (WIN/MAC, presents more than 1,000 poems by 150 poets). Voyager, 1994.

Edward Lear's Book of Nonsense. Maxima New Media, 1996.

Multimedia World of Children's Poetry. Young Digital Poland, 1997.

VIDEOS:

Poetry Hall of Fame. Monterey Home Video, 1993. (Celebrity performers take viewers on a journey through great poetry)

Singing Time! Lightyear Entertainment, 1996. (Animated. Includes poems by Dickinson, Wordsworth, and Browning)

Spoon River Anthology and a Poetic Portrait Gallery. Nebraskans for Public Television, 1997. (Excerpts from "Spoon River Anthology"; part of the Master Poets Collection)

WEB SITES

Carol Hurst's Children's Literature Site (Information and links) www.carolhurst.com/index.html

Children's Literature Web Guide (Links) www.acs.ucalgary.ca/~dkbrown/index.html

Kristine George's Children's Poetry Corner (Information and ideas) www.home.earthlink.net/~froggie1/

Poetry For Kids (Poetry and links) www.nesbitt.com/poetry/poems.html

➤ **SEE ALSO THESE RELATED PATHFINDERS**

Caldecott Books; Newbery Books

Prairie (Grassland)

In regions where the climate is too dry and the soil too poor to grow trees, only grasses grow. These areas are called grasslands. In North America these regions are called prairies. The prairies are generally level, and were originally grass-covered and treeless plains stretching from Ohio to the Great Plains. The prairies are sometimes called the vanishing grasslands, because farmers have turned them into agricultural regions. In South America grasslands are called pampas and llanos. In Eurasia they are called steppes. And in South Africa, grasslands are called savanna. Grasslands support a variety of grazing and burrowing wild life.

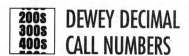 **DEWEY DECIMAL CALL NUMBERS**

577.44 Prairie

508.73 Geographic descriptions, Travel and surveys

574.909 Geographical treatment

917.1 Geography and travel in North America

 SEARCH TERMS

Prairies
Prairie ecology
Prairie animals
ecology
Grasslands
Grassland ecology
Grassland animals
Great Plains
Savannah

 NONFICTION/REFERENCE BOOKS

America's Prairies (Carolrhoda Books Earth Watch Books) by Frank Staub. Carolrhoda Books, 1994.

An American Safari: Adventures on the North American Prairie by Jim Brandenburg. Walker & Co., 1995.

Grasslands (Habitats of the World) by Sheri Amsel. Raintree/Steck Vaughn, 1993.

Prairies by Dorothy Hinshaw Patent. Holiday House, 1996.

Prairies and Grasslands (A New True Book) by James P. Rowan. Children's Press, 1983.

African Savanna by Donald M. Silver. Learning Triangle Press, 1997.

FICTION

By the Shore of Silver Lake by Laura Ingalls Wilder. HarperCollins, 1973.

Chinook Christmas by Rudy Wiebe. Red Deer College Press, 1992.

If You're Not from the Prairie by David Bouchard.
Atheneum Books for Young Readers, 1995.

Little House on the Prairie by Laura Ingalls Wilder. HarperCollins, 1973

On the Banks of Plum Creek by Laura Ingalls Wilder. HarperCollins, 1973.

One Day in the Prairie by Jean Craighead George. Crowell, 1986.

A Prairie Boy's Winter by William Kurelek. Houghton Mifflin Co., 1973.

Skylark by Patricia MacLachlan. HarperCollins, 1994.

MULTIMEDIA

 ### VIDEOS:

Kiki and the Cuckoo (Key Concepts in Personal Development). Marsh Media/Marshfilms Enterprises, 1993.

Plains (Our Natural Heritage). Hollywood Select Video, 1987.

Prairie Wildlife (Life Science: Nature). Natural History Educational, 1995.

Sarah, Plain and Tall and **Skylark**. Republic Home Video, 1993.

Tallgrass Prairie: An American Story. National Geographic Educational, 1997.

 ## WEB SITES

Ecosystems of Our World—Grasslands
www.tqd.advanced.org/2988/grassland.htm
Ecosystems of Our World—Savannah
www.tqd.advanced.org/2988/savannah.htm
Grasslands Biome
www.mobot.org/MBGnet/vb/grasslnd/index.htm

➤ SEE ALSO THESE RELATED PATHFINDERS
Biomes; Ecology

Prehistoric Life

Anything which occurred before history was recorded or written is considered prehistoric. Prehistoric life begins with the origins of life on earth and continues through 16,000 B.C., the time of the earliest known cave paintings and through 3,000 B.C., the earliest known writing. Scientists called paleontologists first learned about prehistoric life by studying ancient plant and animal fossils. Some of the most well known prehistoric creatures are dinosaurs, saber-toothed tigers, and prehistoric humans.

DEWEY DECIMAL CALL NUMBERS

200s
300s
400s

930 Ancient history
560 Paleontology

SEARCH TERMS

Prehistoric
Neanderthal
Stone age
Iceman
Fossils
History of civilization
Origins of life

NONFICTION/REFERENCE BOOKS

Dinosaur Valley by Mitsuhiro Kurokawa. Chronicle Books, 1992.

Discovering the Iceman by Shelley Tanaka. Hyperion, 1996.

An Ice Age Hunter (Everyday Life of... series). Peter Bedrick Books, 1992.

In the Beginning... The Nearly Complete History of Almost Everything by Richard Platt. Dorling Kindersley, 1995.

Over 6,000 Years Ago—In the Stone Age by Hazel Martell. Maxwell Macmillan International, 1992.

The People by Robert Pickering. Millbrook Press, 1996.

Rand McNally Picture Atlas of Prehistoric Life by Tim Hayward. Rand McNally, 1992.

Stone Age Farmers Beside the Sea by Caroline Arnold. Clarion Books, 1997.

When Clay Sings by Byrd Baylor. Scribner, 1972.

FICTION

Boy of the Painted Cave by Justin Denzel. Philomel Books, 1988.

The First Dog by Jan Brett. Harcourt Brace Jovanovich, 1988.

Malu's Wolf by Ruth Craig. Orchard Books, 1995.

Mike's Mammoth by Roy Gerrard. Farrar Straus Giroux, 1990.

The Ogs Invent the Wheel by Felicity Everett. Usborne, 1995.

One Small Blue Bead by Byrd Baylor. Scribner, 1992.

Stanley by Syd Hoff. HarperTrophy, 1992.

MULTIMEDIA

CD-ROMS:

Dinosaurs and Prehistoric Life. Factfinder, 1997.

Eyewitness Children's Encyclopedia. Dorling Kindersley, 1996.

Eyewitness Prehistoric Life. Dorling Kindersley, 1995.

Magic School Bus Explores the Age of Dinosaurs. Microsoft, 1996.

VIDEOS:

Eyewitness Prehistoric Life. Dorling Kindersley, 1996.

Awesome Ancestors (Bonehead Detectives of the Paleoworld). Discovery Channel, 1997.

WEB SITES

Strange Science—The Rocky Road to Modern Paleontology and Biology (Fun amateur site with prehistoric discoveries time line and a "goof gallery" of mistaken prehistoric discoveries)
www.turnpike.net/~mscott/index.htm

Neanderthal Heaven (Good information on Neanderthal humans; glossary, references, links)
www.iinet.net.au/~chawkins/heaven.htm

➤ SEE ALSO THIS RELATED PATHFINDER

Dinosaurs

Quilts

Quilting is a particular process of sewing a blanket or coverlet. A quilt is made using two layers of fabric with a layer of cotton, wool, feathers, or down between them. The layers are firmly stitched together using decorative patterns all across the quilt. The tops of quilts are made by sewing togeth er pieces of fabric that have been cut to create geometric patterns, usually forming a square of fabric. These squares, or quilt blocks, are then sewn together to form the top layer of the quilt. Quilt making has been done for centuries in many different cultures and countries. It is an important par of our American heritage.

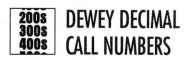

DEWEY DECIMAL CALL NUMBERS

746.4 Needle and handwork (quilting)

SEARCH TERMS

Quilting
Quilts
Needlework

NONFICTION/REFERENCE BOOKS

Eight Hands Round: A Patchwork Alphabet by Ann Paul. HarperCollins, 1991.

Kids Can Quilt by Barbara J. Eikmeier. That Patchwork Place, 1997.

The Quilt-Block History of Pioneer Days: With Projects Kids Can Make by Mary Cobb. Millbrook Press, 1995.

The Seasons Sewn: A Year in Patchwork by Ann Whitford Paul. Browndeer Press, 1996.

Stitching Stars: The Story Quilts of Harriet Powers by Mary E. Lyons. Scribner, 1993.

With Needle and Thread: A Book about Quilts by Raymond Bial. Houghton Mifflin Co., 1996.

FICTION

Aunt Skilly and the Stranger by Kathleen Stevens. Ticknor & Fields, 1994.

Bess's Log Cabin Quilt by D. Anne Love. Bantam Books Doubleday Dell, 1996.

The Canada Geese Quilt by Natalie Kinsey-Warnock. Cobblehill Books, 1989.

Cemetery Quilt by Kent and Alice Ross. Houghton Mifflin Co., 1995.

The Dream Quilt by Amy Zerner & Jessie Spicer Zerner. Charles E. Tuttle Co., 1995.

The Josefina Story Quilt by Eleanor Coerr. Harper & Row, 1986.

The Keeping Quilt by Patricia Polacco. Simon & Schuster, 1988.

The Log Cabin Quilt by Ellen Howard. Holiday House, 1996.

Luka's Quilt by Georgia Guback. Greenwillow Books, 1994.

The Mountains of Quilt by Nancy Willard. Harcourt Brace Jovanovich, 1997.

Patchwork Island by Karla Kuskin. HarperCollins, 1994.

The Patchwork Quilt by Valerie Flournoy. Dial Books for Young Readers, 1985.

The Quilt by Ann Jonas. Greenwillow Books, 1984.

The Quilt Story by Tony Johnston. G. P. Putnam's Sons, 1985.

Sam Johnson and the Blue Ribbon Quilt by Lisa Ernst. Lothrop, Lee & Shepard, 1983.

Selina and the Bear Paw Quilt by Barbara Smucker. Crown, 1995.

Sewing Quilts by Ann Turner. Macmillan, 1994.

Sweet Clara and the Freedom Quilt by Deborah Hopkinson. Random House, 1993.

MULTIMEDIA

 ### CD-ROM:

Better Homes and Gardens Cool Crafts Interactive. Multicom, 1994.

 ### VIDEOS:

Gathered in Time. Bonneville, 1997.
The Keeping Quilt. Philomel, 1993.
Patchwork: A Kaleidoscope of Quilts. Her Own Words Productions, 1989.

 ## WEB SITES

Country Quilt Maker
www.members.xoom.com/Quilt_Maker/
Quilt-Town USA
www.quilttownusa.com/
World Wide Quilting Page (Instructions on how to make a quilt, patterns, links)
www.ttsw.com/MainQuiltingPage.html

➤ **SEE ALSO THIS RELATED PATHFINDER**
Pattern

Rain Forest

A tropical rain forest is a dense, evergreen forest in a tropical region near the equator where it rains at least 100 inches each year. Rain forests cover less than 10 percent of the earth, but they are home to more than half of all animal and plant species in the world. All the conditions of the rain forest encourage life. They are wet and warm, and when it isn't raining, they are filled with bright sunshine.

 DEWEY DECIMAL CALL NUMBERS

577.34 Rainforest

338.1 Production (economic goods and services)

674.5 Lumber, wood, cork technologies

508.315 Geography, descriptions (travels and surveys)

574.5 Ecology (relationships of organisms to their environment)

 SEARCH TERMS

Rain forests
Rain forest ecology
Rain forest animals
Rain forest plants
Rain forest ecology, Amazon River Region
Biological diversity
Ecology
Amazon River Region
Rain forests, Brazil
International Children's Rain Forest (Costa Rica)
Rain forest conservation, Costa Rica
Conservation of natural resources

 NONFICTION/REFERENCE BOOKS

Welcome to the Green House by Jane Yolen. G. P. Putnam's Sons, 1993.

Bats, Bugs, and Biodiversity: Adventures in the Amazonian Rain Forest by Susan E. Goodman. Atheneum Books for Young Readers, 1995.

The Brazilian Rain Forest by Alexandra Siy. Maxwell Macmillan International, 1992.

Children Save the Rain Forest by Dorothy Hinshaw Patent. Cobblehill Books, 1996.

Here is the Tropical Rain Forest by Madeleine Dunphy.
Hyperion Books for Children, 1994.

Inside the Amazing Amazon by Don Lessem. Crown, 1995.

Journey Through a Tropical Jungle by Adrian Forsyth.
Simon & Schuster Books for Young Readers, 1988.

Nature's Green Umbrella: Tropical Rain Forests by Gail Gibbons.
Morrow Junior Books, 1994.

Tropical Rain Forests (A New True Book) by Emilie U. Lepthien.
Children's Press, 1993.

FICTION

Where the Forest Meets the Sea by Jeanie Baker. Greenwillow Books, 1987.

Antonio's Rain Forest adapted by Anna Lewington. Carolrhoda Books, 1993.

The Great Kapok Tree: A Tale of the Amazon Rain Forest by Lynne Cherry. Harcourt Brace Jovanovich, 1990.

Jaguar in the Rain Forest (A Just for a Day Book) by Joanne Ryder. Morrow Junior Books, 1996.

Journey of the Red-eyed Tree Frog by Martin and Tanis Jordan. Green Tiger Press, 1992.

One Day in the Tropical Rain Forest by Jean Craighead George. Crowell, 1990.

MULTIMEDIA

 CD-ROMS:

Destination, Rain Forest Interactive Multimedia. Edmark, 1996.
Magic School Bus Explores the Rainforest. Microsoft, 1997.
Rainforest Explorer Interactive Multimedia: Discover the Wonder of Nature. New Media Schoolhouse, 1995.
U*X*L Science. Gale, 1997.
Zurk's Rainforest Lab Interactive Multimedia. Soleil Software, 1995.

 VIDEOS:

Adventures of the Rain Forest. Video Treasures, 1994.
America's Rainforest. Cambridge Career Products, 1992.
Animals of the Rainforest (Rainforest for Children). Schlessinger, 1996.
People of the Rainforest (Rainforest for Children). Schlessinger, 1996.
Rain Forest (Earth at Risk). Schlessinger, 1993.
Tropical Rain Forest. Holiday Films, 1992.

 WEB SITES

Rainforest Action Network
www.ran.org/ran/
Ecosystems of Our World—Tropical Rain Forest
www.tqd.advanced.org/2988/trforest.htm
Ecosystems of Our World—Tropical Dry Forest
www.tqd.advanced.org/2988/tdforest.htm
Amazon Interactive
www.eduweb.com/amazon.html

➤ SEE ALSO THIS RELATED PATHFINDER
Biomes

Reptiles

Reptiles are dry-skinned, usually scaly, cold-blooded, vertebrate animals. Reptiles live in warm and temperate areas and can be as small as two-inch-long lizards and as large as 30-foot-long snakes. Most reptiles have bodies that are close to the ground and have long tails and four short legs, except snakes which do not have any legs. Most reptiles live on land, although a few live in the water. All reptiles breathe air through their lungs and have thick, waterproof skins. Some of the more common reptiles are turtles, alligators, crocodiles, lizards, and snakes.

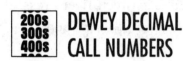 **DEWEY DECIMAL CALL NUMBERS**

598.1   Reptiles
568.1   Fossil Sauropsida (reptiles)

 SEARCH TERMS

Reptiles
Lizards
Skinks
Crocodiles
Alligators
Crocodilia
Snakes
Turtles
Tortoises
Dinosaurs
Prehistoric animals
Evolution
Search by specific breed of snakes, for example: Cobra

 NONFICTION/REFERENCE BOOKS

How Dinosaurs Came To Be by Patricia Lauber.
Simon & Schuster Books for Young Readers, 1996.

Scaly Babies: Reptiles Growing Up by Ginny Johnston and Judy Cutchins.
Morrow Junior Books, 1988.

Revolting Reptiles (Creepy Creatures) by Steve Parker. Raintree/Steck Vaughn, 1994.

Roaring Reptiles (Creatures All Around Us) by D. M. Souza. Carolrhoda Books, 1992.

Scaly Facts by Ivan Chermayeff. Harcourt Brace Jovanovich, 1995.

What is a Reptile? by Robert Snedden. Sierra Club Books for Children, 1995.

What On Earth is a Skink? (What On Earth Series) by Edward R. Ricciuti.
Blackbirch Press, 1994.

FICTION

Nate the Great and the Tardy Tortoise by Marjorie Weinman Sharmat and Craig Sharmat. Bantam Doubleday Dell Books for Young Readers, 1997.

The Reptile Ball by Jacqueline K. Ogburn. Dial Books for Young Readers, 1997.

MULTIMEDIA

 ### CD-ROMS:

The World of Reptiles Interactive Multimedia. REMedia, 1994.

Amphibians & Reptiles Interactive Multimedia (Junior Nature Guides Series). ICE Integrated Communications & Entertainment, 1996.

Animals and How They Grow Interactive Multimedia. National Geographic Society, 1994.

Multimedia Exotic Pets Interactive Multimedia: Horses, Birds, Aquatics, and Pocket Pets. Inroads Interactive, 1995.

The San Diego Zoo Presents the Animals! 2.0 Interactive Multimedia. Arnowitz Studios, 1994.

 ### VIDEOS:

Amphibians and Reptiles (Animal Classes). National Geographic Film & TV, 1996.

Cool Creatures: Reptiles. Rainbow Educational Video, 1994.

Exploring the World of Reptiles (Shamu and You). Video Treasures, 1992.

Eyewitness Reptile (Eyewitness Natural World). Dorling Kindersley Videos, 1995.

Prehistoric Animals, Reptiles, and Amphibians (Tell Me Why). TMW Media Group, 1987.

Reptiles and Insects: Leapin' Lizards (Bill Nye, the Science Guy). Disney Home Video, 1995.

What Is A Reptile? (Now I Know). Troll Assoc., 1993.

 ## WEB SITES

Jason's Snake and Reptile Page www.snakesandreptiles.com/index.html

Animal Omnibus (Reptile links) www.birminghamzoo.com/ao/reptile.htm

The National Zoo (Photos of reptiles, and other animals, with captions) www.si.edu/organiza/museums/zoo/photos/pintrset.htm

➤ *SEE ALSO THESE RELATED PATHFINDERS*
Animals; Dinosaurs

Revolutionary War, American

The American Revolution is also called the American War of Independence. It was fought by the American colonists against Britain, their mother country. The war began near Boston, Massachusetts, in 1775. On July 4, 1776, the American colonists issued their Declaration of Independence. The final battle was fought at Yorktown, Virginia, in 1781. With the American victory, the 13 colonies became 13 independent states.

 DEWEY DECIMAL CALL NUMBERS

973.3 Revolution and confederation, 1775-1789

973.4 Constitutional period, 1789-1809

 SEARCH TERMS

American Revolution
Revolutionary War
Colonial America
Thirteen Colonies
British Colonialism
American History
United States Revolutionary History
Boston Tea Party
Declaration of Independence
Battle of Concord
Battle of Lexington
Battle of Yorktown
Valley Forge
Search by names of significant people or places, for example: Paul Revere *or* Williamsburg, Va.

 NONFICTION/REFERENCE BOOKS

Buttons for General Washington by Peter and Connie Roop. Carolrhoda Books, 1986.

Concord and Lexington by Judy Nordstrom.
Dillon Press/Maxwell Macmillan International, 1993.

The Revolutionary War: A Sourcebook on Colonial America edited by Carter Smith.
Millbrook Press, 1991.

Scholastic Encyclopedia of the Presidents and Their Times by David Rubel.
Scholastic Professional Books, 1994.

The Winter at Valley Forge: Survival and Victory by James E. Knight.
Troll Assoc., 1982.

Valley Forge (Cornerstones of Freedom) by R. Conrad Stein. Children's Press, c1994.

A Young Patriot: The American Revolution as Experienced by One Boy by Jim Murphy. Clarion Books, 1996.

FICTION

The Boston Coffee Party (An I Can Read Book) by Doreen Rappaport. HarperTrophy, 1990.

Changes for Felicity: A Winter Story (The American Girls Collection, Book 6) by Valerie Tripp. Pleasant Co., 1992.

Johnny Tremain by Esther Forbes. Houghton Mifflin Co., 1962.

The Seekers by Ellis Dillon Press. Scribner, 1986.

Toliver's Secret by Esther Wood Brady. Random House, 1993.

Why Don't You Get a Horse, Sam Adams? by Jean Fritz. PaperStar Book, 1996.

MULTIMEDIA

CD-ROMS:

Founding of America: Colonization, Revolution, and Independence. Entrex, 1998.
New Nation—The Constitution to the War of 1812. MultiEducator, 1998.
Revolutionary War: Birth of a Nation. MultiEducator, 1998.

VIDEOS:

A&E Biography (series). **Benedict Arnold** (1998); **Biography:Thomas Jefferson—Philosopher of Freedom** (1996); **George Washington** (1995); **Patrick Henry** (1998); **Paul Revere** (1996). A&E Entertainment.
American History for Children—American Independence and **United States Flag.** Schlessinger, 1996.
Liberty! The American Revolution. PBS Home Video, 1998.
Revolutionary War. Discovery Comm., 1998.
Revolutionary War. Simitar Video, 1993.

WEB SITES

Internet Resources about Colonial America from the Madison Metropolitan School District
www.danenet.wicip.org/mmsd-it/colonialamerica.html
Life of Washington (Information about his slaves, tour of Mt. Vernon, images of Washington—a little wordy, but very informative)
www.mountvernon.org/education/
MultiEducator—America's Revolutionary War (Samples of information from their CD-ROM)
www.multied.com/revolt/
On-Line Guide and Resources for the PBS series: Liberty—The American Revolution. (Includes time lines, historic documents, and illustrations.)
www.pbs.org/ktca/liberty/
The Revolutionary War—A Journey Towards Freedom (A comprehensive site for teachers and students, with primary sources, games, and teacher resources)
www.library.advanced.org/10966/

➤ *SEE ALSO THESE RELATED PATHFINDERS*
Colonial Life, American; Thirteen Colonies

Sea Animals

Nearly three-quarters of the earth is covered by oceans and seas, and within these waters is a variety of sea life. The oceans are home to sharks and dolphins, whales and fish, shellfish, starfish, and octopuses. Plankton are the tiniest of sea animals, but without them, no other animals would survive.

200s 300s 400s DEWEY DECIMAL CALL NUMBERS

591.92 Zoology, Hydrographic (marine and freshwater biology)

597 Anamnia (frogs, toads, salamanders, newts, etc.)

599.74 Mammals (whales, dolphins, porpoises)

574.5 Biology, Ecology

 SEARCH TERMS

Ocean
Sea life
Ocean ecology
Marine animals
Aquatic biology
Seashore biology
Search by names of specific sea animals, for example: Whales

 NONFICTION/REFERENCE BOOKS

Beneath the Waves: Exploring the Hidden World of the Kelp Forest by Norbert Wu. Chronicle Books, 1992.

Fearsome Fish (Creepy Creatures) by Steve Parker. Raintree/Steck Vaughn, 1994.

Ocean Animals in Danger by Gary Turbak. Northland Pub., 1994.

Sea Life (Picturepedia) by Malcolm MacGarvin. Dorling Kindersley, 1992.

Seals by Eric S. Garce. Sierra Club/Little, Brown & Co., 1991.

Sharks and Other Creatures of the Deep (See & Explore Library) by Philip Steele. Dorling Kindersley, 1991.

A Swim Through the Sea by Krinstin Joy Pratt. Dawn, 1994.

Where the Waves Break: Life at the Edge of the Sea by Anita Malnig. Carolrhoda Books, 1985.

Young Explorer's Guide to Undersea Life by Pam Armstrong. Monterey Bay Aquarium Press, 1996.

FICTION

A House by the Sea by Joanne Ryder. Morrow Junior Books, 1994.

A House for Hermit Crab by Eric Carle. Simon & Schuster Books for Young Readers, 1987.

In the Swim: Poems and Paintings by Douglas Florian. Harcourt Brace Jovanovich, 1997.

The Magic School Bus on the Ocean Floor by Joanna Cole. Scholastic, 1992.

My Visit to the Aquarium by Aliki. HarperCollins, 1993.

Sea Watch by Jane Yolen. Philomel Books, 1996.

MULTIMEDIA

CD-ROMS:

Amazing Animals Interactive Multimedia. DK Multimedia, 1997.

Destination, Ocean Interactive Multimedia (Imagination Express). Edmark, 1995.

Eyewitness Children's Encyclopedia Interactive Multimedia. DK Multimedia, 1997.

Oceans Interactive Multimedia. World Book in association with Two Can, 1997.

20,000 Leagues Under the Sea Interactive Multimedia (Talking Storybook Series) by Rory Kelsch, original story by Jules Verne. New Media Schoolhouse, 1994.

U*X*L Science. Gale, 1997.

WEB SITES

Ocean Link—Marine Science Information and Interaction
www.oceanlink.island.net/main.html

NetVet—Marine Mammals (Links to additional sites)
www.netvet.wustl.edu/marine.htm

VIDEOS:

Breakfast, Lunch, and Dinner (Seahouse One). Rainbow Educational Video, 1991.

Creatures of the Blue (Sierra Club Kids). Sierra Club Kids, 1995.

Deep and Dark (Seahouse Two). Rainbow Educational Video, 1992.

Deep Sea Dive (Really Wild Animals). National Geographic Home Video, 1994.

Dolphin (Seahouse Two). Rainbow Educational Video, 1992.

Exploring the World of Fish (Shamu and You). Video Treasures, 1992.

Eyewitness Fish (Eyewitness Natural World). Dorling Kindersley Videos, 1995.

Fish (Animal Classes). National Geographic Film & TV, 1997.

Fish, Shellfish, and Other Underwater Life (Tell Me Why). TMW Media Group, 1987.

Marine Madness (Zoo Life With Jack Hanna). Time-Life Education, 1992.

Sea Animals (See How They Grow). Sony Wonder, 1996.

➤ *SEE ALSO THESE RELATED PATHFINDERS*
Animals; Dolphins; Ocean; Sharks; Whales

Seasons

There are four natural divisions, or seasons, of the year: spring, summer, autumn (or fall), and winter. These seasons are only experienced fully in the North and South Temperate zones of the earth. Each season has its own climatic changes and natural events. For example, cold weather or snow in wintertime and new growth of plants in the springtime. Each season is marked by an equinox or a solstice, which is determined by the earth's position during its annual movement around the sun.

DEWEY DECIMAL CALL NUMBERS

508.2 Seasons
525 Earth astronomy (seasons)

SEARCH TERMS

Seasons
Four seasons
Autumn
Fall
Spring
Summer
Winter

NONFICTION/REFERENCE BOOKS

Fall by Ron Hirschi. Cobblehill Books, 1991.

The Kids' Nature Book by Susan Milord. Williamson Pub. Co., 1989.

Winter by Ron Hirschi. Puffin Books, 1996.

Seasons Across America (series) by Seymour Simon. **Autumn Across America** (1993); **Spring Across America** (1996); **Winter Across America** (1994). Hyperion for Children.

Spring by Ron Hirschi. Puffin Unicorn Books, 1996.

The Reasons for Seasons by Gail Gibbons. Holiday House, 1995.

Sunshine Makes the Seasons by Franklyn M. Branley. Harper & Row, 1986.

Snowflakes Can Fall in Summer and Other Facts About Seasons (You'd Never Believe It, But) by Helen Taylor. Copper Beech Books, 1998.

FICTION

Autumn: An Alphabet Acrostic by Steven Schnur. Clarion Books, 1997.

An Autumn Tale by David Updike. Pippin Press, 1988.

The Big Snow by Berta and Elmer Hader. Aladdin Paperbacks, 1993.

A Circle of Seasons by Myra Cohn Livingston. Holiday House, 1982.

Gather up, Gather in: A Book of Season by M. C. Helldorfer. Viking, 1994.

The Happy Day by Ruth Krauss. Harper & Row, 1989.

Henry and Mudge in the Sparkle Days: The Fifth Book of Their Adventures by Cynthia Rylant. Simon & Schuster Books for Young Readers, 1988.

Henry and Mudge Under the Yellow Moon: The Fourth Book of Their Adventures by Cynthia Rylant. Bradbury Press, 1988.

In for Winter, Out for Spring by Arnold Adoff. Harcourt Brace Jovanovich, 1990.

In the Eyes of the Cat: Japanese Poetry for All Seasons selected and illustrated by Demi, translated by Tze-si Huang. Henry Holt & Co., 1994.

My Mama had a Dancing Heart by Libba Moore Gray. Orchard Books, 1995.

Thirteen Moons on Turtle's Back: A Native American Year of Moons by Joseph Bruchac and Jonathan London. Philomel Books, 1992.

MULTIMEDIA

 ### CD-ROMS:

Changes Around Us Interactive Multimedia. Edunetics Interactive, 1996.
Seasons Interactive Multimedia. National Geographic Society, 1994.
U*X*L Science. Gale, 1997.

 ### VIDEOS:

Barney—Barney's 1-2-3-4 Seasons. Lyons Group, 1996.
Climate & Seasons (Weather Fundamentals). Schlessinger, 1998.
Which Way Weather? Tapeworm, 1995.

 ## WEB SITES

World Book Encyclopedia: The Seasons (Articles on the four seasons) www.worldbook.com/fun/seasons/ html/seasons.htm
The Four Seasons www.4seasons.org.uk/
Four Seasons www.dlk.com/stories98/fourseasons.html

➤ *SEE ALSO THESE RELATED PATHFINDERS*
Earth; Weather

Shapes

The form of an object is called its shape. Some familiar shapes are: circles, squares, rectangles, and triangles.

 DEWEY DECIMAL CALL NUMBERS

372.6 Elementary education, Communication skills

372.7 Elementary education, Mathematics

516 Geometry

 SEARCH TERMS

Shapes
Geometry
Form
Search by names of specific shapes, for example: Triangle

 NONFICTION/REFERENCE BOOKS

The Amazing Book of Shapes by Lydia Sharmon. Dorling Kindersley, 1994.

Everyday Mysteries by Jerome Wexler. Dutton Children's Books, 1995.

Frank Lloyd Wright for Kids by Kathleen Thorne-Thomsen. Chicago Review Press, 1994.

The Hands-On Marvelous Ball Book by Bradford Hansen-Smith. Scientific American, 1995.

Making Shapes by Gary Gibson. Copper Beech Books, 1995.

Sea Shapes by Suse MacDonald. Harcourt Brace Jovanovich, 1994.

Shape Space by Cathryn Falwell. Clarion Books, 1992.

Shapes by Sally Hewitt. Raintree/Steck Vaughn, 1996.

Shapes, Shapes, Shapes by Tana Hoban. Greenwillow Books, 1986.

When a Line Bends—a Shape Begins by Rhonda Gowler Greene. Houghton Mifflin Co., 1997.

FICTION

Beach Ball by Peter Sis. Greenwillow Books, 1990.

Bedtime for Frances by Russell Hoban. HarperCollins, 1996.

Brown Rabbit's Shape Book by Alan Baker. Kingfisher Books, 1994.

Color Farm by Lois Ehlert. Lippincott, 1990.

Color Zoo by Lois Ehlert. Lippincott, 1989.

Cyndy Szerkes' I Love My Busy Book: About the Alphabet, Counting, Colors, Opposites, Shapes, and Much, Much More. Scholastic, 1997.

Oh! by Josse Goffin. Harry N. Abrams, 1991.

Round and Around by James Skofield. HarperCollins, 1993.

MULTIMEDIA

CD-ROMS:

Mighty Math Carnival Countdown. Edmark, 1996.

Millie's Math House Interactive. Edmark, 1995.

Richard Scarry's Best Math Program. Paramount Interactive, 1997.

The Rabbits at Home Interactive. Brimax, 1994.

VIDEOS:

Hullabaloo! All about Shapes. Dorling Kindersley Videos, 1995.

Barney's Colors and Shapes. Lyons Group, 1997.

Clifford's Fun With Shapes. Family Home Entertainment, 1988.

Colors, Shapes and Counting. Rock 'n Learn, 1997.

Opposites. National Geographic Film & TV, 1991.

Richard Scarry's Best Learning Songs Video Ever. Sony Wonder, 1993.

Using a Model; Estimating and Checking. Educational Activities, 1993.

WEB SITES

The Cartoon Factory
www.cartoonfactory.net/

Wonderful World of Geometry
www.cedar.evansville.edu/~m202web/Projects/group5/

➤ SEE ALSO THESE RELATED PATHFINDERS

Pattern; Quilts

Sharks

Sharks are marine fishes and are carnivorous, which means they eat other sea animals. Some sharks are very large and aggressive. The tiger shark and the great white shark have even been known to attack people.

200s 300s 400s **DEWEY DECIMAL CALL NUMBERS**

597.3 Sharks

574.92 Hydrographic biology (marine and freshwater biology)

591.92 Zoology

597 Anamnia (fish, amphibians)

 SEARCH TERMS

Sharks
Marine animals
Marine life
Search by specific breed of shark, for example: Hammerhead shark

 NONFICTION/REFERENCE BOOKS

The Best Way to See a Shark (Rookie Read-about Science) by Allan Fowler. Children's Press, 1995.

Hungry, Hungry Sharks (Step Into Reading. Step 2 Book) by Joanna Cole. Random House, 1986.

Marine Biologist: Swimming With the Sharks (Risky Business) by Keith Elliot Greenberg. Blackbirch Press, 1996.

Outside and Inside Sharks by Sandra Markle. Atheneum Books for Young Readers, 1996.

A Sea Full of Sharks by Betsy Maestro. Scholastic, 1990.

Sharks by Ruth Berman. Carolrhoda Books, 1995.

Sharks by Seymour Simon. HarperCollins, 1995.

Sharks by Russell Freedom. Holiday House, 1985.

Sharks and Other Creatures of the Deep (See & Explore Library) by Philip Steele. Dorling Kindersley, 1991.

FICTION

Shark In the Sea (A Just for a Day Book) by Joanne Ryder. Morrow Junior Books, 1997.

The Story of the Three Kingdoms by Walter Dean Myers. HarperCollins, 1995.

The Great White Man-Eating Shark: A Cautionary Tale (Picture Puffin Books) by Margaret Mahy. Puffin Pied Piper Books, 1996.

MULTIMEDIA

 ### CD-ROMS:

Amazing Animals Interactive Multimedia. DK Multimedia, 1997.
Eyewitness Children's Encyclopedia. Dorling Kindersley, 1997.
Grolier Multimedia Encyclopedia. Grolier Interactive, 1998.
Compton's Interactive Encyclopedia. Compton's, 1997.

 ### VIDEOS:

Big Five Little Five: Sharks (Kratt's Creatures). PBS Video, 1996.
Creatures of the Blue (Sierra Club Kids). Sierra Club Kids, 1995.
Deep Sea Dive (Really Wild Animals). National Geographic Home Video, 1994.
Eyewitness Shark (Eyewitness Natural World). Dorling Kindersley Videos, 1995.
Fish, Shellfish, and Other Underwater Life (Tell Me Why). TMW Media Group, 1987.
Life in the Sea. Questar Video Comm., 1995.
Shark (Seahouse Two). Rainbow Educational Video, 1992.

 ## WEB SITES

Shark Surfari!—National Geographic (online quiz for kids)
www.nationalgeographic.com/ features/97/sharks/side.html
Sharks of Hawaii
www.aloha.com/~lifeguards/sharintr.html
The Ocean of Know—Sharks
www.oceanofk.org/sharks/introShark.html

➤ SEE ALSO THESE RELATED PATHFINDERS

Animals; Ocean; Sea Animals

Shelter

A shelter is a place that gives protection from the weather, the outside world, or predatory creatures. A shelter may be made by people, or it may be found in nature. Some examples of shelters would be houses, nests, dens, caves, or even a turtle's shell.

 DEWEY DECIMAL CALL NUMBERS

392 Homes, Customs
591.5 Zoology, Habitat (where animals live)
720 Architecture

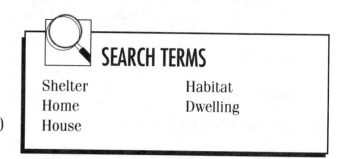 **SEARCH TERMS**

Shelter   Habitat
Home   Dwelling
House

NONFICTION/REFERENCE BOOKS

Animal Homes by Barbara Taylor. Dorling Kindersley, 1996.

The Apartment Book by Leo Hartas. Dorling Kindersley, 1995.

Children Just Like Me by Barnabas and Anabel Kindersley. Dorling Kindersley, 1995.

Colonial American Home Life by John F. Warner. Franklin Watts, 1993.

Come Home With Me: A Multicultural Treasure Hunt by Aylette Jenness. W. W. Norton, 1993.

The Egyptians by Roger Coote. Thomson Learning, 1993.

Everyday Life in Viking Times by Hazel Martell. Franklin Watts, 1994.

Finding Shelter by Daphne Butler. Raintree/Steck Vaughn, 1996.

First Houses: Native American Homes and Sacred Structures by Ray Williamson and Jean Monroe. Houghton Mifflin Co., 1993.

Frontier Home by Raymond Bial. Houghton Mifflin Co., 1993.

The Gift of the Tree by Alvin Tresselt. Lothrop, Lee & Shepard, 1992.

House Through the Ages by Philip Steele. Troll Assoc., 1994.

Houses: Structures, Methods, and Ways of Living by Piero Ventura. Houghton Mifflin Co., 1993.

Houses and Homes by Ann Morris. Lothrop, Lee & Shepard, 1992.

Houses of Bark: Tipi, Wigwam and Longhouse by Bonnie Shemie. Tundra Books, 1990.

Houses of Snow, Skin and Bones: Native Dwellings, the Far North by Bonnie Shemie. Tundra Books, 1989.

The Igloo by Charlotte and David Yue. Houghton Mifflin Co., 1988.

Monticello by Leonard Everett Fisher. Holiday House, 1988.

Think of a Beaver by Karen Wallace. Candlewick Press, 1995.

Visual Encyclopedia. Dorling Kindersley, 1996.

FICTION

Bam, Bam, Bam by Eve Merriam. Henry Holt & Co., 1995.

The Coldest Winter by Elizabeth Lutzeier. Oxford University Press, 1991.

Evan's Corner by Elizabeth Starr Hill. Puffin Books, 1993.

I Have an Aunt on Marlborough Street by Kathryn Lasky. Macmillan, 1992.

In My Mother's House by Ann Nolan Clark. Puffin Books, 1992.

Kiki: A Cuban Boy's Adventures in America by Hilda Perera. Pickering Press, 1992.

Mushroom in the Rain by Mirra Ginsburg. Aladdin Books, 1990.

My Fabulous New Life by Sheila Greenwald. Browndeer Press, 1993.

My House Has Stars by Megan McDonald. Orchard Books, 1996.

Pagoo by Holling Clancy Holling. Houghton Mifflin Co., 1985.

Town Mouse, Country Mouse by Jan Brett. G. P. Putnam's Sons, 1994.

MULTIMEDIA

CD-ROM:
Davidson's Kid CAD Interactive Multimedia. Davidson, 1994.

VIDEOS:
Cool Cats, Raindrops, and Things That Live in Holes. National Geographic Society, 1994.

Michael the Visitor (based on Tolstoy's tale "Truths We Live By"). Fast Forward Video, 1996.

Reefs. Rainbow Educational Video, 1991.

The Three Little Pigs. Walt Disney, 1932.

Wilderness Bob's Outdoor Survival Video. Tapeworm 1996.

The Wonderful World of Houses. Tapeworm, 1993.

WEB SITES

The Cliff Dwellings of Palatki
www.aztec.asu.edu/aznha/palatki/palruins.html

Desert Life
www.desertusa.com/life.html

Native American Dwellings (A second grade class project—good for ideas)
www.bridge.ci.lexington.ma.us/classroom/Projects/Abban/NativeAmericaDwellings/index.html

➤ SEE ALSO THIS RELATED PATHFINDER

Architecture

Shoshoni Indians

The Shoshoni are a Native American people who lived in portions of Wyoming, Utah, Nevada, and Idaho. Their stronghold was originally in the Snake River area of Idaho, but hostile tribes eventually pushed them into the mountains. Today, most Shoshoni Indians live on reservations.

 DEWEY DECIMAL CALL NUMBERS

970.1 Indians of North America
979 Pacific Coast States (Great Basin)
970.004 History, North America (1800-1900)
398.2 Folk literature
973 History, United States

 SEARCH TERMS

Shoshoni Indians
Bannock Indians
Great Basin Indians
Native Americans
Shoshoni Indians folklore
Bannock Indians folklore
Sacagawea, 1786-1884
Lewis and Clark Expedition (1804-1806)
Indians of North America

 NONFICTION/REFERENCE BOOKS

Sacajawea: The Journey West (Drawing America) by Elaine Raphael and Don Bolognese. Scholastic, 1994.

Sacagawea by Jan Gleiter. Raintree/Steck Vaughn, 1995.

Sacagawea by Judith St. George. G. P. Putnam's Sons, 1997.

The Shoshone (Indians of North America) by Kim Dramer and Frank W. Porter. Chelsea House, 1996.

The Shoshone Indians (Junior Library of American Indians) by Nathaniel B. Moss. Chelsea House, 1997.

The Shoshoni (First Books) by Alden R. Carter. Franklin Watts, 1989.

The Shoshoni by Dennis Fradin. Children's Press, 1988.

The Story of Sacajawea by Della Rowland. Dell, 1989.

FICTION

Brave as a Mountain Lion by Ann Herbert Scott. Clarion Books, 1996.

Jenny of the Tetons by Kristiana Gregory. Harcourt Brace & Co., 1989.

Naya Nuki, Girl Who Ran by Kenneth Thomasma. Baker Book House, 1983.

Old Bag of Bones: A Coyote Tale by Janet Stevens. Holiday House, 1996.

Sage Smoke: Tales of the Shoshoni-Bannock Indians by Eleanor B. Heady. Silver Burdett Press, 1993.

MULTIMEDIA

 ### VIDEOS:

Lewis and Clark: The Journey of the Corps of Discovery (Ken Burns). PBS Video, 1997.

Song of Sacajawea (American Heroes and Legends). Rabbit Ears, 1992.

WEB SITES

Native Nevada Classroom
www.unr.edu/nnap/
Desert Peoples—Native Americans
www.desertusa.com/ind1/
du_peo_native2.html
Sacajawea
www.powersource.com/powersource/
gallery/womansp/shoshoni.html

 ## ➤ SEE ALSO THIS RELATED PATHFINDER

Native Americans

Sioux Indians

The Dakota Indians, commonly called Sioux, are a group of Native American peoples who lived in the northern Great Plains, west of the Great Lakes. They are divided into three cultural groups: Dakota, Nakota, and Lakota. The Dakota hunted, fished, and gathered food from the lake and forest areas, including wild rice. Today Sioux live mainly in North and South Dakota.

DEWEY DECIMAL CALL NUMBERS

970.1 Indians of North America
970.004 History, North America (1800-1900)
398.2 Folk literature
973.8 History, United States (1800-1900)
978 Western United States

SEARCH TERMS

Sioux Indians
Lakota Indians
Dakota Indians
Native Americans
Plains Indians
Wounded Knee
Indians of North America
Dakota Indians folklore
Sitting Bull
Indians of North America Great Plains

NONFICTION/REFERENCE BOOKS

A Boy Becomes a Man at Wounded Knee by Ted Wood with Wanbli Numpa Afraid of Hawk. Walker & Co., 1994.

If You Lived with the Sioux Indians by Ann McGovern. Scholastic, 1992.

A Picture Book of Sitting Bull by David A. Adler. Holiday House, 1993.

The Sioux (A New True Book) by Alice Osinski. Children's Press, 1994.

The Sioux (Journey into Civilization) by Robert Nicholson. Chelsea House, 1994.

The Sioux (First Americans Book) by Virginia Driving Hawk Sneve. Holiday House, 1993.

FICTION

The Great Race of the Birds and Animal by Paul Goble. Macmillan, 1991.

Moonstick: The Seasons of the Sioux by Eve Bunting. HarperCollins, 1997.

MULTIMEDIA

CD-ROM:

Vision Quest: Men, Women and Sacred Sites of the Sioux Nation (based on Don Doll's book). Crown, 1996.

VIDEOS:

People of the Plains (Native Americans). Rainbow Educational Video, 1993.

Yankton Sioux (Indians of North America). Schlessinger, 1993.

WEB SITE

The Sioux Indians
www.scf.usc.edu/%7Emmcmahan/indian.html

➤ SEE ALSO THESE RELATED PATHFINDERS

Native Americans; Plains Indians

Solar System

A solar system consists of a sun and the planets which orbit (or circle) around it. The planets in our solar system are: Mercury, Venus, Earth, Mars, Jupiter, Saturn, Uranus, Neptune, and Pluto.

 DEWEY DECIMAL CALL NUMBERS

523.2 Solar system
523.4 Planets
523.7 Sun
520 Astronomy
523 Descriptive astronomy (celestial bodies, groupings, phenomena)
550 Earth

 SEARCH TERMS

Solar System	Planets
Galaxy	Sun
Astronomy	Moon
Outer space	

Search by names of particular planets, for example: Pluto

 NONFICTION/REFERENCE BOOKS

Asteroids, Comets, and Meteors (Gateway Solar System) by Gregory L. Vogt. Millbrook Press, 1996. See additional titles in this series: **Earth** (1996); **Jupiter** (1996); **Mars** (1994); **Mercury** (1994); **Neptune** (1993); **Saturn** (1993); **The Sun** (1996); **Uranus** (1993); **Venus** (1994).

Can You Find a Planet by Sidney Rosen. Carolrhoda Books. 1992.

The Children's Space Atlas: A Voyage of Discovery by Robin Kerrod. Millbrook Press, 1992.

The Earth and Sky by Jean-Pierre Verdet. Scholastic, 1992.

Mars by Seymour Simon. Mulberry Books, 1990.

Neptune by Seymour Simon. Mulberry Books, 1997.

Night Sky by Carole Stott. Dorling Kindersley, 1993.

Our Planetary System by Isaac Asimov. Gareth Stevens Pub., 1994.

Our Solar System by Seymour Simon. Morrow Junior Books, 1992.

The Planets by Gail Gibbons. Holiday House, 1993.

Planets in Our Solar System by Franklyn M. Branley. HarperCollins, 1987.

Planets, Moons, and Meteors (Young Stargazer's Guide to the Galaxy) by John Gustafson. J. Messner, 1992.

Postcards from Pluto: A Tour of the Solar System by Loreen Leedy. Holiday House, 1993.

Saturn by Seymour Simon. Mulberry Books, 1990.

Space Probes to the Planets by Fay Robinson. Albert Whitman & Co., 1993.

Stars and Planets. Time-Life Books, 1996.

The Story of Astronomy by Carole Stott. Troll Assoc., 1994.

Uranus by Seymour Simon. Mulberry Books, 1990.

NONFICTION/REFERENCE BOOKS CONTINUED

Venus: Magellan Explores Our Twin Planet by Franklyn M. Branley. HarperCollins, 1994.

Voyager: An Adventure to the Edge of the Solar System by Sally Ride and Tam O'Shaughnessy. Crown, 1992.

FICTION

Blast-Off!: A Space Counting Book by Norma Cole. Charlesbridge Pub., 1994.

Dogs in Space by Nancy Coffelt. Harcourt Brace Jovanovich, 1993.

The Magic School Bus Lost in the Solar System by Joanna Cole. Scholastic, 1990.

The Universe is My Home by Bill Fletcher. Science & Art Pub., 1992.

MULTIMEDIA

CD-ROMS:

3-D Tour of the Solar System. LPI, 1997.

Exploring the Solar System and Beyond. National Geographic Society, 1994.

Eyewitness Encyclopedia of Space and the Universe. Dorling Kindersley, 1996.

The Magic School Bus Explores the Solar System. Microsoft, 1994.

Planetary Taxi. Voyager, 1993.

VIDEOS:

Exploring Our Solar System. National Geographic Society, 1990.

Inner Planets. Allied Video, 1992.

Magic School Bus Gets Lost in Space. Kid Vision, 1995.

Our Solar System. January Prod., 1993.

Outer Planets. Allied Video, 1992.

Solar System. Gareth Stevens Pub., 1994.

What's Out There? Exploring the Solar System. Rainbow, 1987.

WEB SITES

Athena: Space and Astronomy
www.athena.ivv.nasa.gov/curric/space/index.html

Eric's Treasure Trove of Astronomy
www.astro.virginia.edu/%7Eeww6n/astro/astro0.html

Expanding Universe (Search tool for amateur astronomy)
www.mtrl.toronto.on.ca/centres/bsd/astronomy/520.HTM

Exploring Our Solar System
www.hq.nasa.gov/office/oss/solar_system/

The Nine Planets
www.anu.edu.au/physics/nineplanets/

Views of the Solar System
www.hawastsoc.org/solar/eng/homepage.htm

➤ SEE ALSO THESE RELATED PATHFINDERS

Astronomy; Planets; Space Travel & Outer Space

Southwest Indians

The Native peoples of Southwestern America spoke languages and had a culture similar to the Aztecs further south. They were known for their basket making, pottery making, and developed farming methods. Some Southwest Indian tribes include the Anasazi cliff dwellers, the Apache, the Navaho, and the Pueblo.

DEWEY DECIMAL CALL NUMBERS

970.1 Indians of North America

970.004 History, North America (1800-1900)

973 History, United States

721.044 Architecture (cliff dwellings, pueblos, terraced community houses)

979 Pacific Coast states

398.2 Folk literature

SEARCH TERMS

Southwest Indians

Indians of North American

Indian folklore

Search by names of Native American tribes, for example: Apache

NONFICTION/REFERENCE BOOKS

American Indian Children of the Past by Victoria Sherrow. Millbrook Press, 1997.

Houses of Adobe: Native Dwellings: The Southwest by Bonnie Shemie. Tundra Books, 1995.

The Navajos: People of the Southwest by Nancy Bonvillain. Millbrook Press, 1995.

Pueblo Indian (American Pastfinder) by Steven Cory. Lerner Pub. Co., 1996.

The Pueblo Indians by Liza N. Burby. Chelsea House, 1994.

Navajo: Visions and Voices Across the Mesa by Shonto Begay. Scholastic, 1995.

The Anasazi (A New True Book) by David Petersen. Children's Press, 1991.

Mesa Verde National Park (A New True Book) by David Petersen. Children's Press, 1992.

FICTION

Coyote: A Trickster Tale from the American Southwest by Gerald McDermott. Harcourt Brace Jovanovich, 1994.

Annie and the Old One by Miska Miles. Little, Brown & Co., 1971.

The Goat in the Rug by Charles L. Blood & Martin Link. Aladdin Books, 1990.

The Shepherd Boy by Kristine L. Franklin. Atheneum, 1994.

The World in Grandfather's Hands by Craig Kee Strete. Clarion Books, 1995.

MULTIMEDIA

CD-ROM:

Native Americans 2 Interactive Multimedia: Southwest, Northwest Coast, and Arctic. National Geographic Society, 1995.

VIDEOS:

500 Nations: The Ancestors. Warner-Pa, 1995.

Mystery of the Ancient Ones (New Explorers). PBS Video, 1996.

Navajo (Indians of North America). Schlessinger, 1993.

Paths of Life: American Indians of the Southwest. Tapeworm, 1997.

Pueblo (Indians of North America, Two). Schlessinger, 1994.

People of the Desert (Native Americans). Rainbow Educational Video, 1993.

WEB SITES

Indian Pueblo Cultural Center
www.hanksville.phast.umass.edu/defs/
independent/PCC/PCC.html

Native American Website for Children
www.nhusd.k12.ca.us/ALVE/
NativeAmerhome.html/
nativeopeningpage.html

➤ SEE ALSO THESE RELATED PATHFINDERS

Apache Indians; Native Americans

Space Travel & Outer Space

Outer Space is the vast expanse we see when we look up into the sky at night. It is the universe that surrounds us, filled with planets, stars, and other celestial bodies. It is everything that lies beyond the earth's atmosphere. To leave our atmosphere and travel to another planet, a space station, or simply into the outer space around the earth is called space travel. In 1926, an American engineer named Robert Goddard launched the first liquid fuel rocket and gave birth to the space age.

 DEWEY DECIMAL CALL NUMBERS

200s 300s 400s

629.4   Astronautics (space flight)

520   Astronomy

523   Descriptive astronomy (planets, stars, celestial groupings, phenomena)

523.1   Astronomy, Universe

521   Astronomy (theoretical)

567.9   Fossils

574.99   Biology (extraterrestrial worlds)

 SEARCH TERMS

Outer space
Space
Space travel
Space flight
Astronaut
NASA
Sputnik
Interplanetary voyages
Project Apollo
Moon exploration

Space station
Space shuttle
Space exploration
Rocketry
Spacecraft
Planets
Celestial bodies
Interstellar matter
Galaxies

Search by names of astronauts or scientists, for example: Robert Goddard
Search by names of space travel missions, for example: Apollo 11

 NONFICTION/REFERENCE BOOKS

Adventure in Space: The Flight to Fix the Hubble by Elaine Scott. Hyperion, 1995.

The Children's Space Atlas: A Voyage of Discovery by Robin Kerrod. Millbrook Press, 1992.

Comets, Meteors, and Asteroids by Seymour Simon. Morrow Junior Books, 1994.

Countdown to the Moon by Susan Dudley Gold. Crestwood House, 1992.

Exploring Space by Lesley Sims. Raintree/Steck Vaughn, 1994.

How Far is a Star? by Sidney Rosen. Carolrhoda Books, 1992.

Let's Visit a Space Camp by Edith Alston. Troll Assoc., 1990.

Life on Mars by David Getz. Henry Holt & Co. 1997.

Planets, Moons, and Meteors (Young Stargazer's Guide to the Galaxy) by John Gustafson. J. Messner, 1992.

Spacecraft by Ian Graham. Raintree/Steck Vaughn, 1995.

To Space and Back: The Story of the Shuttle by Susan Dudley Gold. Crestwood House, 1992.

The Third Planet: Exploring the Earth from Space by Sally Ride and Tam O'Shaunessy. Crown, 1994.

Voyager: An Adventure to the Edge of the Solar System by Sally Ride and Tam O'Shaughnessy. Crown, 1992.

FICTION

Astronauts are Sleeping by Natalie Standiford. Knopf, 1996.

Dogs in Space by Nancy Coffelt. Harcourt Brace Jovanovich, 1993.

Fat Men from Space by Daniel Pinkwater. Dell, 1984.

Guys from Space by Daniel Pinkwater. Aladdin Books, 1992.

I Want to be an Astronaut by Byron Barton. HarperCollins, 1992.

The Magic School Bus Lost in the Solar System by Joanna Cole. Scholastic, 1990.

Regards to the Man in the Moon by Ezra Jack Keats. Collier Books, 1985.

Richie's Rocket by Joan Anderson. Morrow Junior Books, 1993.

Wallpaper from Space by Daniel Pinkwater. Atheneum, 1996.

What Next, Baby Bear by Jill Murphy. Dial Books, 1986.

Zoom! Zoom! Zoom! I'm Off to the Moon by Dan Yaccarino. Scholastic, 1997.

MULTIMEDIA

CD-ROMS:

Exploring the Solar System and Beyond. National Geographic Society, 1994.

Eyewitness Encyclopedia of Space and the Universe. Dorling Kindersley, 1996.

The Magic School Bus Explores the Solar System. Microsoft, 1994.

Planetary Taxi. Voyager, 1993.

Space Facts. Goldhil Home Media, 1997.

VIDEOS:

Exploring Our Solar System. National Geographic Society, 1990.

Inner Planets. Allied Video, 1992.

Magic School Bus Gets Lost in Space. Kid Vision, 1995.

Outer Planets. Allied Video, 1992.

Space Exploration. Gareth Stevens Pub., 1995.

Space Exploration: The Rockets. United Learning, 1994.

Story of Living in Space. Hawkhill Assoc., 1994.

What's Out There? Exploring the Solar System. Rainbow Educational Video, 1987.

WEB SITES

Athena: Space and Astronomy
www.athena.ivv.nasa.gov/curric/space/index.html

Eric's Treasure Trove of Astronomy
www.astro.virginia.edu/%7Eeww6n/astro/astro0.html

Exploring Our Solar System
www.hq.nasa.gov/office/oss/solar_system/

History of Space Exploration (Lots of text and information)
www.hawastsoc.org/solar/eng/history.htm

Kids Space (NASA site for kids)
www.liftoff.msfc.nasa.gov/kids/

NASA Historical Archive
www.ksc.nasa.gov/history/history.html

Welcome to Star Child—A Learning Center for Young Astronauts
www.heasarc.gsfc.nasa.gov/docs/StarChild/StarChild.html

➤ *SEE ALSO THESE RELATED PATHFINDERS*
Astronomy; Solar System

Sports

Sports are active games. Some, such as football, baseball, basketball, and hockey, are team sports; while others, such as skiing, golf, and bowling, are played by individuals competing against each other. Mastery of a sport usually requires skill and a great deal of practice. However most sports may be enjoyed by any level of player.

 DEWEY DECIMAL CALL NUMBERS

794 Indoor sports
796 Outdoor sports
797 Water sports
798 Horsemanship/racing
799 Fishing/hunting

 SEARCH TERMS

Sports
Athletes
Athletics
Olympics
Olympic Games
Search by names of particular sports, for example: Rodeo

 NONFICTION/REFERENCE BOOKS

Also see these sports biography series: **Today's Heroes** (Zondervan Pub.); **Sports Heroes** (Zondervan Pub.); **Sports Legends** (Chelsea House); **Race Car Legends** (Chelsea House); **Sports Achievers** (Lerner Pub. Co.); and **Hockey Superstars** (Beech Tree Books).

Babe Ruth by William R. Sanford and Carl Green. Crestwood House, 1992.

Beginning Sports (series—each volume features a different sport) by Julie Jensen. Lerner Pub. Co., 1995.

Comeback!: Four True Stories by Jim O'Connor. Random House, 1992.

Encyclopedia Brown's Book of Wacky Sports by Donald J. Sobol. William Morrow & Co., 1984.

Jesse Owens by Rick Rennert. Chelsea Juniors, 1992.

Lives of the Athletes: Thrills, Spills (and What the Neighbors Thought) by Kathleen Krull. Harcourt Brace Jovanovich, 1997.

Olympics! by B. G. Hennessy. Viking, 1996.

Sports (Now Hiring) by Staci Bonner. Crestwood House, 1994.

Sports Lab: How Science Has Changed Sports by Robert Sheely. Silver Moon Press, 1994.

Superstars of Women's Figure Skating by Pohla Smith. Chelsea House, 1997.

Superstars of Women's Tennis by Martin Schwabacher. Chelsea House, 1997.

Track and Field by Bert Rosenthal. Raintree/Steck Vaughn, 1994.

Wilma Unlimited: How Wilma Rudolph Became the World's Fastest Woman by Kathleen Krull. Harcourt Brace Jovanovich, 1996.

The Young Track and Field Athlete by Colin Jackson. Dorling Kindersley, 1996.

FICTION

Baseball, Football, Daddy, and Me by David Friend. Puffin Books, 1992.

The Bicycle Man by Allen Say. Parnassus Press, 1982.

The Hit-Away Kid by Matt Christopher. Little, Brown & Co., 1988.

Last One in is a Rotten Egg by Leonard Kessler. Harper & Row, 1969.

Running Girl: The Diary of Ebonee Rose by Sharon Mathis. Browndeer Press, 1997.

The Sluggers Club: A Sports Mystery by Paul Walker. Harcourt Brace Jovanovich, 1993.

Sports Pages (poems) by Arnold Adoff. Harper & Row, 1990.

Woodsie by Bruce Brooks. HarperCollins, 1997.

MULTIMEDIA
CD-ROMS:

Awesome Athletes. Creative Multimedia, 1995.

Everything You Wanted to Know About Sports Encyclopedia. Creative Multimedia, 1994.

Baseball Encyclopedia. Macmillan, 1996.

Kristi Yamaguchi Fantasy Ice Skating. Morning Star Multimedia, 1997.

Olympic Gold: A 100 Year History of the Summer Olympics. SEA, 1995

Tim McCarver's The Way Baseball Works. Simon & Schuster Interactive, 1996.

VIDEOS:

America's Greatest Olympians. Warner, 1996.

Animalympics. United American Video, 1998.

Biography: Joe DiMaggio. A&E Entertainment, 1994.

Slimey's World Games. Sesame Street, 1996.

Sports and Games. TMW Media Group, 1989.

WEB SITES

A&E Biography Series (Searchable database with brief biographical entries)
www.biography.com

All Sports (Information on many, if not all, sports—includes rules)
www.allsports.com

Locker Room: Sports for Kids (Information on several different sports)
www.members.aol.com/msdaizy/
sports/locker.html

Major League Baseball (Kids' page)
www.majorleaguebaseball.com/kids/
index.htm

Major League Soccer
www.mlsnet.com

National Basketball Association (History page)
www.nba.com/history/

National Football League (Kids' page)
www.nfl.com/playfootball/pfmain.html

➤ SEE ALSO THESE RELATED PATHFINDERS
Famous People; Famous Women

States

There are 50 states that comprise the United States of America. Forty-eight of these states are contiguous, which means that they are joined border to border. The other two states are Alaska and Hawaii. Each state of the United States of America has its own governing body and a state capital. They also are represented within the federal government, which is the governing body for the 50 United States.

DEWEY DECIMAL CALL NUMBERS

917 Geography and travel in North America
974 Northeastern United States
975 Southeastern United States
976 South central United States
977 North central United States
978 Western United States

SEARCH TERMS

United States of America
North America
Search by names of particular states, for example: Texas

NONFICTION/REFERENCE BOOKS

See also these series on states: **Hello USA** (Lerner Pub. Co.) and **From Sea to Shining Sea** (Children's Press); both series have volumes on almost all 50 states.

Facts about the States. H. W. Wilson, 1993.

Greetings from America: Postcards from Donovan and Daisy by Ray Nelson. Beyond Words, 1995.

It Happened in America: True Stories from the Fifty States by Lila Perl. Henry Holt & Co., 1996.

The Kingfisher Books Young People's Encyclopedia of the United States. Kingfisher Books, 1994.

The Usborne First Book of America by Louisa Somerville. Usborne, 1990.

Wish You Were Here: Emily's Guide to the 50 States by Kathleen Krull. Doubleday, 1997.

FICTION

Akiak: A Tale from the Iditarod by Robert J. Blake. Philomel Books, 1997.

All Aboard! by James Stevenson. Greenwillow Books, 1995.

The Armadillo from Amarillo by Lynne Cherry. Harcourt Brace Jovanovich, 1994.

An Occasional Cow by Polly Horvath. Farrar Straus Giroux, 1989.

Once We Had a Horse by Glen Rounds. Holiday House, 1996.

Once Upon America (series—stories of different events in American history). Puffin Books, dates vary.

The Ring by Lisa Maizlish. Greenwillow Books, 1996.

Riddle City, USA by Marco Maestro. HarperCollins, 1994.

Tar Beach by Faith Ringgold. Crown, 1996.

Thimble Summer by Elizabeth Enright. Dell, 1984.

The Tree That Would Not Die by Ellen Levine. Scholastic, 1995.

MULTIMEDIA

 ### CD-ROMS:

Rand McNally Children's Atlas of the United States. GameTek, 1995.
See the USA. Compu Teach, 1998.
State by State: A History of America's Fifty. MultiEducator, 1998.
Talking USA Map. MicroMedia, [nd].

 ### VIDEOS:

United States of America. Ernst Interactive Media, 1993.
Alaska and Hawaii. National Geographic Educational, 1983.
Video Visits Discovering the USA. Ivn Entertainment, 1994.

 ### WEB SITES

50 States and Capitals
www.50states.com
A Brief Guide to State Facts
www.phoenix.ans.se/freeweb/holly/
state.html

Technology

Scientists and inventors continue to discover new and better things. When a new discovery is used to improve the way things are done or made, it is called technology. It includes the development of new materials and machinery that improve how things are made, or a process that improves the way something is done. Throughout history, the development of new technology has changed the way people live, work, and play. Recent technological advances include the development of computers and the invention of the laser.

 DEWEY DECIMAL CALL NUMBERS

600 Technology (Applied sciences)
500 Natural sciences and mathematics
621.382 Applied physics

 SEARCH TERMS

Technology
Technological developments
Electronics
Invention
Search by names of technologies, for example: Fiber optics

 NONFICTION/REFERENCE BOOKS

Click! A Story about George Eastman by Barbara Mitchell. Carolrhoda Books, 1986.

Electronic Communication by Chris Oxlade. Franklin Watts, 1998.

Eureka! It's an Automobile by Jeanne Bendick. Millbrook Press, 1992.

Flight and Flying Machines by Steve Parker. Dorling Kindersley, 1993.

Great Inventions. Time-Life Books, 1995.

How Things Work by Ian Graham. Time-Life Books, 1996.

The Internet for Kids by Charna and Tom Kazunas. Children's Press, 1997.

Light: A Bright Idea by Siegfried Aust. Lerner Pub. Co., 1992.

Mistakes that Worked by Charlotte Foltz Jones. Doubleday, 1991.

Personal Computers by Charnan and Tom Kazunas. Children's Press, 1997.

The Renaissance: The Invention of Perspective by Lillo Canta. Chelsea House, 1995.

Steven Caney's Invention Book by Steven Caney. Workman Pub., 1985.

Techno Lab: How Science is Changing Entertainment by Carol D. Anderson. Silver Moon Press, 1995.

TV's Forgotten Hero: The Story of Philo Farnsworth by Stephanie Sarmmartino McPherson. Carolrhoda Books, 1996.

Until I Met Dudley: How Everyday Things Really Work by Roger McGough. Walker & Co., 1997.

What's the Difference Between Lenses and Prisms and other Scientific Things? by Gary Soucie. Wiley, 1995.

Who?: Famous Experiments for the Young by Robert W. Wood. TAB Books, 1995.

Wizard of Sound: A Story about Thomas Edison by Barbara Mitchell. Carolrhoda Books, 1991.

FICTION

Bravo Minski by Arthur Yorinks. Farrar Straus Giroux, 1988.

The Day-Off Machine by John Himmelman. Silver Press, 1990.

Dog for a Day by Dick Gackenbach. Clarion Books, 1987.

Dream Cars by Jack C. Harris. Crestwood House, 1988.

The Gadget War by Betsy Duffey. Puffin Books, 1991.

I Gave Thomas Edison My Sandwich by Floyd C. Moore. Albert Whitman & Co., 1995.

Tiny for a Day by Dick Gackenbach. Clarion Books, 1993.

MULTIMEDIA

 CD-ROMS:

Invention Studio Interactive. Discovery Channel Multimedia, 1996.

The Way Things Work 2.0. DK Multimedia, 1996.

 VIDEOS:

Artificial Intelligence: Mankind's Mind-Child. Unapix Entertainment, 1997.

Magic School Bus Taking Flight. Warner, 1997.

Rocket Men: Goddard Space Exploration. Fast Forward Video, 1994.

Science of Star Trek. PBS Video, 1995.

The Wrong Trousers (Wallace & Gromit). Twentieth Century Fox, 1995.

 WEB SITES

Concoctions and Inventions
www.members.aol.com/acalendar/
February/11th.html
Invention Dimension
www.web.mit.edu/invent/
Virtual Library For History of Science, Technology & Medicine
www.asap.unimelb.edu.au/hstm/
hstm_ove.htm

➤ *SEE ALSO THESE RELATED PATHFINDERS*

Computers; Inventions; Inventors

Thirteen Colonies

The 13 colonies were the original settlements of British immigrants to America from 1607 to 1775. The earliest colonies were at Jamestown and Williamsburg, Virginia. These colonies were subject to Britain and were part of the British Empire until 1775 when the colonist fought for their independence. These colonies eventually became the states of New Hampshire, Massachusetts, Rhode Island, Connecticut, New York, New Jersey, Pennsylvania, Delaware, Maryland, Virginia, North Carolina, South Carolina, and Georgia.

DEWEY DECIMAL CALL NUMBERS

200s
300s
400s

973.2 United States History, Colonial period, 1607-1775

974 New England and Mid Atlantic states

975 South Atlantic states

SEARCH TERMS

Thirteen colonies
Colonial America
Colonists
Virginia
Jamestown
Williamsburg
Puritans
Pilgrims
Search by names of particular colonists, for example: John Smith
Search by names of colonial settlements, for example: Williamsburg

NONFICTION/REFERENCE BOOKS

Life in the Thirteen Colonies, 1650-1750 by Stuart Kallen. Abdo & Daughters, 1990.

The Thirteen Colonies by Dennis B. Fradin. Children's Press, 1988.

The Jamestown Colony (Cornerstones of Freedom) by Gail Sakurai. Children's Press, 1997.

African-Americans in the Thirteen Colonies (Cornerstones of Freedom) by Deborah Kent. Children's Press, 1996.

Making Thirteen Colonies (A History of the United States) by Joy Hakim. Oxford University Children's Books, 1993.

A Nation is Born: Rebellion and Independence in American, 1700-1820 by Richard Steins. Twenty First Century Books, 1993.

Book of the American Colonies (Brown Paper School USKids History) by Howard Egger-Bovet and Marlene Smith-Branzini. Little, Brown & Co., 1996.

FICTION

Finding Providence: The Story of Roger Williams by Avi. HarperCollins, 1997.

My Brother, My Enemy by Madge Harrah. Simon & Schuster Books for Young Readers, 1997.

Colonial Days by David King. Wiley, 1998.

MULTIMEDIA

CD-ROMS:

American History v 4.2s. MultiEducator, 1998.

Founding of America: Colonization, Revolution, and Independence. Entrex, 1997.

Life in Colonial America. Queue, 1996.

VIDEOS:

A&E Biography (series). **Benedict Arnold** (1998); **Biography: Thomas Jefferson—Philosopher of Freedom** (1996); **George Washington** (1995); **Patrick Henry** (1998); **Paul Revere** (1996). A&E Entertainment.

Colonial Life for Children Video Series. Schlessinger, 1998.

Early Settlers (American History for Children). Schlessinger, 1996.

Independence: Birth of a Nation (National Park Series). Eastern National, [nd].

Where America Began: Jamestown, Colonial Williamsburg, Yorktown (History in America). American Heritage. Holiday Films, 1988.

WEB SITES

The Revolutionary War—A Journey Towards Freedom (A comprehensive site for teachers and students, with primary sources, games, and teacher resources) www.library.advanced.org/10966/

Life of Washington (Information about his slaves, tour of Mt. Vernon, images of Washington—a little wordy, but very informative) www.mountvernon.org/education/

Internet Resources about Colonial America from the Madison Metropolitan School District www.danenet.wicip.org/mmsd-it/ colonialamerica.html

On-Line Guide and Resources for the PBS series: Liberty—The American Revolution. (Includes time lines, historic documents, and illustrations) www.pbs.org/ktca/liberty/

➤ SEE ALSO THESE RELATED PATHFINDERS

Colonial Life, American; Pilgrims; Revolutionary War, American

Transportation

Transportation involves moving people or things from one place to another. There are many different modes of transportation, but all travel by land, or air, or water. There has always been some form of transportation, but as technologies develop so have the methods of transportation.

 ## DEWEY DECIMAL CALL NUMBERS

629.04 Transportation engineering
625 Engineering of railroads and roads
629.2 Motor land vehicles, and cycles
629.22 Types of vehicles (cars, trucks, etc.)

 ## SEARCH TERMS

Transportation
Wheels
Transportation history
Search by modes of transportation, for example: Train

 ## NONFICTION/REFERENCE BOOKS

Aircraft (Pointers) by Bob Munro. Raintree/Steck Vaughn, 1994.

Airplane (Mighty Machines) by Christopher Maynard. Dorling Kindersley, 1995.

Airplanes (What if–) by Steven Parker. Copper Beech Books, 1995.

Amazing Bikes (Eyewitness Juniors; 22) by Trevor Lord. Random House, 1992.

The Big Book of Things That Go. Dorling Kindersley/Houghton Mifflin Co., 1994.

Big Book of Trains. Dorling Kindersley, 1998.

Boats (What's Inside?). Dorling Kindersley, 1992.

Boats, Ships, Submarines, and Other Floating Machines (How Things Work) by Ian Graham. Kingfisher Books, 1993.

Cars (Eye Openers) by Angela Royston. Aladdin Books, 1991.

Dorling Kindersley Visual Timeline of Transportation by Anthony Wilson. Dorling Kindersley, 1995.

Eureka! It's An Automobile! (Inventing) by Jeanne Bendrick. Millbrook Press, 1992.

Ship by David Macauley. Houghton Mifflin Co., 1993.

Things That Go (Unicorn Paperback) by Anne Rockwell. Dutton, 1991.

Travel (Stepping Through History) by Peggy Burns and Peter Chrisp. Thomson Learning, 1995.

Trains by Gail Gibbons. Holiday House, 1987.

Transportation (Picturepedia). Dorling Kindersley, 1993.

Wheels Around by Shelley Rotner. Houghton Mifflin Co., 1995.

FICTION

The Boats on the River by Marjorie Flack. Viking, 1991.

Chitty Chitty Bang Bang; the Magical Car by Ian Fleming. Random House, 1964.

Country Crossing by Jim Aylesworth. Aladdin Paperbacks, 1995.

The Cut-ups Crack Up (Picture Puffin Books) by James Marshall. Puffin Books, 1994.

Freight Train by Donald Crews. Greenwillow Books, 1978.

I Spy a Freight Train: Transportation in Art by Lucy Micklethwait. Greenwillow Books, 1996.

Pigs Ahoy! by David McPhail. Dutton Children's Books, 1995.

Pippi Goes on Board by Astrid Lindgren, trans. by Florence Lamborn. Viking, 1985.

The Return of Freddy Legrand by John Agee. Farrar Straus Giroux, 1994.

Richard Scarry's Cars and Trucks and Things That Go (Golden Books) by Richard Scarry. Western Pub. Co., 1996.

Sheep on a Ship by Nancy Shaw. Houghton Mifflin Co., 1989.

MULTIMEDIA
 ### CD-ROMS:
Invention Studio Interactive Multimedia. Discovery Channel Multimedia, 1996.
Putt-Putt Saves the Zoo Interactive Multimedia (Junior Adventures). Humongous Entertainment, 1995.

 ### VIDEOS:
Cars! Cars! Cars! Mothers Lode Entertainment, 1996.
Come Fly With Us. Adventure Video, 1994.
How a Car Is Built. Think Media Productions, 1995.
Trains, Lots of Trains. Tapeworm Video, 1995.

 ## WEB SITES
Art Cars in Cyberspace
www.artcars.com/
Fox River Trolley Museum
www.foxtrolley.org/membership.htm
The Komoka Railway Museum
www.komokarail.ca/index1.html
National Air and Space Museum
www.nasm.edu/

➤ *SEE ALSO THIS RELATED PATHFINDER*
Technology

Trees

Trees are tall plants with woody trunks and leaves. There are three types of trees: broad-leaved trees, needle-leafed trees, and palm trees. Most broad-leaved trees are deciduous, which means they lose their leaves seasonally. Most needle-leafed trees, or evergreens, are conifers and produce pine cones. The tallest trees in the world grow in Redwood National Park. The oldest known tree was more than 5,100 years old—a bristlecone pine in Nevada.

DEWEY DECIMAL CALL NUMBERS

200s
300s
400s

582.16 Trees
582 Seed-bearing plants
583 Flowering plants
634 Orchards, fruits, nuts, forestry

SEARCH TERMS

Trees
Broad-leaved
Needle-leafed
Deciduous
Palm trees
Conifers
Forests
Logging
Search by species of tree, for example:
Live Oak

NONFICTION/REFERENCE BOOKS

A B Cedar: An Alphabet of Trees by George Lyon. Orchard Books, 1996.

Crinkleroot's Guide to Knowing the Trees by Jim Arnosky. Bradbury Press, 1991.

Dinosaur Tree by Douglas Henderson. Bradbury Press, 1994.

Discovering Trees by Keith Brandt. Troll Assoc., 1982.

Giant's in the Land by Diane Appelbaum. Houghton Mifflin Co., 1993.

Green Giants: Twelve of the Earth's Tallest Trees by Sneed B. Collard. Northwood Press, 1994.

Mangrove Wilderness: Nature's Nursery by Bianca Lavies. Dutton Children's Books, 1994.

Plants (DK Picturepedia). Dorling Kindersley, 1993.

Sky Tree: Seeing Science Through Art by Thomas Locker. HarperCollins, 1995.

Sugaring Time by Kathryn Lasky. Macmillan, 1986.

A Tree is Nice by Janice May Udry. HarperCollins, 1984.

Tree of Life: The World of the African Baobab by Barbara Bash. Sierra Club, 1989.

Trees by Jonathan Pine. HarperCollins, 1995.

The Tremendous Tree Book by Barbara Brenner. Caroline House, 1992.

FICTION

An Autumn Tale by David Updike. Pippin Press, 1988.

Chita's Christmas Tree by Elizabeth Fitzgerald Howard. Aladdin Books, 1993.

Have You Seen Trees? by Joanne Oppenheim. Scholastic, 1995.

Johnny Appleseed: A Poem by Reeve Lindbergh. Joy Street Books, 1990.

Red Leaf, Yellow Leaf by Lois Ehlert. Harcourt Brace & Co., 1991.

The Tree that Would Not Die by Ellen Levine. Scholastic, 1995.

The Way of the Willow Branch by Emery Bernhard. Harcourt Brace & Co., 1996.

MULTIMEDIA

 CD-ROMS:

Amazon Trail. MECC, 1997.
Living Lab—Plants. MindPlay. 1997.
Living Deserts & Rainforests. Bytes of Learning, 1997.
A World of Plants Interactive. National Geographic Society, 1994.

 VIDEOS:

Eyewitness Tree. Dorling Kindersley, 1996.
First Look at Trees. AIMS Media, 1991.
Flowers, Plants and Trees (Tell Me Why Video Encyclopedia). Bennett Marine Video, 1987.
In Celebration of Trees. Discovery Channel, 1991.
My First Nature Video. Sony Wonder, 1992.
Ancient Forests: Rage Over Trees.

 WEB SITES

Forests Are For Kids
www.idahoforests.org/kids1.htm
Gardening for Kids
www.geocities.com/EnchantedForest/
Glade/3313/
Kids For Trees
www.inhs.uiuc.edu/chf/pub/tree_kit/
Botany.Com (Online botanical encyclopedia—not many pictures, but lots of information)
www.botany.com/Common~1.html
Dragonfly Magazine On-line—Trees
www.muohio.edu/dragonfly/trees.htmlx

➤ *SEE ALSO THESE RELATED PATHFINDERS*

Forests; Plants; Rain Forest

The Unknown

There are many things that explorers have discovered and that scientists understand. However, other things remain a mystery. These are things that are considered unknown. Many things and events that are not completely understood have existed for years and years, and many stories have been created about them. Theses stories are very much like modern-day mythology. There are stories about ghosts, the supernatural, UFOs, Big Foot, and many other incredible things.

200s 300s 400s DEWEY DECIMAL CALL NUMBERS

001.9 Curiosities, mysteries, hoaxes, superstitions
133 Parapsychology and occultism

SEARCH TERMS

Supernatural
UFO
Unidentified flying objects
Paranormal
Ghosts
Yeti
Sasquatch

Roswell
Abominable Snowman
Bermuda Triangle
Stonehenge
Parapsychology
Curiosities and wonders
Urban myths

NONFICTION/REFERENCE BOOKS

The Abominable Snowman (Great Unsolved Mysteries) by Barbara Antonopulos. Raintree/Steck Vaughn, 1996.

Alien Abductions: Opposing Viewpoints (Great Mysteries) by Patricia D. Netzley. Greenhaven, 1996.

Beastly Tales: Yeti, Bigfoot, and the Loch Ness Monster (Eyewitness Readers. Level 3) by Malcolm Yorke. Dolring Kindersley, 1998.

The Bermuda Triangle by Jim Collins. Raintree/Steck Vaughn, 1983.

Bringing UFOs Down to Earth (Young Readers) by Philip J. Klass. Prometheus Books, 1997.

Could UFO's Be Real (The UFO Library). Capstone Press, 1991.

The Curse of Tutankhamen (Mysteries of Science) by Elaine Landau. Millbrook Press, 1996.

Dead Giveaways: How Real Life Crimes Are Solved by Amazing Scientific Evidence, Personality Profiling and Paranormal Investigations by Andrew Donkin. Element, 1998.

ESP (Mysteries of Science) by Elaine Landau. Millbrook Press, 1996.

Fortune Telling (Mysteries of Science.) by Elaine Landau. Millbrook Press, 1996.

Frauds, Myths, and Mysteries: Science and Pseudoscience in Archaeology by Kenneth L. Feder. Mayfield Pub. Co., 1996.

The Ghost of Elvis and Other Celebrity Spirits by Daniel Cohen. Minstrel Books, 1997.

Great Mysteries (Info Adventure) by Robert Nicholson, Caroline Clayton, and Damian Kelleher. World Book, 1995.

NONFICTION/REFERENCE BOOKS CONTINUED

The Mystery of UFOs by Judith Herbst. Atheneum Books for Young People, 1997.

Sasquatch: Wild Man of the Woods (Mysteries of Science) by Elaine Landau. Millbrook Press, 1993.

Scary Science: The Truth Behind Vampires, Witches, UFOs, Ghosts and More by Sylvia Funston. Owl Comm., 1996.

The Supernatural by Jillian Powell. Copper Beech Books, 1996.

UFOs (Mysteries of Science) by Elaine Landau. Millbrook Press, 1995.

UFOs: True Mysteries or Hoaxes? by Isaac Asimov. Gareth Stevens Pub., 1995.

World's Best "True" UFO Stories by Jenny Randles. Sterling Pub., 1994.

Yeti: Abominable Snowman of the Himalayas (Mysteries of Science) by Elaine Landau. Millbrook Press, 1993.

FICTION

The 13th Floor: A Ghost Story by Sid Fleischman. Yearling Books, 1997.

The Boggart and the Monster by Susan Cooper. Margaret K. McElderry Books, 1997.

Cam Jansen and the Mystery of the U.F.O. by David Adler. Puffin Books, 1991.

The Doom Stone by Paul Zindel. Hyperion, 1996.

The Ghosts' Trip to Loch Ness by Jacques Duquennoy. Harcourt Brace Jovanovich, 1996.

Sasquatch by Roland Smith. Hyperion, 1998.

UFO Diary by Satoshi Kitamura. Farrar Straus Giroux, 1989.

MULTIMEDIA

VIDEOS:

Bermuda Triangle. NOVA, 1976.

Escape to Witch Mountain. Walt Disney, 1975.

Ghostly Thrillers (Halloween Horror Series). Family Home Entertainment, 1986.

Isaac Asimov's Library of the Universe (Includes UFOs and life on other planets). Gareth Stevens Pub., 1995.

Secrets of the Psychics. NOVA, 1997.

Secrets of the Unknown (Series includes: Big Foot, Lake Monsters, and UFOs). Mpi, 1989.

WEB SITES

Alien Chaser
www.geocities.com/Area51/Hollow/8827/

Alien Research Site
www.soltec.net/~mako/main2.sht

How to Create Fake Photos of Ghosts
www3.sympatico.ca/roddy/ghost.html

Obiwan's UFO-Free Paranormal Page
(Stories, folklore, haunted places, links to other sites)
www.ghosts.org/

U.S. Government

The United States government is a democracy. It is organized into three branches of government: the executive branch, the judicial branch, and the legislative branch. Many of the people who hold positions within these branches are elected by the citizens of the United States, while others are appointed by the President. The President of the United States oversees the executive branch.

DEWEY DECIMAL CALL NUMBERS

200s 300s 400s

320.4 United States Politics and government

973.3 Revolution and confederation, 1775-1789

324 Electoral Process

324.973 Voting

328.73 United States, Congress

347.307 United States, Supreme Court

347.3022 United States, Constitutional Convention (1787)

SEARCH TERMS

United States Government
Federal Government
Democracy
Executive branch
Legislative branch
Judicial branch
Checks and balances
House of Congress
Senate
Judiciary
Supreme Court
President
Elections
Constitution
Declaration of Independence

NONFICTION/REFERENCE BOOKS

Our Congress (I Know America) by Michael Weber. Millbrook Press, 1994.

Our Constitution (I Know America) by Linda Carlson Johnson. Millbrook Press, 1992.

Our Declaration of Independence (I Know America) by Jay Schleifer. Millbrook Press, 1992.

Our Elections (I Know America) by Richard Steins. Millbrook Press, 1994.

The Supreme Court (Places in American History) by Catherine Reef. Maxwell Macmillan International, 1994.

Take a Stand!: Everything You Never Wanted to Know About Government by Daniel Weizmann. Price Stern Sloan, 1996.

The Voice of the People: American Democracy in Action by Betsy Maestro and Giulio Maestro. Lothrop, Lee & Shepard, 1996.

FICTION

Next Stop, the White House! by Judy Delton. Hyperion Paperbacks for Children, 1995.

MULTIMEDIA

 ### CD-ROMS:

We the People. MultiEducator, 1997.
Vote America. Virtual Knowledge, 1996.
History of the United States for Young People. American Heritage, 1996.

VIDEOS:

Election Day. Schlessinger, 1996.
Our Federal Government—Presidency. Rainbow Educational Video, 1993.
The Congress—Ken Burns's America Collection. PBS Home Video, 1988.
United States Constitution (American History for Children). Schlessinger, 1996.

 ## WEB SITES

Welcome to the White House
www2.whitehouse.gov/WH/Welcome.html
U.S. Senate Web Site
www.senate.gov

➤ *SEE ALSO THIS RELATED PATHFINDER*
U.S. Presidents

U.S. Presidents

The President of the United States is the chief executive of the United States, overseeing the executive branch of the United States government. While the legislative and judicial branches of government are not directly overseen by the President and are considered equal to the executive branch, the President is generally regarded as the leader of the nation. The President lives and works at the White House in the nation's capital, Washington, D.C.. George Washington was the first President of the United States. Presidential elections are held every four years.

DEWEY DECIMAL CALL NUMBERS

920 Collective biography
921 Biography
973 American history

SEARCH TERMS

President
First Lady
White House
United States Government
Search by names of particular presidents, for example: Millard Fillmore

NONFICTION/REFERENCE BOOKS

First Ladies: Women Who Called the White House Home by Beatrice Gormley. Scholastic, 1997.

Our Presidency by Karen Spies. Millbrook Press, 1994.

Presidents by Martin Sandler. HarperCollins, 1995.

The Presidents Almanac by Paula Kessler. Contemporary Books, 1996.

The Scholastic Encyclopedia of the Presidents and their Times by David Rubel. Scholastic, 1994.

The Story of the White House by Kate Waters. Scholastic, 1991.

FICTION

Breakfast at the Liberty Diner by Daniel Kirk. Hyperion, 1997.

Hail to the Chief!: Jokes About the Presidents by Diane and Clint Burns. Lerner Pub. Co., 1989.

Lost at the White House by Lisa Griest. Carolrhoda Books. 1994.

President's Day by Laura Alden. Wing Park, 1994.

Wooden Teeth & Jelly Beans by Ray Nelson. Beyond Words, 1995.

MULTIMEDIA

CD-ROMS:
Atlas of U.S. Presidents. Queue, 1992.

History of the United States for Young People. American Heritage, 1996.

Oval Office: Challenge of the Presidency. Meridian Creative Group, 1996.

Vote America. Virtual Knowledge, 1996.

VIDEOS:
George Washington: The Man Who Wouldn't Be King. PBS, 1995.

Our Federal Government—Presidency. Rainbow Educational Video, 1993.

Portraits of American Presidents Series. NBC News, 1992.

Presidents (Presidential Series). ABC News, 1990.

WEB SITES

Welcome to the White House
www2.whitehouse.gov/WH/Welcome.html
PBS Presidents Page
www.pbs.org/wgbh/pages/amex/Presidents
Presidents of the United States (POTUS)
www.ipl.org/ref/POTUS
United States Presidents Information Page
www.we.got.net/docent/soquel/Pressez.htm

➤ SEE ALSO THESE RELATED PATHFINDERS
Biographies; U.S. Government

War

Fighting which occurs over a period of time between two or more countries, or between opposing groups within one country, is called war. War has always been a significant part of history. Wars are fought to preserve freedom or to expand one nation's dominion by overtaking another nation or region.

DEWEY DECIMAL CALL NUMBERS

909 World history
930 History of ancient world, to ca. 499
940 General history of Europe
940.3 World War I
940.53 World War II
970 General history of North America

SEARCH TERMS

War
Military
Military history
Refugees
Search by names of specific wars, for example: The Trojan War

NONFICTION/REFERENCE BOOKS

Battles that Changed the Modern World by Dale Anderson. Raintree/Steck Vaughn, 1994.

A Bosnian Family by Robin Landew Silverman. Lerner Pub. Co., 1997.

The Boys' War: Confederate and Union Soldiers Talk about the Civil War by Jim Murphy. Clarion Books, 1990.

Conflict in Art by Clare Gogerty. Marshall Cavendish, 1997.

Dorling Kindersley Visual Encyclopedia. Dorling Kindersley, 1995.

The Greeks by Susan Williams. Thomson Learning, 1993.

The Grolier Library of World War I. Grolier Educational, 1997.

If You Lived at the Time of the Civil War by Kay Moore. Scholastic, 1994.

The Kingfisher Books Illustrated History of the World. Kingfisher Books, 1993.

The Korean War (A First Book) by Tom McGowan. Franklin Watts, 1993.

The Mexican War: Manifest Destiny (A First Book) by Alden Carter. Franklin Watts, 1993.

Over 50 Years Ago in Europe: During World War II (History Detective) by Philip Steele. New Discovery Books, 1993.

A Place Called Heartbreak: A Story of Vietnam by Walter Dean Myers. Raintree/Steck Vaughn, 1993.

Rwanda: Fierce Clashes in Central Africa by John Issac. Blackbirch Press, 1997.

Russia at War (WW II 50th Anniversary Series). Crestwood, 1991.

The Soldiers' Voice: The Story of Ernie Pyle by Barbara O'Connor. Carolrhoda Books, 1996.

War Game by Michael Foreman. Arcade Pub., 1993.

FICTION

Cecil's Story by George Ella Lyon. Orchard Books, 1991.

Faithful Elephants: A True Story of Animals, People, and War by Yukio Tsuchiya. Houghton Mifflin Co., 1988.

George Washington's Socks by Elvira Woodruff. Scholastic, 1991.

Hanna's Cold Winter by Trish Marx. Carolrhoda Books, 1993.

The House of Sixty Fathers by Meindert De Jong. HarperTrophy, 1988.

The Kingdom by the Sea by Robert Westall. Farrar Straus Giroux, 1993.

The Little Ships: The Heroic Rescue at Dunkirk in World War II by Louise Borden. Margaret K. McElderry Books, 1997.

Over There! Stories of World War I by Phyllis Fenner. William Morrow & Co., 1961.

Sami and the Time of Troubles by Florence Perry Heide and Judith Heide Gilliland. Clarion Books, 1995.

The Trojan Horse: How the Greeks Won the War by Emily Little. Random House, 1988.

MULTIMEDIA

 CD-ROMS:

Civilization II. Micropose, 1996.
Eyewitness History of the World. DK Multimedia, 1996.
Multimedia World History. Queue/Bureau of Electronic Pub., 1997.

 **VIDEOS:**

Florence Nightingale (Animated Hero Classics). Schlessinger, 1996.
Joan of Arc (Animated Hero Classics). Schlessinger, 1996.
War from the Air. NOVA, 1975.
What Have We Learned Charlie Brown. Paramount, 1983.

 **WEB SITES**

The History Place
www.historyplace.com
What Did You Do in the War, Grandma?
www.stg.brown.edu/Projects/
WWII_Women/tocCS.html

➤ SEE ALSO THESE RELATED PATHFINDERS

Civil War, American; Revolutionary War, American; World War I; World War II

Weather

People are always dependent on the weather. It influences what we eat, what we wear and how our homes are built. The weather is the condition that our atmosphere is in at any given time. We determined weather conditions by measuring temperature, air pressure, humidity, wind, cloudiness, and precipitation.

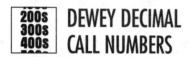 **DEWEY DECIMAL CALL NUMBERS**

551.5 Meteorology

 SEARCH TERMS

Weather	Wind
Meteorology	Clouds
Storms	Hurricanes
Rain	Tornadoes
Rainfall	Weather forecasting
Snow	

 NONFICTION/REFERENCE BOOKS

Storms by Seymour Simon. Morrow Junior Books, 1989.

The Weather: Sun, Wind, Snow, Rain by Colleen Carroll. Abbeville Kids, 1996.

Experiment with Weather by Miranda Bower. Lerner Pub. Co., 1994.

How's the Weather?: A Look at Weather and How it Changes by Melvin and Gilda Berger. Ideals Children's Books, 1993.

The Science Book of Weather by Neil Ardley. Harcourt Brace Jovanovich, 1992.

Weather by Seymour Simon. Morrow Junior Books, 1993.

Weather (Discoveries Library) by Sally Morgan. Time-Life Books, 1996.

Weather Forecasting by Gail Gibbons. Maxwell Macmillan International, 1993.

Weather (Eyewitness Explorers) by John Farndon. Dorling Kindersley, 1992.

FICTION

Heat Wave at Mud Flat by James Stevenson. Greenwillow Books, 1997.

Sail Away by Donald Crews. Greenwillow Books, 1995.

Thunderstorm! Nathanial Tripp. Dial Books for Young Readers, 1995.

Weather (An I Can Read Book) poems selected by Lee Bennett. HarperCollins, 1994.

What a Wonderful Day to be a Cow by Carolyn Lesser. Knopf, 1995.

Boat Ride With Lillian Two Blossom by Patricia Polacco. Philomel Books, 1988.

Cloudy with a Chance of Meatballs by Judi Barrett. Aladdin Books, 1978.

The Long Winter by Laura Ingalls Wilder. Harper, 1953.

Storms at the Shore (The Explorers Club) by Betsy Loredo. Silver Moon/August House, 1993.

What Color Was the Sky Today? by Miela Ford. Greenwillow Books, 1997.

MULTIMEDIA

 ### CD-ROMS:

Our Earth Interactive Multimedia. National Geographic Society, 1994.

Sammy's Science House Interactive Multimedia. Edmark, 1995.

Science Blaster Jr. interactive Multimedia. Davidson & Assoc., 1996.

Weather. Interfact, 1997.

 ### WEB SITES

AccuWeather Main Weather Page
www.accuweather.com/weatherf/index_corp

WeatherNet4—Education
www.home.nbcin.com/nbcin/frames/
WRC_left_blue_dark.html

VIDEOS:

Atmosphere in Motion (Exploring Weather). United Learning, 1993.

Cloudy With A Chance of Meatballs. Live Oak Media, 1987.

Exploring Weather (Exploring Weather). United Learning, 1993.

Weather (Eyewitness). Dorling Kindersley, 1996.

Investigating Weather. United Learning, 1995.

Job of a TV Meteorologist (Exploring Weather). United Learning, 1993.

Magic School Bus Kicks Up a Storm. Kid Vision, 1995.

Rain or Shine: Understanding the Weather. Rainbow Educational Video, 1987.

Story of Climate, Weather, and People. Hawkhill Assoc., 1994.

Telling the Weather. National Geographic Film & TV, 1996.

What Makes the Weather (Now I Know). Troll Assoc., 1988.

➤ *SEE ALSO THESE RELATED PATHFINDERS*

Clouds; Hurricanes; Natural Disasters; Seasons

Westward Expansion

The Westward Expansion refers to the gradual process by which America became populated. From 1607, with the first settlement at Jamestown, to the late 1800s, there was a stead surge of frontiersmen and pioneers who set forth in covered wagons to claim unsettled territory. By 1890, the census determined that there were no areas within the American continent that had not been settled.

DEWEY DECIMAL CALL NUMBERS

910 Geography & travel
917.04 Geography & travel, North America
970.01 General history of North America
978 Western United States

SEARCH TERMS

Westward expansion
Oregon Trail
Frontier life
Pioneer life
History of Western United States
Overland journeys to the Pacific

NONFICTION/REFERENCE BOOKS

Bent's Fort: Crossroads of Cultures on the Santa Fe Trail by Melvin Bacon. Millbrook Press, 1995.

Black Frontiers: A History of African American Heroes in the Old West by Lillian Schlissel. Simon & Schuster, 1995.

Children of the Westward Trail by Rebecca Stefoff. Millbrook Press, 1996.

Frontier Home by Raymond Bial. Houghton Mifflin Co., 1993.

How We Crossed the West: The Adventures of Lewis & Clark by Rosalyn Schanzer. National Geographic Society, 1997.

In Search of the Grand Canyon by Mary Ann Fraser. Henry Holt & Co., 1995.

Pioneers by Martin W. Sandler. HarperCollins, 1994.

The Santa Fe Trail by David Lavender. Holiday House, 1995.

The West: An Illustrated History for Children (based on PBS series) by Dayton Duncan. Little, Brown & Co., 1996.

West by Covered Wagon: Retracing the Pioneer Trails by Dorothy Patent. Walker & Co., 1995.

Westward Ho!: An Activity Guide to the Wild West by Laurie Carlson. Chicago Review Press, 1996.

Westward Ho!: The Story of the Pioneers by Lucille Recht Penner. Random House, 1997.

Westward, Ho, Ho, Ho! by Peter and Connie Roop. Millbrook Press, 1996.

FICTION

Aurora Means Dawn by Scott Sanders. Bradbury Press, 1989.

Flatboats on the Ohio: Westward Bound by Catherine E. Chambers. Troll Assoc., 1984.

Lewis & Clark and Davy Hutchins by Nolan Carlson. Hearth Pub., 1994.

By the Shores of Silver Lake by Laura Ingalls Wilder. Harper & Row, 1971.

The Long Way Westward by Joan Sandin. Harper & Row, 1989.

My Name is York by Elizabeth Van Steenwyck. Rising Moon, 1997.

On the Long Trail Home by Elisabeth Stewart. Clarion Books, 1994.

Train to Somewhere by Eve Bunting. Clarion Books, 1996.

Wagon Train 911 by James Gilson. Lothrop, Lee & Shepard, 1996.

Westward Ho, Carlotta! by Candace Fleming. Atheneum, 1998.

MULTIMEDIA

CD-ROMS:

Go West! Interactive. Edunetics, 1996.
Oregon Trail II. MECC, 1995.
The Westward Movement Interactive. National Geographic Society, 1997.
Yukon Trail Interactive. MECC, 1994.

VIDEOS:

America's Westward Expansion. Knowledge Unlimited, 1996.
Louisiana Purchase: Moving West of the Mississippi. Encyclopaedia Britannica, 1990.
Railroad Builders. Encyclopedia Britannica, 1990.
United States Expansion (American History for Children). Schlessinger, 1996.
West That Was. National Geographic Society, 1996.

WEB SITES

Lewis and Clark (Companion to Ken Burns's film; information, maps, and resources)
www.pbs.org/lewisandclark/
Oregon Trail—The Trail West (Maps and lots of information)
www.ukans.edu/kansas/seneca/oregon/ortrail.html
Pioneer Life in Ohio
www.rootsweb.com/~ohpickaw/life.html
Westward Expansion
www.americanwest.com/pages/wexpansi.htm

➤ *SEE ALSO THESE RELATED PATHFINDERS*
California Gold Rush; Pioneer Life

Whales

Whales are marine mammals, which means they live in the ocean, but they also breathe air and nurse their young. They are shaped like fish and have small front flippers and a tail. There are two groups of whales, Toothed Whales and Baleen (toothless) Whales. The Blue Whale is the largest animal ever, even larger than dinosaurs.

DEWEY DECIMAL CALL NUMBERS

599.5 Mammals, whales, dolphins, porpoises

SEARCH TERMS

Whales
Mammals
Marine mammals
Cetacean
Search by species, for example: Blue Whale

NONFICTION/REFERENCE BOOKS

Big Blue Whale by Nicola Davies. Candlewick Press, 1997.

Humpback Whales by Deborah Hinshaw Patent. Holiday House, 1989.

Whales by Seymour Simon. HarperCollins, 1992.

Baby Whales Drink Milk (Let's-read-and-find-out Science. Stage 1) by Barbara Juster Esbensen. HarperCollins, 1994.

Great Whales: The Gentle Giants (Redfeather Book) by Pieter Folkens. Henry Holt & Co., 1993.

Killer Whale by Caroline Arnold. Morrow Junior Books, 1994.

Whales by Gail Gibbons. Holiday House, 1991.

Whales, Dolphins, and Porpoises by Mark Carwardine. Dorling Kindersley, 1992.

FICTION

All I See by Cynthia Rylant. Orchard Books, 1994.

Amos & Boris by William Steig. Farrar Straus Giroux, 1992.

Moby Dick; or, The White Whale by Herman Melville, adapted by Geraldine McCaughrean. Oxford University Press, 1996.

The Whales' Song by Dyan Sheldon. Dial Books for Young Readers, 1991.

MULTIMEDIA

CD-ROM:

A World of Animals Interactive Multimedia. National Geographic Society, 1994.

VIDEOS:

Deep Sea Dive (Really Wild Animals). National Geographic Home Video, 1994.

Gift of the Whales (Legend). Miramar Productions, 1989.

Gray Whales (In the Wild). PBS Video, 1995.

Great Whales. National Geographic Home Video, 1978.

Humpbacks of Hawaii. National Geographic Film & TV, 1986.

Whales (National Audubon Society Special). Vestron Video, 1987.

WEB SITES

Whale Net (An interactive educational project)
www.whale.wheelock.edu/

Whale Watcher Expert System (Downloadable program of whale video clips)
www.com/ai/demos/whale.html

The Virtual Whale Project (Pacific Humpback Whales)
www.fas.sfu.ca/cs/research/Whales/

Sea World California–J The Gray Whale (Whale sounds and movies)
www.seaworld.org/GrayWhale/current.html

NetVet–Marine Mammals (Many links)
www.netvet.wustl.edu/marine.htm

David's Whale and Dolphin Watch (Photos and sounds of whales, sorted by species)
www.neptune.atlantis-intl.com/dolphins/

Whale Times (Has a kids' page)
www.whaletimes.org/

➤ SEE ALSO THESE RELATED PATHFINDERS
Animals; Dolphins; Sea Animals

Wildlife

Wildlife refers to wild animals and vegetation which live in their natural, undomesticated environment. The term especially refers to wild animals. Today, many species of wildlife are endangered so efforts have been made to protect wild animals and their natural habitats.

200s 300s 400s DEWEY DECIMAL CALL NUMBERS

590   Animals
591   Specific topics in natural history
598   Aves (birds)
599   Mammals
639   Hunting, fishing, conservation

SEARCH TERMS

Wildlife
Undomesticated animals
Rare animals
Mammals
Birds
Natural history

NONFICTION/REFERENCE BOOKS

The African Rhino by Gloria G. Schaepfer and Mary Samuelson. Dillon Press, 1992.

All the King's Animals: The Return of Endangered Wildlife to Swaziland by Christina Kessler. Boyds Mills Press, 1995.

Animal Hullabaloo: A Wildlife Noisy Book by Jakki Wood. Simon & Schuster, 1995.

Animals in Disguise by Martine Duprez. Charlesbridge Pub., 1994.

Apes by Eric S. Grace. Sierra Club Books for Children, 1995.

Back to the Wild by Dorothy Hinshaw Patent. Harcourt Brace Jovanovich, 1997.

Bears by Ian Stirling. Sierra Club Books for Children, 1992.

Birds of Prey by Jill Bailey. Facts on File, 1988.

Dolphin Adventure by Wayne Grover. Beech Tree Books, 1993.

Elephants by Eric Grace. Sierra Club Books for Children, 1993.

Gray Wolf, Red Wolf by Dorothy Hinshaw. Clarion Books, 1996.

How to Babysit an Orangutan by Tara and Kathy Darling. Walker & Co., 1996.

Lions by Caroline Arnold. Morrow Junior Books, 1995.

Monk Seal Hideaway by Diane Ackerman. Crown, 1995.

Secrets of a Wildlife Watcher by Jim Arnosky. Beech Tree Books, 1991.

Snakes by Eric S. Grace. Sierra Club Books for Children, 1994.

Summer Ice: Life Along the Antarctic Peninsula by Bruce McMillan. Houghton Mifflin Co., 1995.

To the Top of the World: Adventures with Arctic Wolves by Jim Brandenburg. Walker & Co., 1993.

Where Once There was a Wood by Denise Fleming. Henry Holt & Co., 1996.

A Walk in the Wild: Exploring a Wildlife Refuge by Lorraine Ward. Charlesbridge Pub., 1993.

FICTION

17 Kings and 42 Elephants by Patricia MacCarthy. Dial Books for Young Readers, 1987.

Aardvarks, Disembark! by Ann Jones. Greenwillow Books, 1990.

Annie and the Wild Animals by Jan Brett. Houghton Mifflin Co., 1985.

The Cabin Key by Gloria Rand. Harcourt Brace Jovanovich, 1994.

Enora and the Black Crane by Arone Raymond Meeks. Scholastic, 1993.

The Great Kapok Tree: A Tale of the Amazon Rain Forest by Lynne Cherry. Harcourt Brace Jovanovich, 1990.

Jackrabbit by Jonathan London. Crown, 1996.

Jaguarundi by Virginia Hamilton. Scholastic, 1995.

Mole's Hill: A Woodland Tale by Lois Ehlert. Harcourt Brace Jovanovich, 1994.

Mowing by Jessie Haas. Greenwillow Books, 1994.

One Sun Rises: An African Wildlife Counting Book by Wendy Hartmann. Dutton Children's Books, 1994.

Sweet Magnolia by Virginia Kroll. Charlesbridge Pub., 1995.

Tigress by Helen Cowcher. Farrar Straus Giroux, 1991.

Toughboy and Sister by Kirkpatrick Hill. Margaret K. McElderry Books, 1990.

Who is the Beast? by Keith Baker. Harcourt Brace Jovanovich, 1990.

The Year of the Panda by Mirian Schlein. HarperTrophy, 1992.

MULTIMEDIA

 ### CD-ROMS:

Amazing Animals Interactive Multimedia. DK Multimedia, 1997.

Animal Planet Interactive. Discovery Channel Multimedia, 1996.

Rand McNally Children's Atlas of World Wildlife Interactive. GameTek, 1995.

 ### VIDEOS:

Creatures of the Blue. Sierra Club Kids, 1995.

Desert Wildlife. Natural History Educational, 1995.

Eyewitness Natural World (series). Dorling Kindersley, 1995.

Prairie Wildlife. Natural History Educational, 1995.

Rocky Mountain Wildlife. Natural History Educational, 1995.

 ## WEB SITES

The Living Planet
www.the-planet.net/

Wildlife Links (Links to wildlife images, sounds, endangered species, zoos, and more)
www.selu.com/~bio/wildlife/links/index.html

U.S. Fish & Wildlife Service (Information center for students and teachers)
www.fws.gov/r9endspp/kid_cor/kid_cor.htm

National Wildlife Federation
www.igc.org/nwf/

> ## SEE ALSO THESE RELATED PATHFINDERS
Animals; Biomes; Zoo Animals

World War I

World War I, also called the Great War, was fought from 1914 to 1918. It was a conflict fought mainly in Europe among most of the world's great powers. The side of the Allies, including Great Britain, France, Russia, Belgium, Italy, Japan, and the United States, fought and defeated the Central Powers: Germany, Austria-Hungary, Turkey, and Bulgaria. The war was primarily caused by the desire of the Central Powers to dominate the European continent, and this was particularly true of Germany. However, it was the nationalistic climate of Austria-Hungary and its declaration of war against Serbia that initiated the world conflict.

DEWEY DECIMAL CALL NUMBERS

940.3 World War I, 1914-1918
940 Europe
941 British Isles
942 England & Wales
943 Central Europe, Germany
944 France & Monaco

SEARCH TERMS

World War (1914-1918)
World War I
WWI
First World War
Doughboys

NONFICTION/REFERENCE BOOKS

America in World War I by Edward F. Dolan. Millbrook Press, 1996.

The Battle of Belleau Wood by Earle Rice, Jr. Lucent Books, 1996.

Causes and Consequences of World War I by Stewart Ross. Raintree, 1998.

The Children's Atlas of the Twentieth Century: Chart the Century from World War I to The Gulf War and from "Teddy" Roosevelt to Nelson Mandela by Sarah Howarth. Millbrook Press, 1995.

First World War edited by John D. Clare. Harcourt Brace Jovanovich, 1995.

In Flanders Fields: The Story of the Poem by John McCrae by Linda Granfield. Doubleday, 1995.

The Grolier Library of World War I. Grolier Educational, 1997.

World War I by Tom McGowen. Franklin Watts, 1993.

FICTION

The Language of Doves by Rosemary Wells. Dial Books, 1996.

Over There! Stories of World War I by Phyllis Fenner. William Morrow & Co., 1961.

War Game by Michael Foreman. Arcade, 1994.

MULTIMEDIA

CD-ROMS:

Chronicle of the 20th Century. DK Multimedia, 1995.

Eyewitness History of the World. DK Multimedia, 1996.

World Discovery Deluxe Great Wave, 1994.

The Causes of World War I. Clearvue, 1997.

Multimedia World History. Queue/Bureau of Electronic Publishing, 1997.

VIDEOS:

All's Quiet on the Western Front. Universal Studios, 1930.

The Guns of August. MCA Home Video, 1993.

Shoulder Arms. Madacy, 1997. (Charlie Chaplin short depicting WWI trench warfare)

WEB SITES

Photos of the Great War
www.members.aol.com/atominfo/
greatwar.htm

World War I
www.info.ox.ac.uk/OUCS/humanities/rose/
war.html

➤ SEE ALSO THESE RELATED PATHFINDERS
War; World War II

World War II

World War II was fought from 1939 to 1945, and involved every major power in the world. The Allied forces of Great Britain, France, the Soviet Union, the United States, China, and others fought and defeated the Axis powers: Germany, Italy, and Japan. The worldwide economic problems brought on by the Great Depression of the 1930s contributed to the developing conflict. However, the war was primarily a result of the totalitarian and militaristic regimes that were becoming more and more powerful in Germany, Italy, and Japan.

DEWEY DECIMAL CALL NUMBERS

940.53 World War II
940.53 World War 2, 1939-1945

940.54 Military history of World War 2
940.5   Europe, 20th century, 1918–
973.91 United States history, early 20th century, 1901-1953
327.12 Spies biography

SEARCH TERMS

World War, 1939-1945
World War, 1939-1945 Europe
World War, 1939-1945 Great Britain
World War, 1939-1945 Germany
World War, 1939-1945 Japan
Japanese Americans, evacuation and relocation, 1942-1945
Hiroshima (Japan) history, bombardment, 1945
Nagasaki (Japan) history, bombardment, 1945

Holocaust, Jewish
Concentration camps, Germany
Frank, Anne, 1929-1945
Dunkirk (France), Battle of, 1940
War correspondents
Pyle, Ernie, 1900-1945
Totalitarianism
Militarism
Search by names of particular events or people, for example: General George S. Patton

NONFICTION/REFERENCE BOOKS

Anne Frank: Life in Hiding by Johanna Hurwitz. Jewish Pub. Society, 1993.

Hiroshima and Nagasaki (Cornerstones of Freedom) by Barbara Silberdick Feinberg. Children's Press, 1995.

Hollywood at War: The Motion Picture Industry and World War II by Charnan Simon. Franklin Watts, 1995.

In the Line of Fire: Eight Women War Spies by George Sullivan. Scholastic, 1996.

Over 50 Years Ago in Europe: During World War II (History Detective) by Philip Steele. New Discovery Books, 1993.

Passage to Freedom: The Sugihara Story by Ken Mochizuki. Lee & Low Books, 1997.

Remember Not to Forget: A Memory of the Holocaust by Norman H. Finkelstein. Mulberry Books, 1993.

The Soldiers' Voice: The Story of Ernie Pyle by Barbara O'Connor. Carolrhoda Books, 1996.

Strange But True Stories of World War II by George Sullivan. Walker & Co., 1983.

Uncle Sam Wants You!: Military Men and Women of World War II by Sylvia Whitman. Lerner Pub. Co., 1993.

NONFICTION/REFERENCE BOOKS CONTINUED

Victims of War by Robin Cross. Thomson Learning, 1993.

War Behind the Lines by Wallace B. Black and Jean Blashfield. Crestwood House, 1992.

When Justice Failed: The Fred Korematsu Story (Stories of America) by Steven A. Chin. Raintree/Steck Vaughn, 1993.

Women and War by Fiona Reynoldson. Thomson Learning, 1993.

World War II by Tom McGowen. Franklin Watts, 1993.

World War II by Stewart Ross. Raintree/Steck Vaughn, 1996.

World War II: The War in Europe by John J. Vail. Lucent Books, 1991.

World War II in the Pacific: "Remember Pearl Harbor" by R. Conrad Stein. Enslow, 1994.

 ## FICTION

American Dreams (Stories of the States) by Lisa Banim. Silver Moon/August House, 1993.

Keep Smiling Through by Ann Rinaldi. Harcourt Brace Jovanovich, 1996.

The Little Ships: The Heroic Rescue at Dunkirk in World War II by Louise Borden. Margaret K. McElderry Books, 1997.

Rose Blanche by Roberto Innocenti, translated by Martha Coventry and Richard Graglia. Creative Education, 1996.

The Shadow Children by Steven Schnur. Morrow Junior Books, 1994.

MULTIMEDIA

 ### CD-ROMS:

Chronicle of the 20th Century. DK Multimedia, 1995.

Eyewitness History of the World. DK Multimedia, 1996.

World Discovery Deluxe. Great Wave, 1994.

The Causes of World War II. Clearvue, 1997.

Multimedia World History. Queue/Bureau of Electronic Pub., 1997.

 ## WEB SITES

ABC Links to World War II
www.chs.chico.k12.ca.us/~mrummens/
marg/WW2/WorldWar2.htm

The History Place
www.historyplace.com/worldwar2

The Holocaust: A tragic legacy
www.library.advanced.org/12663/

The United States Holocaust Memorial Museum www.ushmm.org

 ### VIDEOS:

African-American Heroes of World War II. OnDeck Home Entertainment, 1995.

Hidden Army: Women in World War II. OnDeck Home Entertainment, 1995.

Miracle at Moreaux. WonderWorks. Bonneville Worldwide Entertainment, 1990.

Story of Dwight D. Eisenhower. (Famous Americans of the 20th Century) Questar Video Comm., 1991.

World War II (United States History Series). Schlessinger, 1996.

> ### SEE ALSO THESE RELATED PATHFINDERS
War; World War I

Zoo Animals

Zoos, or zoological gardens, are parks where animals are kept for exhibition and study. Most zoo animals are captured in their natural habitat, but some zoo animals are born in zoos. Many zoos have special programs to breed certain species of animals that are nearing extinction. These species are then reintroduced into the wild. Some of the most notable zoos are in the Bronx (N.Y.), San Diego, Chicago, London, Paris, and Berlin.

DEWEY DECIMAL CALL NUMBERS

590.73 Zoos
590 Zoological science
591 Zoology
599 Mammals

SEARCH TERMS

Zoo animals
Animals
Zoos
Zoological gardens
Endangered Species
Search by group or species of animal, for example: Primate *or* Lemur

NONFICTION/REFERENCE BOOKS

Can Elephants Drink through Their Noses?: The Strange Things People Say about Animals at the Zoo by Deborah Dennard. Carolrhoda Books, 1993.

Cats in the Zoo by Roland Smith. Millbrook Press, 1994.

A Children's Zoo by Tana Hoban. Greenwillow Books, 1985.

The Dorling Kindersley Visual Encyclopedia. Dorling Kindersley, 1996.

Going to the Zoo by Tom Paxton. Morrow Junior Books, 1996.

Let's Visit a Super Zoo by Georgeanne Irvine. Troll Assoc., 1990.

My Visit to the Zoo by Aliki. HarperCollins, 1997.

Popcorn Park Zoo: A Haven with a Heart by Wendy Pfeffer. J. Messner, 1992.

Primates in the Zoo by Roland Smith. Millbrook Press, 1992.

The Visual Dictionary of Animals. Dorling Kindersley, 1996.

Whales, Dolphins, and Porpoises in the Zoo by Roland Smith. Millbrook Press, 1994.

When We Went to the Zoo by Jan Omerod. Lothrop, Lee & Shepard, 1991.

FICTION

Alligator Baby by Robert Munsch. Scholastic, 1997.

Faithful Elephants: A True Story of Animals, People, and War by Yukio Tsuchiya. Houghton Mifflin Co., 1988.

Good Night, Gorilla by Peggy Rathmann. G. P. Putnam's Sons, 1994.

I Went to the Zoo by Rita Golden Gelman. Scholastic, 1993.

If Anything Ever Goes Wrong at the Zoo by Mary Jean Hendrick. Harcourt Brace Jovanovich, 1993.

If I Ran the Zoo by Dr. Seuss. Random House, 1977.

A Lion Named Shirley Williamson by Bernard Waber. Houghton Mifflin Co., 1996.

Peculiar Zoo by Barry Louis Polisar. Rainbow Morning Music, 1993.

Polar Bear, Polar Bear, What Do You Hear? by Bill Martin. Henry Holt & Co., 1991.

Sam Who Never Forgets by Eve Rice. Greenwillow Books, 1977.

Sammy, the Seal by Syd Hoff. HarperTrophy, 1987.

Zoo Doings: Animal Poems by Jack Prelutsky. Greenwillow Books, 1983.

Zoo Dreams by Cor Hazelaar. Frances Foster Books, 1997.

Zoo-Looking by Mem Fox. Mondo Pub., 1996.

MULTIMEDIA

 CD-ROMS:

The Animals! Interactive Multimedia (Featuring San Diego Zoo). Mindscape, 1995.

Animals in their World Interactive. Edunetics, 1996.

Kid's Zoo: A Baby Animal Adventure. Knowledge Adventure, 1993.

Zoo Explorer. Compton's New Media, 1995.

Zookeeper. RomTech, 1996.

 WEB SITES

The Electronic Zoo
www.netvet.wustl.edu/e-zoo.htm
The Micke Grove Zoo
www.mgzoo.com/

 VIDEOS:

Adventures with Baaco: Animal Quest. Kids Trek Prod., 1994.

Animal ABCs. Rainbow Educational Video, 1988.

At Home with Zoo Animals. National Geographic Film & TV, 1992.

Beyond the Bars: Zoos and Zoo Animals. Rainbow Educational Video, 1987.

Zoo Life with Jack Hanna. Time-Life Video, 1992.

Zoofari. Whitetree Pictures, 1995.

➤ *SEE ALSO THESE RELATED PATHFINDERS*
Animals; Biomes; Birds; Endangered Species

CHAPTER 4

Ways to Research

► INTRODUCTION TO RESEARCH METHODS

Every day people ask questions and seek out answers. This is research in its most basic form. Where is the bathroom? What should I have for lunch? Where's the new park with the baseball field?

When the need and interest are enough of a motivation, we find the answer we are looking for from whatever sources are available. We look first for something we can refer to—a person, a map, a telephone book—but we don't think of them as "reference materials." We probably even have some sort of research method or process that we go through, but it comes so naturally that we aren't aware of it.

The process for finding answers to everyday questions is basic: 1) You have a question: "Where's the bathroom?" 2) You look for the answer: "Excuse me, do you know where the bathroom is?" 3) You find an answer: "Yes, it's through those doors." Then you make use of the informa-

tion: You go through the doors and look for the bathroom! This is the framework for every good method of research. So then the question follows: "If finding answers to questions comes so naturally, why is 'research' so hard?"

For many reasons, the natural flow of questions and answers is lost when a child is faced with a research assignment. What may have been a simple query, suddenly becomes a looming task. Wonder becomes stifled and confusion sets in. The entire project becomes overwhelming.

This is where a good research method becomes useful. A research method gives us direction. It helps us organize our approach and our thoughts. It helps us find the best resources to address our particular needs.

For our simple, daily-life questions, we find most of our answers without an awareness of a particular method. With hindsight, we may see that we "took the long way" to get an answer to a simple question. Perhaps if we had thought more about our approach, we could have solved the problem more quickly.

When young children begin their "research life," their primary resource is Mom, Dad, or Teacher. In the mind of a child, these important people carry unfathomable volumes of information. But as children grow, so should their ability to question and to seek answers. If nurtured, this natural sense of wonder matures and the "research project" can become a natural extension of their wonder, instead of an overwhelming burden. Just as reading and writing skills should develop until they become second nature to a child, so should research skills. It is unnatural to suddenly thrust students into the position of performing organized research projects without first allowing these skills to grow naturally and gently. It's akin to waking up one morning and saying to yourself, "I think today I shall read out loud a book with words in it that I do not know."

The research methods which follow vary in their approach, but the purpose of each is to facilitate the process of finding answers to questions. The more formal research methods, such as the Big6 and the I-Search, were originally created for older students with complex research problems. The third approach, the Alphabet Book, may be most suitable for the youngest students, but could be adapted for use by any age. At their core, all three offer a good basic structure appropriate for any level of research. However, they will be presented in a form best suited for the elementary-aged student.

▷ THE BIG6 APPROACH

The Big6 Skills™ is a problem-solving approach developed by Mike Eisenberg and Bob Berkowitz. This six-step process can be used in any type of problem-solving situation, but the

> If nurtured, this natural sense of wonder matures and the "research project" can become a natural extension of their wonder, instead of an overwhelming burden.

vocabulary used to describe the steps will need to be redefined for the younger child. For complete information on The Big6 Skills™, see their Web site, The Big6.com—Teaching Technology & Information Skills at http://big6.syr.edu/overview/index.html, or refer to their book, **Information Problem-Solving: The Big Six Skills Approach to Library and Information Skills Instruction**, by Michael B. Eisenberg and Bob Berkowitz (Ablex Publishing Corp., 1990). The phrases "Big6 Skills" and "Big6 Skills Curriculum" are all copyrights of Michael B. Eisenberg and Robert E. Berkowitz.

The six steps of the Big6 approach, as defined by Mike Eisenberg and Bob Berkowitz, are 1) Task Definition, 2) Information Seeking Strategy, 3) Location and Access, 4) Use of Information, 5) Synthesis, and 6) Evaluation. These six steps will be redefined for the younger child, with a simpler vocabulary and, at times, a more limited scope.

1 ASK THE QUESTION Think about the question you are trying to answer or the problem you are trying to solve. What do you already know? For example, consider the question "Where does rain come from?" Think about what you already know about rain: It's water, it falls from the sky, it's cloudy when it rains. Read a basic definition of rain.

2 MAKE A PLAN Think of all the possible ways to find information about rain. Make a list. It might be helpful to put a dictionary on your list. Do you think it would be helpful to watch a rain storm? Put that on your list, too. Your library may have books or videos about rain. What about an encyclopedia? Do you know anyone who might know a lot about rain? A weather forecaster or a science teacher? Make a list of all your possible sources of information.

3 FINDING THE INFORMATION If you are using a library, find out where everything is. Where are the books on rain? Where is a dictionary? Where is an encyclopedia? Is there a video collection? Look around the library. Ask the librarian. Draw and label a map of the library showing where everything is. Consider this map your treasure map!

4 USING THE SOURCES THAT YOU HAVE FOUND Read the dictionary or the encyclopedia first. Now look through the book on rain. Read the Table of Contents, the Index, the Glossary. Do they look helpful? Watch the video about weather. If it's raining outside, go to the window and watch. Take notes. Write down any information that is interesting and seems to answer your question. If you want to, make drawings that explain how and why it rains. Make sure you write down where the information comes from, for example, the book called **Rain**, the videotape called **Fun With Extreme Weather**, the name of the meteorologist you interviewed. For more information, refer to the appendix on citing sources.

> It is important to remember that this is not a linear process. You cannot simply begin with the first point and work to the sixth point and be finished.

5 SHOW WHAT YOU KNOW Organize all your notes and drawings into an order that seems to best answer your question. Decide the best way to present you answer: a written explanation, a poster with drawings and notes, or a demonstration involving a fish tank and a watering can. Now, show the class what you have learned.

6 EVALUATE Did you answer your question? Can other people understand what the question was and the answer you found just by looking at what you've done? What about your notes? Did you collect enough information? Could you read them? Would you like to know more about this subject? Is there a question you'd still like answered? Is there anything you would like to do differently next time?

It is important to remember that this is not a linear process. You cannot simply begin with the first point and work to the sixth point and be finished. There should be times when you loop back up to a step. You may get to the fifth step and realize that you do not have all the information you need to completely answer your question. After reading a definition of something, you may realize that there is more to explore. Or you may want to rephrase your question. As your research progresses, your knowledge base broadens. The more you know about something, the more questions you develop.

Very young children may not have complicated questions. There may not be any "looping back" for them. The youngest child will follow the most basic framework of a research strategy: Beginning–Middle–End. In other words, ask the question, search for information, then report what you've found.

As Eisenberg and Berkowitz assert, this six-step system of problem solving is not limited to the classroom or the library. Here is a "real-life" scenario that illustrates how we naturally use this process for everyday problem-solving. It includes a little "looping back."

Everyone starts with a question: "What's for lunch?"

You look around in the usual spots: the refrigerator, the pantry, the fruit bowl on the counter. You find what seems to be the answer—things that look good to you: the bread in the pantry, the apple in the fruit bowl, the peanut butter in the refrigerator. You take all these things out and put them on the counter. Does this look right? It's looking like lunch in progress. But grape jelly would be good, too. Go back to the resources. There's the jelly—in

*the back of the refrigerator. Now, put every-
thing together. Jelly and peanut butter on the
bread. Slice the apple. Now, check out the
results. Is it lunch? One thing missing. Back to
the refrigerator. Find the milk and pour a glass.
How does it all look now? Glass of milk, sandwich, and apple. It looks like lunch!*

➤ THE I-SEARCH

The I-Search is a four-phase method of research
which was originally developed for middle and
high school-aged students by Ken Macrorie and
explained in his book **The I-Search Paper**
(Boynton/Cook Publishers, Heinemann, 1988).
This method focuses on the student's personal
interest and depends on this interest to moti-
vate the student to ask questions and learn
more about a subject. It emphasizes process
over product. It is the process of discovery and
the blow-by-blow recording of that process and
its findings that are important. The product is
the "research story" and not a formal research
paper. Because it is linear in its approach, it is
also appropriate for young children, who tend
to understand and remember a sequence of
events more easily and may not be prepared to
organize thoughts and discoveries into a formal
presentation.

This four-phased process is easily adapted
for simple, individual research tasks as well as
cooperative group explorations.

PHASE ONE: BECOME IMMERSED IN A PARTICULAR
THEME In a classroom setting the teacher can
present a broad overview of a particular topic or
theme. This is a time to build a background of
knowledge that children can later draw from. It
is also a time to explore what is already known
about the theme. By the end of this phase, children should be able to ask a specific question
which has naturally developed from their own
particular interests found within the theme.

At the core of this approach is personal
motivation. The first phase of the project is

especially designed to generate students'
personal interest in a topic. Ultimately, the
research question the students pose is something that is truly interesting to them and
has not been restricted in any way.

Once a topic has been selected, the
researcher undergoes a three-part inquiry: 1)
discover what you already know about the
topic, 2) imagine what you think is true about
the topic, 3) decide what you want to find
out. This inquiry is recorded and becomes
the first part of the "research story."

PHASE TWO: DEVELOP A SEARCH PLAN The more
personally involved the student is in the
search, the better. Talking to people who may
know about their topic or who can refer them
to other sources is one of the best ways to
engage students. Older children might con-
duct part or all of this personal interview
online by sending questions through e-mail to
people with expertise (whether professional
or recreational) in the subject being studied.
This part of the search, the personal interview, in whatever form it takes (mail or e-
mail, fax, person-to-person, or telephone), is
considered one of the most significant methods of discovery.

During this search process, the students
write down the "story" of their discoveries:
how they found things and what they found.
Each new discovery process—i.e., interviews,
reading books and articles, watching videos,
etc.—is followed by a written addition to the
continuing story of what they have found and
how they found it.

PHASE THREE: COMPARE AND DISCOVER
Now the students compare the "story" of their
search with their original inquiry in Phase
One. They compare what they knew and what
they thought they would find with the information they actually have found. And, they
discover whether they have answered any of
the questions they first posed.

PHASE FOUR: REFLECTION

This phase of the project asks the researcher to review the process and its results. First, the students need to consider what they knew and expected to learn about the topic and what they actually learned. They then review the information-gathering process: What were the benefits of doing research in this style? of different techniques (books, interviews, magazines, etc.)? What did they gain from what they learned and experienced?

Cooperative Learning—The "We-Search"

This search method is easily adapted to a cooperative learning environment, or a "We-Search." A group can work on a particular theme, with each student posing an individual question that addresses a specific aspect of the theme. The discovery process will naturally overlap as people begin gathering information. This information can then be shared within the group.

There will be individual "stories" but because they are all within the same theme, they all are interrelated. The final presentation can also be a cooperative experience, through writing, the display of art work, or dramatic presentations.

A Simplified Search For Younger Children

A very young child may use this approach in an even more simplified form, which follows the basic structure of beginning–middle–end:

1 BEGINNING: Ask a question.

2 MIDDLE: Collect information from different sources.

3 END: Tell what you have learned.

This would be a verbal version of the written

"story" of how and what they have discovered.

This process is naturally done as a classroom experience. The teacher of very young children can help them formulate a question. Throughout the day or week, the teacher may then provide a variety of resources that relate in some way to the theme. For example, if on a rainy day, the child wants to know why it rains, the teacher may use this as an opportunity to introduce different resources into the classroom. The teacher may read stories about rain, show a video about rain, or invite a meteorologist to visit the classroom. The teacher may perform a rainmaking experiment or sing rhymes about rain. At the end of this discovery process, or even along the way if the process takes longer than a day, the findings can be reviewed, discussed, and explained by the children as a means of recalling the events and stories of each day. The teacher may even keep a written record which is added to as the process continues, and this "story" can be reread from time to time during the discovery process. In this way, these young students, without even knowing it, have begun to perform research.

▶ CREATING AN ALPHABET BOOK

Another way to introduce research skills to younger students is through the creation of an alphabet book. It is an easy and creative way for them to discover and record information on a particular theme. For example, an alphabet book on the Weather could have the A page as Atmosphere. Students would then need to find information about our atmosphere or words that describe it, as well as find or create pictures of how the atmosphere looks to them. B could be for Barometer, C for Climate, D for Downpour, etc. To create the pages, an assortment of words could be found in a dictionary of weather, or the pages could be filled in randomly as different sources on weather are provided.

A cooperative class effort could produce a single, more densely detailed book by assigning each student or team of students a particular letter of the alphabet. Their job might be to find words relating to the theme that begin with that letter (i.e., weather words beginning with the letter Q) and then to find or create pictures to illustrate their page. At the end of the project, all the pages are assembled into one complete alphabet book.

Appendix A: Research Methods and Library Skills Bibliography

 BOOKS:

Building Reference Skills in the Elementary School by M. Ellen Jan and Hilda L. Jay. Library Professional Publications, 1986.

Developing an Integrated Library Program (Professional Growth Series) by Donna Miller and J'Lynn Anderson. Linworth Publishing, 1996.

Developing Learning Skills Through Children's Literature: An Idea Book for K-5 Classrooms and Libraries by Mildred Knight Laughlin and Letty S. Watt. Oryx Press, 1986.

Elementary School Library Resource Kit by Jerry J. Mallett and Marian R. Bartch. Center for Applied Research in Education, c1984.

Flip It! for Information Literacy Skills (Professional Growth Series) by Alice H. Yucht. Linworth Publishing Company, 1997.

Hi Ho Librario! Songs, Chants, and Stories To Keep Kids Humming by Judy Freeman. Rock Hill Press, 1997.

Information Problem-Solving: The Big Six Skills Approach to Library and Information Skills Instruction by Michael B. Eisenberg and Bob Berkowitz. Ablex Publishing Corporation, 1990.

The I-Search Paper by Ken Macrorie. Boynton/Cook Publishers, Heinemann, 1988.

Library Skills (The Complete Library Skills Series). Instructional Fair, 1994.

Making the Writing and Research Connection with the I-Search Process: A How-to-do-it Manual by Matilyn Z. Joyce and Julie I. Tallman. Neal-Schuman Publishing, c1997.

Power Teaching: A Primary Role of the School Library Media Specialist by Kay E. Vandergrift. American Library Association, 1994.

The Research Project Book: Over 100 Research Reporting Models! by Nancy Polette, et. al., Book Lures, 1992.

Research Strategies for Moving Beyond Reporting (Professional Growth Series) by Sharron L. McElmeel. Linworth Publishing, c1997.

Skills for Life: Library Information Literacy for Grades K-6 (Professional Growth Series) edited by Christine Allen. Linworth Publishing, c1993.

Stepping Into Research!: A Complete Research Skills Activities Program for Grades 5-12 by Margaret A. Berry and Patricia S. Morris. Center for Applied Research in Education, c1990.

Teaching the Research Paper: From Theory to Practice, From Research to Writing edited by James E. Ford. Scarecrow Press, 1995.

Teaching Information Literacy Using Electronic Resources for Grades K-6 (Professional Growth Series) edited by Linda Skeele. Linworth Publishing, c1996.

Teaching Library Skills in Grades K Through 6: A How to Do It Manual (How to Do It Manual for School and Public Librarians, No. 10) by Catharyn Roach and Joanne Moore. Neal Schuman Publishing, 1993.

Tracking the Facts: How to Develop Research Skills by Clarie McInerney. Lerner Publications Company, c1990.

VIDEOS:

Beyond the Stacks: Finding Fun in the Library. Cheshire Book Companions, 1992.

Find It All at the Library. American Library Association Video, 1996.

Information Please! Your Library in Action (Community Helpers). Rainbow Educational Video, 1995.

Library Study Skills. Encyclopaedia Britanica, 1990.

Mysteries Revealed: Basic Research Skills. United Learning, 1996.

What Is a Media Center? Meridian Education, 1995.

Appendix B: Researching on the Internet and Evaluating Web Sites

▷ ABOUT THE INTERNET

The Internet is not child friendly. It may seem fun and engaging at first, but it can quickly become a sluggish, often tedious way to find information. A well-developed Web page may prove a wonderful resource, but finding that page can be sheer misery.

Of course there are times when the World Wide Web is invaluable and the perfect information almost immediately accessible. Where else can you log in to live photos from the surface of Mars, or a simulcast of open heart surgery, or find the latest box scores from that afternoon's game of the World Series? And certainly there are pieces of information that are available only on the Internet, and finding such a rarity (a primary source, for instance) gives you the sense of having struck gold. No actual library in the world could contain the multitude of information (and misinformation) published and contained within the virtual library of the Internet.

▷ USING THE INTERNET

This glorious gift of the information age has occasionally been compared to a library that has exploded. In the explosion all the books have lost their covers and been knocked off the shelves. Information is everywhere, but figuring out where the science books are and then, which ones have anything to do with, say, biology, is a daunting task. Then, when you think you've found what you're looking for, how do you determine the source of the information you've found? Is it from a science text? a reference book? or a speculative essay? Who wrote it? Is it factual, theoretical, or just made up?

For children attempting research, the Internet may prove extremely frustrating. Even skilled researchers can find searching for specific information via a search engine a somewhat irksome task. For instance, a search we recently tried, seeking information on young adult literature, found results that included sites not just totally unrelated but completely inappropriate (for users of any age). Yet, aside from the inappropriate nature of sites accidentally uncovered (an issue which can be addressed by filters), there remains the inescapable organizational problem that comes with keyword searching such a massive and diverse collection.

To make Internet research run smoothly and rewardingly, plan ahead. Locate sites and evaluate them before you ask students to use them as possible sources. Ask yourself, is the information reliable, easy to find, satisfactorily documented? If it is possible, bookmark sites ahead of time so that students can go straight to them. Not only will this speed up the Internet research process, but it will help avoid the ever-present temptation to "surf the Net."

Although many students come into the classroom extremely familiar with the World Wide Web (search engines, FTPs, and the works) others don't even know how to scroll down a page. In the classroom a little basic training can go a long way. If you take the time to give students a brief introduction to the basics (where the address bar is, how to scroll down a page, how to find and use **hyper links**) their time online can be spent efficiently. It would be hard to say how many times even high school students look at a good Web site and decide it has no information because they never scroll past the title or look beyond the opening graphics.

For young children especially, searching for shards of information in the vast glittering expanses of the Internet is impractical. A well-organized book is still a much more useful tool than almost any Web page.

➤ EVALUATING WEB SITES

Anyone can create a Web site. Your next door neighbor, an elementary school class, a company or business—anyone with access to the Internet and a little know-how can do it. It's a great way to share your knowledge and interests with everyone else in the world. But, because just about anyone who wants to can create a Web site, those of us using the Internet as an information resource should approach sites with a discriminating eye. It's possible that the person who owns the site knows absolutely nothing about the subjects on his page. More likely, they do know something, in fact, they probably really like whatever their site is about. Otherwise, they wouldn't spend so much time making their Web page. For example, Melanie and Mike's Etymology Web Page, called "Take Our Word For It," was created by Melanie and Mike because they love words. They aren't getting paid for their work on the Web page, and no one told them they had to do it. They just wanted to. It looks like a good site. It's well organized, they update it frequently, and they tell us who they are. It seems to be credible. But although it looks good, it's still important to be wary of just "taking their word for it." Unlike a book on etymology, Melanie and Mike don't have an editor to check over their work, and they don't have a publishing house standing behind them putting its reputation on the line. They're working alone and they've published themselves.

There are many clues within a Web page to help us decide whether the information it contains is likely to be reliable and its author

credible. The first thing to check is the URL. URL, or Uniform Resource Locator, is the unique address of any Web document. It tells you where a page is and what kind of page it is. URLs generally have four parts: protocol://server name/file path/file name. At the end of every server name there is a three-letter extension, like **.edu** or **.com**, etc. This extension tells us what type of group is hosting, or publishing, the site. Here's a list of different URLs and a brief description of them:

.edu = *educational—institutions such as universities or schools*

.com = *commercial—companies or business usually advertising their company or selling products*

.gov = *government—government organizations usually providing information as a service*

.org = *organization—these are groups other than business and usually are nonprofit*

Educational and government sites generally have reliable, accurate information. Web sites that originate from universities can be especially informative, but often their presentation is too advanced for the elementary school student. Commercial sites are usually designed to sell and advertise products or services. But some of these sites can be very informative. For example, A&E's www.biography.com site, though designed to sell videotapes of the network's programs, contains a good, searchable, biographical encyclopedia. It is a very useful site in spite of its commercial intentions. Nonprofit organizations may have excellent sites also, but may reflect only the group's interests, not the "whole picture."

Another quick way to judge a Web site is by the creation and "last updated" dates listed on it (often at the bottom of the home page). These dates can quickly tell you whether the information is current and whether the author of the page is actively interested in the site. A site may look very good, but if the information hasn't been updated in five years, then you must decide whether it's the kind of information that needs to be updated to remain accurate.

Now check the sophistication level of the site. Is it well put together? Is its information well organized and easy to find? Do the links work? Are the graphics useful? And finally, notice whether the grammar and spelling are correct. Then go on to study the content of the page. Does it give you information that is well developed and useful? Does the information correspond with information you have gathered from other sources on the same subject? Conflicting information should raise a red flag. One of your sources is probably wrong, and it's possible that the Web site is not reliable. Check to see whether the author of the page has included a bibliography. A good bibliography suggests good research. It usually shows that an author has researched the topic well and that the information is reliable.

And finally, find out about the author. The Web page you found on dolphins may be written by the dolphin expert at Sea World, or it may be written by your next-door neighbor, who happens to be a dolphin lover. Hobbyists may or may not have credentials to prove their expertise, but the information they provide could be extremely reliable and insightful. It just might take you a little more leg work to figure this out. Some authors have a section on their Web page that lets you know who they are. And, almost every Web page has an e-mail address. Use this address to ask questions about the site and its author. Also, check to see whether the site has a sponsor. If the dolphin site is sponsored by Sea World, for instance, then you can probably assume the information is accurate.

By using these guidelines to evaluate Web sites, you should be able to get a good idea about their reliability. If everything measures up, then it should be a good resource.

Worksheet for Evaluating Web Sites

1. Address of the site (URL): _____

   What type of site is it?

   .gov = government

   .edu = educational

   .com = commercial

   .org = organization

2. Author or Sponsor of the site: _____

   Is the sponsor nationally known?

   Is the author affiliated with a college or university?

   Has the author written books or articles on the subject?

   Is the author self-taught on the subject?

   Is this subject the author's hobby?

3. How current is the information on the site? When was it last updated? _____

   Does the subject require current information?

4. How well developed is the site?

   Is the information well organized and easy to find?

   Do the links work?

   Are the graphics useful?

   Are grammar and spelling correct?

   Is the information well developed and useful?

   Does the information seem correct?

5. Does the site include a bibliography on the subject?

Appendix C: Creative Citations

Nontraditional citation methods may encourage researchers to use a variety of sources and to think about the many different ways they can gather information. The use of symbols can serve as visual reminders and cues. Each symbol can represent a different type of resource. These symbols can be designed by the class, or they can be provided by the teacher in the form of stickers or rubber stamps or simple, prepared drawings. These symbols can be applied to note cards or in the margins of the I-Search story.

Here are some resource symbol ideas:

Interview   *a stick figure drawing, or a face*
Book   *an image of a book*
TV or Video   *a simple drawing of a television, or the letters "TV" in a box*
Internet   *the letters "WWW" for World Wide Web*
CD-ROM   *a circle representing a CD-ROM*
Periodical   *a picture of a magazine, a simple rectangle*
Audio   *a simple drawing of a boom box or an ear*
Experiment   *a drawing of a test tube or microscope*
Observation   *a picture of an eye*

Just coming up with the symbols would be a good class project, and it would promote the many different ways we can learn about things.

Appendix D: Periodical Indexes for Children's Literature

Children's Magazine Guide. R. R. Bowker. (Indexing 51 popular children's magazines, including **Girl's Life, Muse, Your Big Backyard, American Girl, National Geographic WORLD, Sports Illustrated for Kids, 3-2-1 Contact.**)

Magazine Article Summaries [CD-ROM]. EBSCO. (Searches full text of articles, reports, and special issues from more than 210 of the most wanted K-12 magazines, and abstracts and indexing for more than 500 titles, including most major U.S. news weeklies such as **Consumer Reports.**)

Primary Search [CD-ROM/Online]. EBSCO. (Searches full text from more than 45 of the most wanted K-12 magazines, and abstracts and indexing for more than 120.)

Appendix E: Children's Magazines and Their Websites

Many children's magazines have sites on the Internet. Some of the sites may include a current issue of the magazine, but most sites only list the contents of the magazines. Using the Table of Contents to locate specific articles may be more cumbersome than turning to a subject in a comprehensive index, but it is one way to find articles on a particular theme when traditional periodical indexes are not available.

American Girl (ages 8-12)

www.americangirl.com/ag/ag.cgi

This magazine includes fiction, games, puzzles, sports topics, and party plans. The Web site has fun things to do, but there is not a complete issue of the magazine or an index.

Appleseeds (ages 7-9)

www.cobblestonepub.com/pages/appleseeds-main.htm

The first issue of this magazine was published in September 1998. Its thematic issues are filled with articles, interviews, and stories about geography, history, math, and science. The Web site offers a list of the themes covered in this year's issues. Most topics on the list are accompanied by a paragraph giving more details about the articles in that issue.

Calliope: World History for Young People (ages 8-14)

www.cobblestonepub.com/pages/callmain.htm

This magazine contains mature articles on historic topics. The Web site offers a list of the themes covered in previous and upcoming issues. Most topics on the list are accompanied by a paragraph giving more details about the articles in that issue.

Cobblestone: The History Magazine for Young People (ages 8-14)

www.cobblestonepub.com/pages/cobbmain.htm

Each issue of this magazine is devoted to an historical theme in American history. The Web site offers a list of the themes covered in last year's and this year's issues. Most topics on the list are accompanied by a paragraph giving more details about the articles in that issue.

Cricket (ages 9-14)

www.cricketmag.com/home.html

Cricket addresses a variety of themes. Only the current month's magazine is online.

Dragonfly (elementary-aged children)

miavx1.acs.muohio.edu/~dragonfly/index.htmlx

Dragonfly is published by the National Science Teachers Association. Its mission is to link children and scientists "in an open community of investigation."

Faces: People, Places, and Cultures (ages 9-14)

www.cobblestonepub.com/pages/facemain.htm

Faces teaches children about other places and cultures. The Web site offers a list of the themes covered in last year's and this year's issues. Most topics on the list are accompanied by a paragraph giving more details about the articles in that issue.

Highlights for Children (ages 6-14)

Each issue of *Highlights* contains articles on sports, nature and science, history, literature, crafts, fictional stories, poems, and games. While *Highlights* does not have a Web site, each year's stories are indexed in its December issue.

Ladybug (ages 2-6)

www.cricketmag.com/ladybug/index.html

Ladybug features play-and-sing, read-together, and parents' sections on a variety of topics. Issues are usually developed around a theme, often seasonal. Only the current month's magazine is online.

Muse (ages 9-14)

www.musemag.com/musemag/museframe1.htm

The current issue and at least 10 previous issues of this magazine are online. The themes of this publication include science, nature, and natural history. The magazine does not have a search engine, but each online issue has a content list that links to the pertinent articles.

National Geographic WORLD (ages 8-14)

www.nationalgeographic.com/media/world/index.html

This magazine is all about the earth and contains factual articles on a variety of topics. The site features a search engine for the site (look in the site index), as well as an online index for the *Geographic* collection. A search using this index will produce a list of hits, each linking to a complete description.

New Moon (girls, age 8-14)

www.newmoon.org/

New Moon is an international magazine with stories by and about girls and women all over the world. Each issue is devoted to a theme.

Ranger Rick (ages 6-14)

www.nwf.org/nwf/rrick/index.html

Ranger Rick is a nature magazine created by the National Wildlife Federation. The Web site includes the Table of Contents for all the issues since January 1996, however, the issues themselves are not online.

Skipping Stones: A Multicultural Children's Magazine (all ages)

www.nonviolence.org/skipping/

This multilingual quarterly is sponsored by Parents and Teachers for Social Responsibility in Vermont, Children of the Green Earth, and other groups concerned with ethnic diversity. It "encourages cooperation, creativity and celebration of cultural and environmental richness." The site lists only the contents of the upcoming issue.

Smithsonian Magazine (for older students)

www.smithsonianmag.si.edu/

This magazine deals with a variety of interesting topics and is the parent magazine of **Kids' Castle**. This site has an internal search engine for its online issues.

Smithsonian Magazine Kids' Castle (ages 8-16)

www.kidscastle.si.edu/home.html

Topics of this online magazine include science, animals, personalities, sports, the arts, worldwide history, and air and space. This site has an internal search engine that links to brief articles.

Spider (ages 6-9)

www.cricketmag.com/spider/index.html

Spider magazine addresses a variety of themes. Only the current month's magazine is online.

Index